Ready® Classroom
Mathematics

Grade 4 • Volume 1

Curriculum Associates®

NOT FOR RESALE

Contents

Contents (continued)

UNIT 3

Multi-Digit Operations and Measurement
Multiplication, Division, Perimeter, and Area

Contents (continued)

UNIT 4 — Fractions, Decimals, and Measurement
Addition, Subtraction, and Multiplication

UNIT 5

Geometry and Measurement
Figures, Classification, and Symmetry

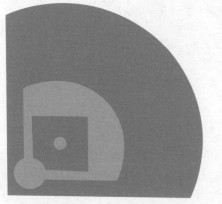

☑ SELF CHECK

Before starting this unit, check off the skills you know below. As you complete each lesson, see how many more skills you can check off!

I can ...	Before	After
Read and write numbers using number names, for example: 495 is *four hundred ninety-five*.	☐	☐
Read and write numbers using expanded form, for example: $352 = 300 + 50 + 2$.	☐	☐
Compare two multi-digit whole numbers, for example: $6{,}131 > 6{,}113$.	☐	☐
Round multi-digit whole numbers, for example: 3,528 rounded to the nearest hundred is 3,500.	☐	☐
Add multi-digit whole numbers, for example: $3{,}966 + 7{,}550 = 11{,}516$.	☐	☐
Subtract multi-digit whole numbers, for example: $25{,}082 - 11{,}919 = 13{,}163$.	☐	☐

Build Your Vocabulary

Math Vocabulary

Define the review word. Work with your partner to clarify.

Review Word	Current Thinking	Revise Your Thinking
place value		

Write a number in the place-value chart.

Hundreds	Tens	Ones

Write a three-digit number and have your partner write another to make the inequality true. Then read each inequality aloud.

1 .... < ....   **2** .... > ....

Academic Vocabulary

Put a check next to the academic words you know. Then use the words to complete the sentences.

☐ compare   ☐ explanation   ☐ clarify   ☐ represent

1 When you .... the problem, it makes it easier to understand.

2 When you look at two numbers to see which is greater, you .... them.

3 An .... makes something easy to understand.

4 In math, you can use symbols to .... operations.

Understand Place Value

Dear Family,

This week your child is exploring place value in numbers.

Our number system is based on a pattern of tens. The value of a digit in a number is based on the place where the digit appears in the number.

A digit in one place has 10 times the value that the same digit would have in the place to its right.

Thousands Period			Ones Period		
Hundred Thousands	Ten Thousands	Thousands	Hundreds	Tens	Ones
7	4	2	5	5	9

This number in **standard form:**	742,559
This number in **word form:**	Seven hundred forty-two thousand, five hundred fifty-nine
This number in **expanded form:**	700,000 + 40,000 + 2,000 + 500 + 50 + 9

Invite your child to share what he or she knows about place value by doing the following activity together.

ACTIVITY PLACE VALUE

Do this activity with your child to explore place value.

The distance from Earth to the moon is about 238,855 miles.

This number in standard form: 238,855.

This number in word form: two hundred thirty-eight thousand, eight hundred fifty-five.

- Write the number 238,855 on a sheet of paper. Show your child the number and have your child read the number aloud in word form (two hundred thirty-eight thousand, eight hundred fifty-five).

- Cover the standard form of the number so that your child cannot see it. Read the number aloud (in word form) and have your child write the number in standard form.

- Now have your child write a six-digit number in standard form without showing you the number. Then have your child tell you the number in word form while you write it in standard form.

- Compare the number you wrote with the number your child wrote.

- Repeat this activity several times, alternating between you and your child giving the six-digit number.

Explore Place Value

What exactly does place value mean?

MODEL IT

Complete the statements below.

1 You can use place-value charts to understand greater numbers. Place value is the value of a digit based on its position in a number. You have seen place-value charts for numbers up to 999. Look at the chart showing 11,111.

Hundred Thousands	Ten Thousands	Thousands	Hundreds	Tens	Ones
	1	1	1	1	1

Describe how each place is related to the place next to it.

a. 10 ones is 1 ....

b. 10 tens is 1 ....

c. 10 hundreds is 1 ....

d. 10 .... is 1 ten thousand.

DISCUSS IT

- Do you and your partner see the same pattern in place values next to each other?

- I think each place value is related to the one next to it because . . .

2 Use the number in the place-value chart to solve the problems.

Hundred Thousands	Ten Thousands	Thousands	Hundreds	Tens	Ones
		3	3	3	3

a. The 3 in the tens place has a value of ....

b. The 3 in the tens place has a value that is

.... times the value of the 3 in the .... place.

MODEL IT

Complete the statements below.

3 Numbers with more than three digits have a comma to separate groups of three digits. Digits in groups of three places are called **periods**.

Thousands Period			Ones Period		
Hundred Thousands	Ten Thousands	Thousands	Hundreds	Tens	Ones
4	6	7	8	8	2

Write the number shown above in **standard form** (the way you usually see it).

.................../....................

4 Use expanded form and word form to understand greater numbers.

a. To say or write the **word form** of a number, you read each group of three digits followed by the period name. You do not say the period name for the ones period.

The word form for the number you wrote in problem 3 is:

four hundred sixty-seven ....,

....

b. Expanded form is a way to write a number to show the place value of each digit. Complete the expanded form below for the number in the place-value chart above.

........00,000 + ...0,000 + ...,000 + ...00 + ...0 + ...

DISCUSS IT

• How did you and your partner decide how to complete the word form and expanded form of the number?

• A place-value chart helps you read numbers because . . .

5 REFLECT

How are the standard form, word form, and expanded form of a number alike and different?

....

....

Prepare for Place Value

1 Think about what you know about place value. Fill in each box. Use words, numbers, and pictures. Show as many ideas as you can.

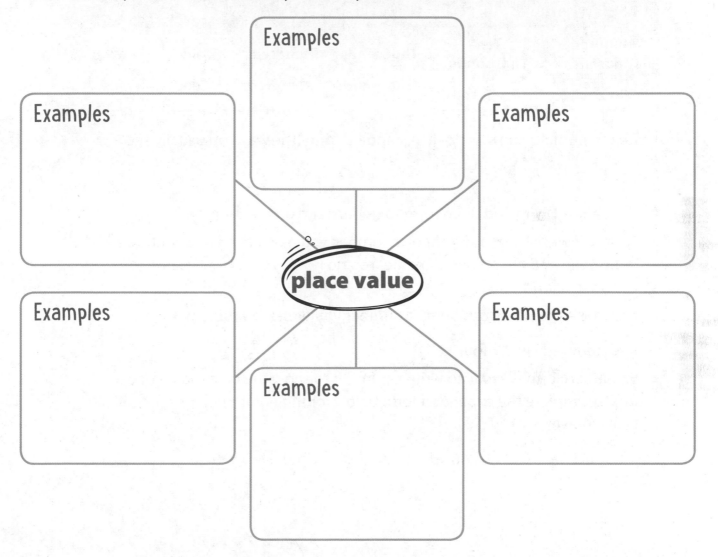

2 Circle a digit in the place-value chart. What is the value of the circled digit?

Hundred Thousands	Ten Thousands	Thousands	Hundreds	Tens	Ones
1	5	6	8	9	3

Solve.

3 Numbers with more than three digits have a comma to separate groups of three digits. Digits in groups of three places are called periods.

Thousands Period			Ones Period		
Hundred Thousands	Ten Thousands	Thousands	Hundreds	Tens	Ones
2	8	4	3	7	1

Write the number shown above in standard form (the way you usually see it).

.................,.................

4 Use expanded form and word form to understand greater numbers.

a. To say or write the word form of a number, you read each group of three digits followed by the period name. You do not say the period name for the ones period.

Complete the word form for the number you wrote in problem 3.

two hundred eighty-four ....,................

b. Expanded form is a way to write a number to show the place value of each digit. Complete the expanded form below for the number in the place-value chart above.

........00,000 + ...0,000 + ...,000 + ...00 + ...0 + ...

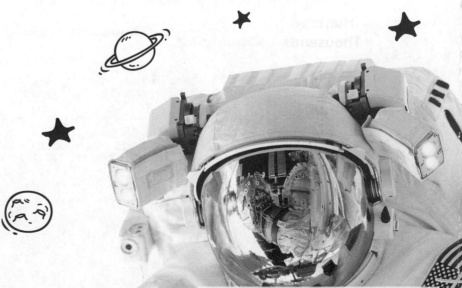

Develop Understanding of Place Value

MODEL IT: PLACE-VALUE CHARTS

Try these two problems.

1 Use a place-value chart to think about greater numbers.

a. Write the number 25,049 in the place-value chart.

Thousands Period			Ones Period		
Hundred Thousands	Ten Thousands	Thousands	Hundreds	Tens	Ones

b. Write the value of each digit.

2: ....   4: ....

5: ....   9: ....

0: ....

2 Think about how the values of the digits change from problem 1.

a. Write the number 250,490 in the place-value chart.

Thousands Period			Ones Period		
Hundred Thousands	Ten Thousands	Thousands	Hundreds	Tens	Ones

b. Write the value of each digit.

2: ....   4: ....

5: ....   9: ....

0: ....   0: ....

> ### DISCUSS IT
>
> • Describe how the values of the digits 2, 5, 0, 4, and 9 in problem 2 compare to their values in problem 1.
>
> • I think a place-value chart helps you understand numbers because . . .

Lesson 1 Understand Place Value   **9**

MODEL IT: EXPANDED FORM

Use expanded form to understand place value.

3 Complete to show the expanded form of 25,049.

25,049 = ... ten thousands + ... thousands + ... hundreds +

.... tens + ... ones

4 Complete to show different ways you can expand and show 25,049.

25,049 = ... thousands + ... hundreds + ... tens + ... ones

25,049 = ... thousands + ... ones

25,049 = ... ones

CONNECT IT

Complete the problems below.

5 What do the expanded form and a place-value chart tell you about a number such as 25,049? How are they alike and different?

6 Complete the expanded form of each number. Think about the value of each digit to help you.

a. 40,389 = 40,000 + 300 + ... + ...

b. 682,902 = ... + ... + ... +

.... + ...

> **DISCUSS IT**
>
> • How does each of the ways in problem 4 show 25,049?
>
> • I think you can show numbers in different ways because . . .

Practice Using Place Value

Study how the Example uses a place-value chart to show the value of the digits in a number. Then solve problems 1–9.

EXAMPLE

Look at the place-value chart below. What is the value of the 3?

Then use place value to explain the value of the 3 if it were in the ten-thousands place.

Hundred Thousands	Ten Thousands	Thousands	Hundreds	Tens	Ones
2	0	3	5	5	4

Standard form: 203,554
Expanded form: 200,000 + 3,000 + 500 + 50 + 4
Word form: two hundred three thousand, five hundred fifty-four

The 3 is in the thousands place, so it has a value of 3,000.
If 3 were in the ten-thousands place, its value would be 30,000.

1 Write 70,681 in the place-value chart at the right.

Hundred Thousands	Ten Thousands	Thousands	Hundreds	Tens	Ones

2 Write 70,681 in expanded form and word form.

3 What would be the value of 7 if it were in the thousands place? ....

4 What is the value of the 6 in 70,681? Explain how you know.

5 Write six hundred ten thousand, twenty-nine in standard form. ....

6 Write 44,910 in expanded form. Do any digits in the number have a value
10 times the value of another digit? Explain.

7 Show some different ways you can make 7,502.

.... hundreds + ... tens + ... ones

.... tens + ... ones

.... ones

8 What are three different ways to make the number 15,638 with only hundreds,
tens, and ones?

9 Solve the following riddle:

I have 30 ones, 2 thousands, 4 hundred thousands, 60 tens, and 100 hundreds.
What number am I?

Show your work.

Refine Ideas About Place Value

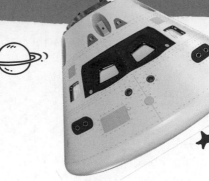

APPLY IT
Complete these problems on your own.

 EXPLAIN

Emma wrote thirty-six thousand, forty-two as 3,642. Explain what she did wrong. Then write the number correctly.

 DEMONSTRATE

Suppose you only have hundreds, tens, and ones blocks. What are two different ways you could make the number 1,718?

 COMPARE

Write 55,555 in expanded form. How does the value of each 5 compare to the value of the 5 to its right?

PAIR/SHARE
Discuss your solutions for these three problems with a partner.

Use what you have learned to complete problem 4.

4 You are playing a game that includes the following cards.

Part A Choose six cards. Circle the cards you choose.

i   Make the greatest number possible using each card once.
Write your answer in standard form and expanded form.

Standard Form: ....

Expanded Form: ....

ii Make the least number possible using the same six cards.
If you have a 0 card, do not use it as the first digit.
Write your answer in standard form and expanded form.

Standard Form: ....

Expanded Form: ....

Part B Look at the standard form of your answers to Part A. Circle a digit
that you used in both numbers. Did the value of the digit change between
the two numbers? Explain.

5 MATH JOURNAL

Choose a six-digit number. Write the number in standard form,
expanded form, and word form.

Compare Whole Numbers

Dear Family,

This week your child is learning how to compare whole numbers.

Your child can use a place-value chart to compare multi-digit numbers. For example, this place-value chart can be used to compare 39,521 and 39,743.

Ten Thousands	Thousands	Hundreds	Tens	Ones
3	9	5	2	1
3	9	7	4	3

To compare the two numbers in the place-value chart above, look down each column in the chart. Start at the left column and compare the digits in each column.

The ten-thousands digits are the same.

The thousands digits are the same.

The hundreds digits are different.

Because 5 hundreds is less than 7 hundreds, the top number, 39,521, is less than the bottom number, 39,743.

Your child is learning to use a symbol to write the comparison:

39,521 < 39,743

Invite your child to share what he or she knows about comparing whole numbers by doing the following activity together.

ACTIVITY COMPARE WHOLE NUMBERS

Do this activity with your child to compare whole numbers.

Famous mountains around the world have the following heights:

> Mount Kilimanjaro: 19,341 feet
>
> K2 (mountain in Asia): 28,251 feet
>
> Mount Everest: 29,035 feet
>
> Denali: 20,310 feet

- Have your child read aloud the mountain heights.

- Ask your child to compare the heights. Encourage your child to use comparison words and symbols as shown in the table below.

symbol	<	>	=
meaning	is less than	is greater than	is equal to

For example, your child could say: *The height of Mount Everest is greater than the height of Denali.*

Or he or she could write 29,035 > 20,310.

Look for other real-life opportunities to compare numbers with your child.

Explore Comparing Whole Numbers

You have already learned how to compare numbers up to 999. Now you will compare numbers in the thousands. Use what you know to try to solve the problem below.

> **Students in Mrs. Allen's math class are divided into teams. Each team collects points by doing projects and playing math games.**
>
> **Team A has 1,347 points. Team B has 1,295 points.**
>
> **Which team has more points?**

Learning Target

• Read and write multi-digit whole numbers using base-ten numerals, number names, and expanded form. Compare two multi-digit numbers based on meanings of the digits in each place, using >, =, and < symbols to record the results of comparisons.

SMP 1, 2, 3, 4, 5, 6, 8

Team A	Team B
1,347	1,295

TRY IT

Math Toolkit
- base-ten blocks
- hundred thousands place-value charts
- number lines
- index cards

DISCUSS IT

Ask your partner: How did you get started?

Tell your partner: I knew . . . so I . . .

CONNECT IT

 LOOK BACK

Which team has more points? Explain which place value shows the team that has more points.

② **LOOK AHEAD**

You can use place value to compare numbers. Start with the greatest place-value position. Sometimes numbers you compare have the same number of digits. Sometimes they have different numbers of digits.

a. Circle the box with the greater number of staples.

b. What place value helps you tell which box has more staples? Explain.

c. Circle the greater price.

d. What place value helps you tell which price is greater? Explain.

③ **REFLECT**

Was it easier to compare the number of staples or the two prices? Explain.

. . . .

. . . .

Prepare for Comparing Whole Numbers

1   Think about what you know about comparing. Fill in each box. Use words, numbers, and pictures. Show as many ideas as you can.

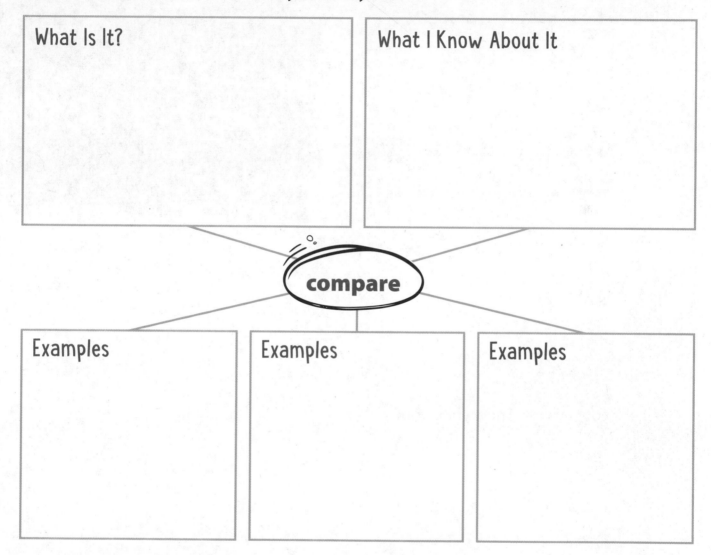

What Is It?	What I Know About It

compare

Examples	Examples	Examples

2   Circle the lesser price. Explain how using place value helps you know this is the lesser price.

 $652    $1,256

Solve the problem. Show your work.

Two teams are competing in a trivia game. Team A has 1,627 points.
Team B has 1,816 points.

Which team has more points?

Solution ....

 Check your answer. Show your work.

Develop Comparing Multi-Digit Numbers

Read and try to solve the problem below.

> There were 23,643 fans at a football game last week and 23,987 fans at a football game this week. Which game had fewer fans?

TRY IT

 **Math Toolkit**
- base-ten blocks
- hundred thousands place-value charts
- number lines
- index cards

DISCUSS IT

Ask your partner: Do you agree with me? Why or why not?

Tell your partner: I started by . . .

Explore different ways to understand how to compare multi-digit numbers.

> There were 23,643 fans at a football game last week and 23,987 fans at a football game this week. Which game had fewer fans?

MODEL IT

You can use a place-value chart to compare multi-digit numbers.

When the numbers are in a place-value chart, it is easy to look down the columns and compare the digits. Start at the greatest place value.

Ten Thousands	Thousands	Hundreds	Tens	Ones
2	3	6	4	3
2	3	9	8	7

The ten-thousands digits are the same. The thousands digits are the same. The hundreds digits are different. So, compare the digits in the hundreds place.

6 hundreds $<$ 9 hundreds

MODEL IT

You can break apart numbers by place value to compare multi-digit numbers.

23,643 = **20,000 + 3,000 + 600 +** 40 + 3

23,987 = **20,000 + 3,000 + 900 +** 80 + 7

Compare the numbers place by place.
The ten thousands and thousands are the same.
The hundreds are different.

600 $<$ 900

CONNECT IT

Now you will use the problem from the previous page to help you understand how to use place value to compare multi-digit numbers.

 Write the numbers 23,643 and 23,987 so that they line up by place value. Explain how to line them up.

 In what place-value position do you begin comparing the two numbers?

3 What is the first place in which the numbers are different?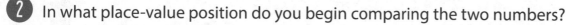

4 Explain how to compare the numbers. Then write the comparison using > or <. Tell which game had fewer fans.

 REFLECT

Look back at your **Try It**, strategies by classmates, and **Model Its**. Which models or strategies do you like best for comparing multi-digit numbers? Explain.

APPLY IT

Use what you just learned to solve these problems.

6 There are two baby macaw parrots at a zoo. Zeke has a mass of 1,582 grams, and Tao has a mass of 819 grams. Which bird has a greater mass? Use >, <, or = to write a comparison. Show your work.

Solution ....

7 Write the symbol that makes the statement true. Show your work.

91,146 ◯ 908,043

8 Which statements correctly compare two numbers?

Ⓐ 37,046 > 37,064

Ⓑ 37,064 < 37,046

Ⓒ 37,046 < 37,064

Ⓓ 37,064 > 37,046

Ⓔ 37,064 = 37,046

Practice Comparing Multi-Digit Numbers

Study the Example showing one way to compare multi-digit numbers.
Then solve problems 1–6.

EXAMPLE

Cara flies an airplane 30,825 feet high on one flight. She flies 30,750 feet high on another flight. Compare how high Cara flies on the two flights.

Hundred Thousands	Ten Thousands	Thousands	Hundreds	Tens	Ones
	3	0	8	2	5
	3	0	7	5	0

The ten-thousands and thousands digits are the same.
The hundreds digits are different. **8 hundreds** > **7 hundreds**
    30,825 > 30,750

 1 In a certain year, 50,266 runners finished the New York City Marathon and 38,879 runners finished the Chicago Marathon. Compare these numbers by lining up the place values. Explain which number is greater.

2 Explain how to compare the two numbers shown in expanded form.

        60,000 + 2,000 + 500 + 80 + 3

        60,000 + 7,000 + 200 + 40 + 5

3 Write the symbol (>, <, =) that makes each statement true.

a.   8,035 ◯ 894

b.   62,999 ◯ 63,000

c.   142,073 ◯ 143,750

d.   501,348 ◯ 500,348

4 Walnut Elementary raises $1,950 for new technology in their school. Grove Elementary raises $1,890. Which school raises more money? Explain how you know.

5 Select all the numbers that are greater than 98,765.

Ⓐ 100,100

Ⓑ 89,975

Ⓒ 99,132

Ⓓ 987,650

Ⓔ 87,956

6 Select >, <, or = to complete a true comparison for each pair of numbers.

	>	<	=
33,003 ☐ 33,030	Ⓐ	Ⓑ	Ⓒ
524,980 ☐ 52,498	Ⓓ	Ⓔ	Ⓕ
279,615 ☐ 279,615	Ⓖ	Ⓗ	Ⓘ
100,000 ☐ 99,999	Ⓙ	Ⓚ	Ⓛ

Refine Comparing Whole Numbers

Complete the Example below. Then solve problems 1–9.

EXAMPLE

Millennium Force and Formula Rossa are two famous roller coasters. Millennium Force is 6,595 feet long and Formula Rossa is 6,562 feet long. Which roller coaster is shorter? Use >, <, or = to write a comparison.

Look at how you could show your work using a place-value chart.

Thousands	Hundreds	Tens	Ones
6	5	9	5
6	5	6	2

Solution ....

....

The student used a place-value chart to compare the digits in the two numbers.

PAIR/SHARE
How else could you solve this problem?

APPLY IT

1 A tile factory shipped 342,085 ceramic tiles in 2016. In 2017, it shipped 342,805 tiles. In which year did the tile factory ship more tiles? Use >, <, or = to write a comparison. Show your work.

What is the first place in which the digits are different?

Solution ....

PAIR/SHARE
How did you and your partner decide where to start comparing?

2 Val's Video Games sells 11,806 new games and 10,899 used games from May to July. Does Val's Video Games sell more new games or more used games? Use >, <, or = to write a comparison. Show your work.

I think the comparison can be shown in different ways.

Solution ....

....

3 Kara has twenty-four thousand, five hundred sixty stickers in her album. Raul has 20,000 + 4,000 + 500 + 60 stickers in his collection.

Which statement correctly compares Kara's and Raul's stickers? Who has more stickers?

Ⓐ 2,456 < 24,560; Raul has more stickers.

Ⓑ 24,560 > 24,506; Kara has more stickers.

Ⓒ 24,560 < 24,650; Raul has more stickers.

Ⓓ 24,560 = 24,560; They each have the same number.

Anna chose Ⓐ as the correct answer. How did she get that answer?

To compare the two numbers, I can write them both in standard form.

4 Dalton has 1,168 marbles, Juan has 1,079 marbles, Gilbert has 967 marbles, and Lydia has 199 marbles. Who has the greatest number of marbles?

Ⓐ Dalton

Ⓑ Juan

Ⓒ Gilbert

Ⓓ Lydia

5 A company makes 189,909 stuffed animals one year. The company makes 198,909 stuffed animals the next year. Which statements correctly compare the numbers of stuffed animals the company makes?

Ⓐ 189,909 > 198,909

Ⓑ 198,909 < 189,909

Ⓒ 189,909 < 198,909

Ⓓ 198,909 = 189,909

Ⓔ 198,909 > 189,909

6 Mr. Hunter writes the following comparison on the board:

96,341 < ▢▢,▢▢▢

Use the digits in the tiles below to find a number that makes the comparison true. Fill in the boxes in the comparison using each digit below only once.

2 3 5 6 9

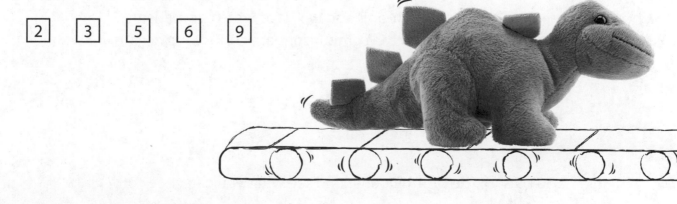

7 Selena organizes her music files into four online albums. Album A has one thousand eleven songs, Album B has $1,000 + 100 + 10$ songs, Album C has 1,101 songs, and Album D has eleven hundred songs.

Write the number of songs in the four albums in the place-value chart. Which album has the most songs?

	Thousands	Hundreds	Tens	Ones
Album A				
Album B				
Album C				
Album D				

Solution ....

8 North Elementary School collects 14,128 cans of soup during a food drive. South Elementary School collects 14,210 cans. Which school collects more cans? Use $>$, $<$, or $=$ to write a comparison. Show your work.

Solution ....
....

9 MATH JOURNAL

Choose 2 six-digit numbers. Use symbols and words to write comparison statements. Explain how you know the comparisons are correct.

☑ SELF CHECK Go back to the Unit 1 Opener and see what you can check off.

Round Whole Numbers

Dear Family,

This week your child is learning to round whole numbers.

An apple orchard harvests 47,382 apples one season.

You can use a number line to help you round a number such as 47,382 to the nearest thousand.

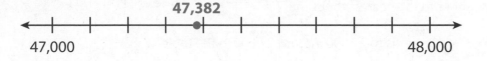

47,382

47,000   48,000

The number line shows the closest thousands less than and greater than 47,382.

The number 47,382 rounded to the nearest thousand is 47,000 because 47,382 is closer to 47,000 than to 48,000.

But what if you want to round 47,500 to the nearest thousand? 47,500 is *exactly halfway* between 47,000 and 48,000. In this case, you would *round up*. So, 47,500 rounded to the nearest thousand is 48,000.

Invite your child to share what he or she knows about rounding whole numbers by doing the following activity together.

ACTIVITY ROUND WHOLE NUMBERS

Do this activity with your child to round whole numbers.

Materials 0–9 digit cards, scissors, bag, tables shown below

Cut out the digit cards below or write each digit from 0–9 on its own index card. Place the cards in a bag. Each player takes five turns.

- Draw five digit cards and record them in the table as a five-digit number in the order drawn. Draw again if 0 is the first card drawn.

  Example: You draw 2, 7, 4, 1, 9 and record 27,419.

- Round the number to the nearest thousand.

  Example: 27,419 rounds to 27,000. Record 27,000 in the table.

- Replace the cards in the bag. Now have your child draw five cards and follow the directions above to round to the nearest thousand.

Player 1		Player 2	
Five-digit number	**Rounded to the nearest thousand**	**Five-digit number**	**Rounded to the nearest thousand**

0 1 2 3 4

5 6 7 8 9

Explore Rounding Whole Numbers

Learning Target

- Use place value understanding to round multi-digit whole numbers to any place.

SMP 1, 2, 3, 4, 5, 6, 7, 8

You have learned how to round three-digit numbers to the nearest ten or hundred. Take a look at rounding greater numbers. Use what you know to try to solve the problem below.

> A toothpaste company surveys 36,219 customers about their favorite toothpaste flavor. The data is used to help the company decide what flavors to continue making. To the nearest thousand, about how many customers does the company survey?

TRY IT

Math Toolkit
- hundred thousands place-value charts
- number lines
- index cards

DISCUSS IT

Ask your partner: Do you agree with me? Why or why not?

Tell your partner: I agree with you about ... because ...

CONNECT IT

1 LOOK BACK

To the nearest thousand, about how many customers does the

toothpaste company survey? ....

2 LOOK AHEAD

You round to **estimate** and to make numbers easier to work with
when you do not need an exact answer.

a. Mark and label 36,219 on the number line below.

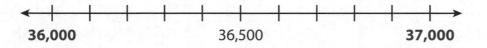

36,000   36,500   **37,000**

b. Between which two thousands is the number 36,219? Write both numbers

of thousands as numerals. .... and ....

c. Is 36,219 closer to 36,000 or 37,000 on the number line? ....

d. The rule for rounding numbers states that if a number is exactly halfway
between, round up. What is 36,500 rounded to the nearest thousand?

....

3 REFLECT

Use the rounding rule stated in problem 2d to explain how to round 1,550
to the nearest hundred.

....

....

....

Prepare for Rounding Whole Numbers

1 Think about what you know about rounding numbers. Fill in each box.
Use words, numbers, and pictures. Show as many ideas as you can.

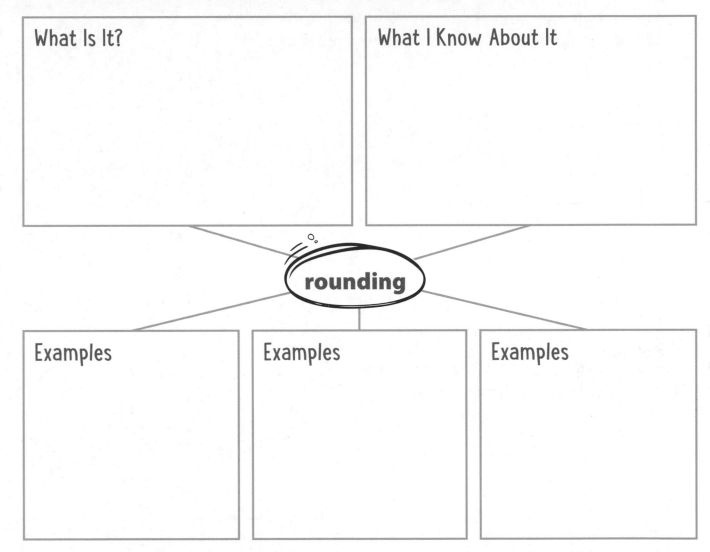

What Is It?

What I Know About It

rounding

Examples

Examples

Examples

2 Round 52,741 to the nearest thousand. Use the number line to help explain
your answer.

Solve the problem. Show your work.

A chewing gum company surveys 25,526 customers about their favorite chewing gum flavors. The data is used to help the company decide what flavors to continue making. To the nearest thousand, about how many customers does the company survey?

Solution ....

 Check your answer. Show your work.

Develop Rounding Whole Numbers

Read and try to solve the problem below.

> Last year Tanaka's Toys spent $117,290 developing a new video game. Mia rounds the amount spent to the nearest ten thousand. Jon rounds the amount spent to the nearest thousand. What amounts do Mia and Jon each round to?

TRY IT

Math Toolkit
- hundred thousands place-value charts
- number lines
- index cards

DISCUSS IT

Ask your partner: Can you explain that again?

Tell your partner: I do not understand how . . .

Explore different ways to understand how to solve a problem that involves rounding a multi-digit number.

> **Last year Tanaka's Toys spent $117,290 developing a new video game. Mia rounds the amount spent to the nearest ten thousand. Jon rounds the amount spent to the nearest thousand. What amounts do Mia and Jon each round to?**

MODEL IT

You can use a number line to round $117,290 to the nearest ten thousand.

Find the closest ten thousands that are less than 117,290 and greater than 117,290.

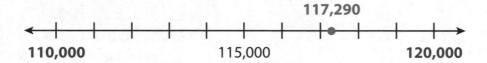

117,290 is between **110,000** and **120,000**.

MODEL IT

You can use place value to round $117,290 to the nearest thousand.

Find the closest thousands that are less than 117,290 and greater than 117,290.

Hundred Thousands	Ten Thousands	Thousands	Hundreds	Tens	Ones
1	1	7	0	0	0
1	1	7	2	9	0
1	1	8	0	0	0

117,290 has **7** thousands, so it is between **117,000** and **118,000**.

There are 10 hundreds in each thousand. Halfway between 0 hundreds and 10 hundreds is 5 hundreds. The number **117,290** has **2** hundreds.

CONNECT IT

Now you will use the problem from the previous page to help you understand how to solve problems that involve rounding multi-digit numbers.

 Look at the first Model It. Which ten thousand is 117,290 closer to: 110,000 or 120,000? ....

 Which ten thousand does 117,290 round to? ....

 To the nearest ten thousand, what amount does Mia round $117,290 to?

....

 Look at the second Model It. Which thousand does 117,290 round to, 117,000 or 118,000? You can compare the number of hundreds in 117,290 to 5 hundreds to help you know whether to round up or down. ....

 To the nearest thousand, what amount does Jon round $117,290 to?

....

 Choose any five-digit number. Write it here. ....

Explain how to round a five-digit number to the nearest ten thousand.

 REFLECT

Look back at your Try It, strategies by classmates, and Model Its. Which models or strategies do you like best for rounding greater numbers? Explain.

....

....

....

Lesson 3 Round Whole Numbers   **39**

APPLY IT

Use what you just learned to solve these problems.

8 Mr. Ruiz's company collects 32,376 water bottles to recycle. Mr. Ruiz rounds this amount to the nearest ten thousand. What number does Mr. Ruiz round the number of water bottles to? Show your work.

Solution

9 Jo's Book Mart sells 468,500 books this year. To the nearest thousand, how many books does the store sell? Show your work.

Solution

10 Round 649,418

to the nearest ten: ....

to the nearest hundred: ....

to the nearest thousand: ....

to the nearest ten thousand: ....

to the nearest hundred thousand: ....

Practice Rounding Whole Numbers

Study the Example showing how to round a multi-digit number. Then solve problems 1–6.

EXAMPLE

Round 651,970 to the nearest thousand.

Hundred Thousands	Ten Thousands	Thousands	Hundreds	Tens	Ones
6	5	1	9	7	0

651,970 has 1 thousand, so it is between 651,000 and 652,000.
There are 9 hundreds in 651,970.
Because 9 hundreds is greater than 5 hundreds, round up.
So, 651,970 rounded to the nearest thousand is 652,000.

1 Look at the Example above.

a. Round 651,970 to the nearest ten thousand. ....

b. Round 651,970 to the nearest hundred thousand. ....

2 Round 45,621 to each place given below.

a. to the nearest ten ....

b. to the nearest hundred ....

c. to the nearest thousand ....

d. to the nearest ten thousand ....

3 Round 452,906 to each place given below.

a. to the nearest hundred thousand ....

b. to the nearest ten thousand ....

c. to the nearest thousand ....

d. to the nearest hundred ....

e. to the nearest ten ....

4 The table below shows driving distances between U.S. cities.
Round each number to the nearest hundred.

	Actual distance (mi)	Rounded distance (mi)
Atlanta, GA to Los Angeles, CA	2,173	
Los Angeles, CA to Seattle, WA	1,135	
Atlanta, GA to Chicago, IL	716	
Chicago, IL to San Francisco, CA	2,131	

5 Look at the table in problem 4. Alex drove a distance between two cities
in the table. He said that he drove about 2,000 miles. Which cities
could Alex have driven between? Show your work.

Solution ....

....

6 Write numbers in the boxes below to show rounding on a number line.
What place value are you rounding to?

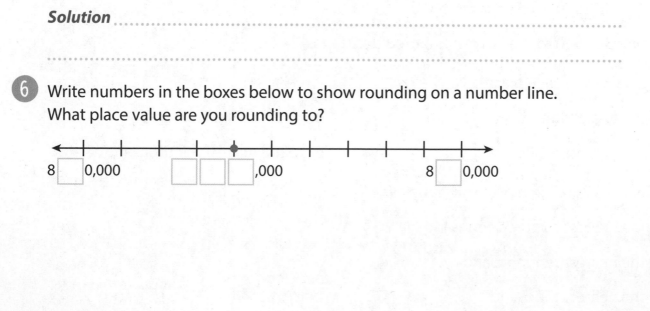

8 ☐ 0,000   ☐ ☐ ☐ ,000   8 ☐ 0,000

Solution ....

Practice Rounding Whole Numbers

Study the Example showing how to round a multi-digit number. Then solve problems 1–6.

EXAMPLE

Round 651,970 to the nearest thousand.

Hundred Thousands	Ten Thousands	Thousands	Hundreds	Tens	Ones
6	5	1	9	7	0

651,970 has 1 thousand, so it is between 651,000 and 652,000.
There are 9 hundreds in 651,970.
Because 9 hundreds is greater than 5 hundreds, round up.
So, 651,970 rounded to the nearest thousand is 652,000.

1. Look at the Example above.

   a. Round 651,970 to the nearest ten thousand. ....

   b. Round 651,970 to the nearest hundred thousand. ....

2. Round 45,621 to each place given below.

   a. to the nearest ten ....   **b.** to the nearest hundred ....

   c. to the nearest thousand ....   **d.** to the nearest ten thousand ....

3. Round 452,906 to each place given below.

   a. to the nearest hundred thousand ....

   b. to the nearest ten thousand ....

   c. to the nearest thousand ....

   d. to the nearest hundred ....

   e. to the nearest ten ....

4 The table below shows driving distances between U.S. cities. Round each number to the nearest hundred.

	Actual distance (mi)	Rounded distance (mi)
Atlanta, GA to Los Angeles, CA	2,173	
Los Angeles, CA to Seattle, WA	1,135	
Atlanta, GA to Chicago, IL	716	
Chicago, IL to San Francisco, CA	2,131	

5 Look at the table in problem 4. Alex drove a distance between two cities in the table. He said that he drove about 2,000 miles. Which cities could Alex have driven between? Show your work.

Solution

6 Write numbers in the boxes below to show rounding on a number line. What place value are you rounding to?

8 ☐ 0,000   ☐ ☐ ☐ ,000   8 ☐ 0,000

Solution

Refine Rounding Whole Numbers

Complete the Example below. Then solve problems 1–9.

EXAMPLE

The tallest building in Martin's city is 1,729 feet tall.
The tallest building in Peggy's city is 1,065 feet tall.
To the nearest hundred feet, what is the height of
each building?

Look at how you could show your work using number lines.

Round each number to the nearest hundred.

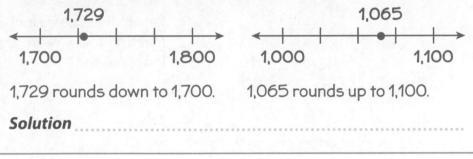

1,729 rounds down to 1,700.   1,065 rounds up to 1,100.

Solution ....

The student used number lines to find which number of hundreds each height is closest to.

PAIR/SHARE
How can you decide which two hundreds a number is between?

APPLY IT

1 Smallville has 12,548 people registered to vote. To the nearest thousand, how many people are registered to vote? Show your work.

How can you use the number of hundreds to round to the nearest thousand?

Solution ....

PAIR/SHARE
How did you decide whether to round up or round down?

2 A company makes wooden golf tees. One year they make 380,285 tees. To the nearest ten thousand, how many tees do they make? Show your work.

Which two ten thousands is 380,285 between?

Solution ....

3 A website streams 264,398 movies to its customers one year. To the nearest ten, how many movies does the website stream?

Ⓐ 264,300

Ⓑ 264,390

Ⓒ 264,400

Ⓓ 265,000

Which two tens is 264,398 between?

Elin chose Ⓒ as the correct answer. Explain how she got her answer.

4 The distances four hot air balloons travel are listed below.

Balloon A: 6,559 kilometers   Balloon B: 6,547 kilometers
Balloon C: 6,545 kilometers   Balloon D: 6,553 kilometers

Leah rounds the distances the balloons travel to the nearest ten. Which distance does NOT round to 6,550 kilometers?

Ⓐ 6,559 kilometers

Ⓑ 6,545 kilometers

Ⓒ 6,547 kilometers

Ⓓ 6,553 kilometers

5 Phoebe's Bait and Tackle sells 102,278 live worms one month. To the nearest thousand, how many worms does Phoebe's Bait and Tackle sell that month?

Ⓐ 100,000

Ⓑ 102,000

Ⓒ 102,300

Ⓓ 103,000

6 Determine whether each original number is rounded to the nearest 100 or to the nearest 1,000 to make the new number.

Original	New	Nearest 100	Nearest 1,000
1,445	1,400	Ⓐ	Ⓑ
12,500	13,000	Ⓒ	Ⓓ
29,607	30,000	Ⓔ	Ⓕ
341,389	341,400	Ⓖ	Ⓗ

7 A is an unknown number. When you round A to the nearest thousand, you get 21,000. When you round A to the nearest hundred, you get 20,500.

Write A in the box that shows its location on the number line.

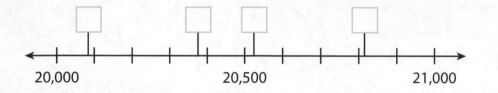

8 Round 5,563 to the nearest thousand, to the nearest hundred, and to the nearest ten. Suppose you can pay a $5,563 bill with a rounded amount. Which place value would you round to? Suppose you win a $5,563 prize and you can choose a rounded amount. Which place value would you round to? Show your work.

9 MATH JOURNAL

Choose a five-digit number that rounds to a six-digit number. Tell what place you round to and why your choice of five-digit number rounds to a six-digit number.

 SELF CHECK Go back to the Unit 1 Opener and see what you can check off.

Add Whole Numbers

Dear Family,

This week your child is learning to add whole numbers using the standard algorithm.

One way your child is adding is by using place value in an addition problem such as 6,859 + 2,703.

In this problem, you can use place value to add. Add ones to ones, tens to tens, hundreds to hundreds, and thousands to thousands.

$$
\begin{array}{r}
6,859 \\
+\ 2,703 \\
\hline
12 \\
50 \\
1,500 \\
8,000 \\
\hline
9,562
\end{array}
$$

Your child is also learning to use the standard algorithm for addition to add and to show **regrouping** above an addition problem. An **algorithm** is a set of steps used to solve a problem.

$$
\begin{array}{r}
^1\ \ ^1 \\
6,859 \\
+\ 2,703 \\
\hline
9,562
\end{array}
$$

Invite your child to share what he or she knows about adding whole numbers by doing the following activity together.

ACTIVITY ADD WHOLE NUMBERS

Do this activity with your child to add whole numbers.

- Ask your child to come up with a four-digit number that is less than 5,000. This will be the "special" number.

  Example: Your child picks 3,854.

- Have your child ask a family member for a four-digit number less than 5,000.

  Example: The family member picks 2,093.

- Have your child add the two numbers.

  Example:

$$\begin{array}{r} \overset{1}{3,854} \\ + \ 2,093 \\ \hline 5,947 \end{array}$$

- Then have your child round each number to the nearest thousand to check that his or her sum is reasonable.

  Example: 3,854 rounds to 4,000.
  2,093 rounds to 2,000.
  4,000 + 2,000 = 6,000
  Because 6,000 is close to 5,947, your child's sum is reasonable.

- Repeat the activity. Use the "special" number and have a family member choose another four-digit number that is less than 5,000.

- Look for real-life opportunities to add numbers with your child.

Prepare for Adding Whole Numbers

1   Think about what you know about algorithms. Fill in each box. Use words, numbers, and pictures. Show as many ideas as you can.

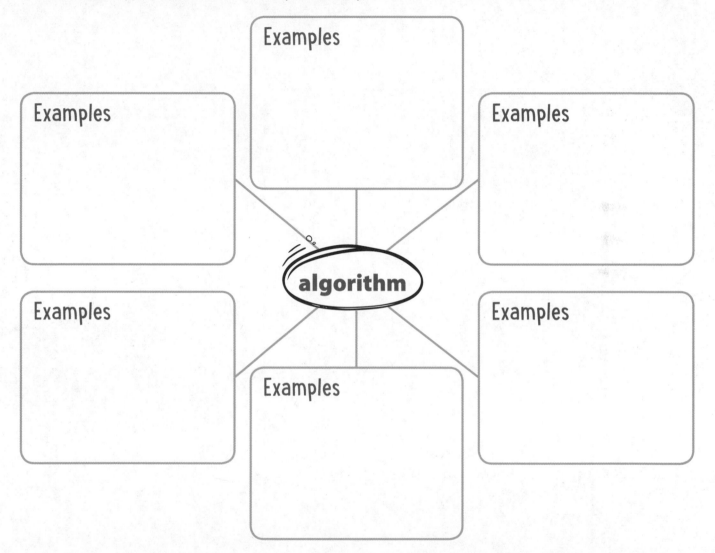

Examples

Examples

Examples

algorithm

Examples

Examples

Examples

2   Describe the steps of an algorithm you can use to add 4,562 and 3,679.

3 Solve the problem. Show your work.

Alfonso earns 1,075 points in a video game, and Ana earns 892 points in the same video game. How many points do Alfonso and Ana earn in all?

Solution ....

4 Check your answer. Show your work.

Develop Using Strategies to Add

Read and try to solve the problem below.

> At a fair, 4,657 ride tickets are sold on Saturday
> and 3,804 tickets are sold on Sunday.
> How many tickets are sold in all during
> those two days? Use any strategy to add.

TRY IT

Math Toolkit
- base-ten blocks
- hundred thousands
  place-value charts
- grid paper

DISCUSS IT

Ask your partner: Why did
you choose that strategy?

Tell your partner: The
strategy I used to find the
answer was . . .

Explore different ways to understand adding four-digit numbers.

> At a fair, 4,657 ride tickets are sold on Saturday and
> 3,804 tickets are sold on Sunday. How many tickets are
> sold in all during those two days? Use any strategy to add.

MODEL IT

**You can use place value to add. Add ones to ones, tens to tens,
hundreds to hundreds, and then thousands to thousands.**

```
   4,657
 + 3,804
```
$\quad\quad$ 11 $\longrightarrow$ 7 ones + 4 ones = 11 ones, or 1 ten + 1 one
$\quad\quad$ 50 $\longrightarrow$ 5 tens + 0 tens = 5 tens
$\quad$ 1,400 $\longrightarrow$ 6 hundreds + 8 hundreds = 14 hundreds, or 1 thousand + 4 hundreds
$+$ 7,000 $\longrightarrow$ 4 thousands + 3 thousands = 7 thousands
$\quad$ 8,461

MODEL IT

You can record the sums by showing regrouping above the problem.

You **regroup** when the sum of the digits in a place is 10 or greater.

```
    ¹
   4,657
 + 3,804
```
$\quad\quad$ 1 $\longrightarrow$ **7 ones + 4 ones** = 11 ones, or **1 ten + 1 one**

```
    ¹
   4,657
 + 3,804
```
$\quad\quad$ 61 $\longrightarrow$ **1 ten + 5 tens + 0 tens = 6 tens**

```
   ¹ ¹
   4,657
 + 3,804
```
$\quad$ 461 $\longrightarrow$ **6 hundreds + 8 hundreds** = 14 hundreds, or **1 thousand + 4 hundreds**

```
   ¹ ¹
   4,657
 + 3,804
```
$\quad$ 8,461 $\longrightarrow$ **1 thousand + 4 thousands + 3 thousands = 8 thousands**

CONNECT IT

Now you will use the problem from the previous page to help you understand how to add four-digit numbers.

$$\begin{array}{r} {\scriptstyle 1\ \ 1}\\ 4,657 \\ +\ 3,804 \\ \hline 8,461 \end{array}$$

1 Here is the second **Model It** showing all the steps at once using the addition algorithm.

The sum of the ones is 11. Where do you see 11 in the addition above?

2 The sum of the hundreds is 1,400. Where do you see 1,400?

3 Why is there a 1 above the tens place and above the thousands place?

4 Explain how to add two four-digit numbers if you need to regroup ones and hundreds.

5 REFLECT

Look back at your **Try It**, strategies by classmates, **Model Its**, and **Connect It** problem 1. Which models or strategies do you like best for adding four-digit numbers? Explain.

....

....

....

....

APPLY IT

Use what you just learned to solve these problems.

6 A video game company sells 5,680 copies of its new game on the first day and 3,235 copies on the second day. In those two days, how many copies of the game does the company sell? Show your work.

Solution ....

7 Find the sum of 12,713 and 9,604. Show your work.

Solution ....

8 What is the missing digit that makes the sum correct?

```
   8,2 4 5
+ 1,5 6 9
  9,□1 4
```

Ⓐ 6

Ⓑ 7

Ⓒ 8

Ⓓ 9

Practice Using Strategies to Add

**Study the Example showing two ways to add multi-digit numbers.
Then solve problems 1–6.**

EXAMPLE

On Friday, 1,150 people attend the school play. On Saturday, 2,987 people attend the play. How many people attend the play on those two days?

Use a place-value strategy.   Use the standard algorithm.

$$
\begin{array}{r}
1{,}150 \\
+\,2{,}987 \\
\hline
\end{array}
$$

7 ⟶ 0 ones + 7 ones = 7 ones

130 ⟶ 5 tens + 8 tens = 13 tens or 1 hundred + 3 tens

1,000 ⟶ 1 hundred + 9 hundreds = 10 hundreds or 1 thousand

+ 3,000 ⟶ 1 thousand + 2 thousands = 3 thousands

4,137

$$
\begin{array}{r}
\overset{1\ 1}{1{,}150} \\
+\,2{,}987 \\
\hline
4{,}137
\end{array}
$$

4,137 people attend the play.

---

1 Show two ways to add 7,315 and 1,890.

2 Find the sum.

$$
\begin{array}{r}
1{,}025 \\
+\,4{,}589 \\
\hline
\end{array}
$$

3 Last summer Mia's family drove 1,024 miles from Grand Canyon National Park to Mount Rushmore National Memorial. Then they drove 1,389 miles from Mount Rushmore to Yosemite National Park. How many miles did they drive in all? Show your work.

Solution

4 Use the tiles below to find a number that makes each addition problem true. You may use a tile more than once.

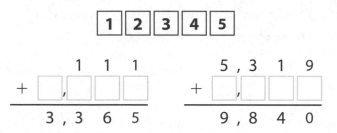

5 On Monday, Calvin runs 4,250 meters. On Tuesday, he runs 4,980 meters. How many meters does he run on Monday and Tuesday? Show your work.

Solution

6 Sam adds 6,152 and 379 and gets a sum of 9,942. Explain why Sam's addition is incorrect and find the correct sum of 6,152 + 379.

Develop Using the Standard Algorithm to Add Greater Numbers

Read and try to solve the problem below.

> **Find the sum of 57,541 and 23,098. Use the standard algorithm for addition. Then estimate to check whether your answer is reasonable, or makes sense.**

TRY IT

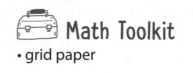 **Math Toolkit**
• grid paper

DISCUSS IT

Ask your partner: Do you agree with me? Why or why not?

Tell your partner: I disagree with this part because . . .

Explore how to use the addition algorithm to add and how to check your answer.

> **Find the sum of 57,541 and 23,098. Use the standard algorithm for addition. Then estimate to check whether your answer is reasonable, or makes sense.**

MODEL IT

You can use the addition algorithm to add.

Line up the numbers. Add from right to left.

$$\begin{array}{r} \overset{1}{5}7,541 \\ + 23,098 \\ \hline 39 \end{array}$$

Add the **ones**.

Add the **tens**.

Regroup if you need to.

Write the regrouped **1 hundred** above.

Then add hundreds, thousands, and ten thousands.

MODEL IT

You can estimate the sum to check your answer for reasonableness.

Round each number to the same place. Then add.

To the nearest thousand, 57,541 rounds to 58,000.

To the nearest thousand, 23,098 rounds to 23,000.

58,000 + 23,000 = 81,000

CONNECT IT

Now you will use the problem from the previous page to understand how to use the addition algorithm and how to check your answer.

$$\begin{array}{r} \square \quad {}^{1} \\ 5\ 7,5\ 4\ 1 \\ +\ 2\ 3,0\ 9\ 8 \\ \hline \square\square,\square\ 3\ 9 \end{array}$$

1 Finish solving the problem in the first **Model It**. Write your answers in the boxes.

2 Why do you need to regroup a second time?

3 Look at the second **Model It**. Is the estimate of 81,000 close to the sum

you wrote in problem 1? .... Is your answer reasonable? ....

4 In the second **Model It**, each number is rounded to the nearest thousand. Could you estimate in different ways? For example, what are the benefits and drawbacks of rounding to the nearest ten instead of to the nearest thousand?

 REFLECT

Look back at your **Try It**, think about your discussion with classmates, and look back at the first **Model It** and **Connect It** problem 1. Describe what you like or do not like about using the standard algorithm compared to other strategies you have seen in this lesson or used in the past to solve addition problems.

....

....

....

....

Lesson 4 Add Whole Numbers   **61**

APPLY IT

Use what you just learned to solve these problems.

6 Xavier is playing a video game. His score is 21,405 points in the first level and 17,865 points in the second level. What is Xavier's total score for both levels? Estimate to check that your answer is reasonable. Show your work.

Solution

7 Find the sum of the three numbers. Show your work.

2,591   43,218   75,043

Solution

8 What is the sum of 50,603 and 46,925?

Ⓐ 97,538

Ⓑ 97,528

Ⓒ 96,628

Ⓓ 96,528

Practice Using the Standard Algorithm to Add Greater Numbers

Study the Example showing how to use the addition algorithm to add five-digit numbers. Then solve problems 1–5.

EXAMPLE

Use the addition algorithm to find the sum of 72,160 and 44,983. Then estimate to check whether your answer is reasonable.

$$\begin{array}{r} {}^{1}{}^{1} \\ 72{,}160 \\ +\ 44{,}983 \\ \hline 117{,}143 \end{array}$$

Step 1: Line up the numbers by place value.
Step 2: Add the ones digits. Regroup if needed.
Step 3: Repeat **Step 2** for all other place values.

Estimate to check: 72,000 + 45,000 = 117,000
117,000 is close to 117,143.
The answer is reasonable.

The sum of 72,160 and 44,983 is 117,143.

1 Add.

$$\begin{array}{r} 36{,}159 \\ +\ 42{,}903 \\ \hline \end{array}$$

2 Find the sum.

$$\begin{array}{r} 65{,}296 \\ +\ 8{,}172 \\ \hline \end{array}$$

3. Find the sum. Then estimate to check that your answer is reasonable.
Show your work.

$$
\begin{array}{r}
70{,}234 \\
11{,}592 \\
+\ 16{,}890 \\
\end{array}
$$

4. Use the tiles below to find a number that makes each addition problem true.
You may use a tile more than once.

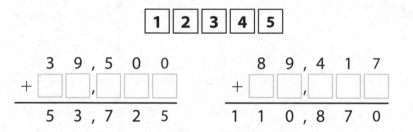

5. There is a mistake in the addition shown. Explain how the mistake was made.
Then find the correct sum.

$$
\begin{array}{r}
\overset{1\ 1}{22{,}365} \\
+\ 53{,}908 \\
\hline
75{,}373 \\
\end{array}
$$

Refine Adding Whole Numbers

Complete the Example below. Then solve problems 1–9.

EXAMPLE

Find the sum of 130,985 and 277,409.

Look at how you could show your work using the addition algorithm.

$$
\begin{array}{r}
\overset{1\ \ 1\ \ \ 1}{277{,}409} \\
+\ 130{,}985 \\
\hline
408{,}394
\end{array}
$$

Solution ....

The student regrouped three times to solve the problem.

PAIR/SHARE
How can you check that your answer is reasonable?

APPLY IT

1. The population of Turtle Valley is 407,989. The population of Art Creek is 86,966. What is the total population of the two cities? Show your work.

How can you line up the numbers to solve this problem?

PAIR/SHARE
To estimate the sum, what place can you round to?

Solution ....

2 Find the sum of the three numbers below.

13,728   15,419   12,399

Show your work.

Do you need to regroup?

Solution ....

PAIR/SHARE
In what order did you add the numbers?

3 Which equation can help you check the reasonableness of the answer to 361,788 + 65,235?

Ⓐ 30,000 + 70,000

Ⓑ 36,000 + 65,000

Ⓒ 360,000 + 70,000

Ⓓ 360,000 + 700,000

Tyrone chose Ⓓ as the correct answer. How did he get that answer?

You can round each number to estimate a sum.

PAIR/SHARE
Does Tyrone's answer make sense?

4 Which equation can help you estimate the sum of 59,106 and 22,477?

   Ⓐ 6,000 + 2,000 = 8,000

   Ⓑ 60,000 + 2,000 = 62,000

   Ⓒ 60,000 + 20,000 = 80,000

   Ⓓ 100,000 + 20,000 = 120,000

5 What is the missing digit that makes the problem correct?

```
    3 2 9,0 4 5
    1 □ 7,6 2 0
  +   7 4,9 1 6
  ─────────────
    5 6 1,5 8 1
```

   Ⓐ 4

   Ⓑ 5

   Ⓒ 6

   Ⓓ 7

6 Select all the correct addition equations.

   Ⓐ 3,538 + 5,491 = 9,029

   Ⓑ 411,603 + 17,850 = 429,553

   Ⓒ 6,771 + 20,293 = 27,064

   Ⓓ 9,729 + 1,385 = 1,114

   Ⓔ 43,719 + 27,185 = 70,904

7 Parkwood School has 1,165 students in seventh grade and 1,027 students in eighth grade. How many students are in both grades?

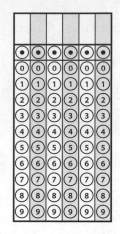

8 Find the sum of 9,618 and 132,501. Then estimate to check that your answer is reasonable. Show your work.

Solution ....

9 MATH JOURNAL

Write an addition problem that has no regrouping. Each addend must have at least four digits. Explain why you do not need to regroup.

☑ SELF CHECK Go back to the Unit 1 Opener and see what you can check off.

Subtract Whole Numbers

Dear Family,

This week your child is learning to subtract whole numbers using the standard algorithm.

One way your child is learning to subtract is to use place value in a subtraction problem such as 6,001 − 3,528.

In this problem, you need to regroup in order to subtract. A place-value chart can show the regrouping.

Thousands	Hundreds	Tens	Ones
6	0	0	1

Thousands	Hundreds	Tens	Ones	
5	10	0	1	6 thousands = 5 thousands + 10 hundreds
5	9	10	1	10 hundreds = 9 hundreds + 10 tens
5	9	9	10 + 1 = 11	10 tens = 9 tens + 10 ones

Now you can subtract.

	Thousands	Hundreds	Tens	Ones
	5	9	9	11
−	3	5	2	8
	2	4	7	3

Instead of using a place-value chart, your child is also learning to use the standard algorithm for subtraction to show regrouping above a subtraction problem.

$$
\begin{array}{r}
{\scriptstyle 5\ \ 9\ \ 9} \\
{\scriptstyle 5\ 10\ 10\ 11} \\
6,001 \\
-\ 3,528 \\
\hline
2,473
\end{array}
$$

Invite your child to share what he or she knows about subtracting whole numbers by doing the following activity together.

ACTIVITY SUBTRACTING WHOLE NUMBERS

Do this activity with your child to subtract whole numbers.

- Ask your child to come up with a four-digit number that is greater than 5,000. This will be the "special" number.

    Example: Your child picks 7,864.

- Have your child ask a family member for a four-digit number less than 5,000.

    Example: The family member picks 3,219.

- Have your child subtract the two numbers.

    Example:

$$\begin{array}{r} \overset{5\,14}{7,8\cancel{6}\cancel{4}} \\ -\ 3,219 \\ \hline 4,645 \end{array}$$

- Then have your child round each number to the nearest thousand to check that his or her difference is reasonable.

    Example: 7,864 rounds to 8,000, and 3,219 rounds to 3,000.
    $8,000 - 3,000 = 5,000$
    Since 5,000 is close to 4,645, your child's difference is reasonable.

- Finally, have your child use addition to check that his or her answer is correct.

    Example: $4,645 + 3,219 = 7,864$; your child's answer is correct!

- Repeat the activity. Use the "special" number and have a family member choose another four-digit number that is less than 5,000.

- Look for real-life opportunities to subtract numbers with your child.

Explore Subtracting Whole Numbers

In this lesson, you will use place-value understanding, basic facts, and an algorithm to subtract numbers. Use what you know to try to solve the problem below.

> **In a display for a flower show, there are 2,425 carnations and 625 roses. How many more carnations than roses are in the display?**

TRY IT

Math Toolkit
• base-ten blocks
• number lines
• hundred thousands place-value charts
• grid paper

DISCUSS IT

Ask your partner: Do you agree with me? Why or why not?

Tell your partner: I agree with you about . . . because . . .

CONNECT IT

 LOOK BACK

How can you find how many more carnations than roses are in the display?

 LOOK AHEAD

Sometimes you need to regroup when you subtract. To find 1,734 − 582, you can subtract 2 ones from 4 ones, but you cannot subtract 8 tens from 3 tens.

a. A place-value chart can help you regroup so you have enough tens to subtract. Look at the chart at the right to fill in the blanks:

Thousands	Hundreds	Tens	Ones
1	⑦	3	4
1	⑥	10 + 3	4

7 hundreds is regrouped as .... hundreds and .... tens.

b. Complete the chart below to find 1,734 − 582.

	Thousands	Hundreds	Tens	Ones
	1	6	13	4
−				

c. Fill in the boxes below to use the standard algorithm for subtraction.

$$\begin{array}{r} {}^{6}{}^{13} \\ 1,\,\cancel{7}\,\cancel{3}\,4 \\ -5\,8\,2 \\ \hline \square,\square\square\square \end{array}$$

 REFLECT

Do you always need to regroup when you subtract? How do you know?

....

....

Prepare for Subtracting Whole Numbers

1 Think about what you know about regrouping. Fill in each box. Use words, numbers, and pictures. Show as many ideas as you can.

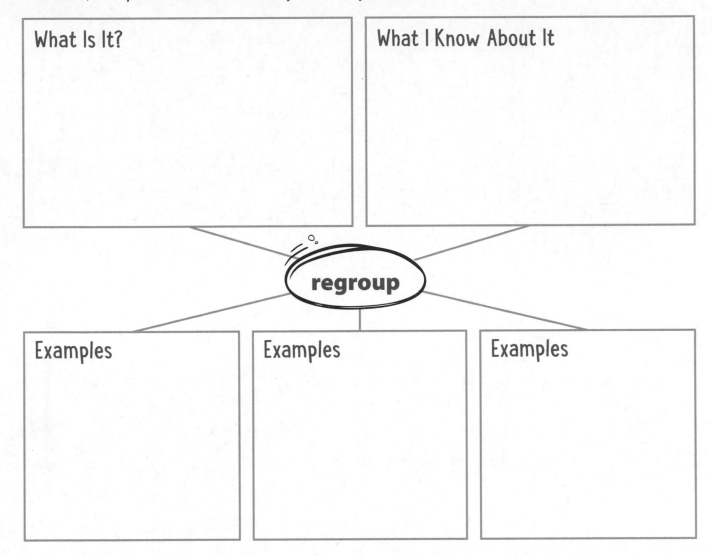

What Is It?

What I Know About It

regroup

Examples

Examples

Examples

2 Do you need to regroup to subtract 881 from 4,986? How do you know?

3 Solve the problem. Show your work.

There are 3,284 cookies and 924 muffins in a bakery. How many more cookies than muffins are in the bakery?

Solution ....

4 Check your answer. Show your work.

Develop Using Strategies to Subtract

Read and try to solve the problem below.

Mr. Diaz travels 4,002 miles for work in April. He travels 2,153 miles in May. How many more miles does Mr. Diaz travel in April than in May? Use any strategy to subtract.

TRY IT

Math Toolkit
- base-ten blocks
- number lines
- hundred thousands place-value charts
- grid paper

DISCUSS IT

Ask your partner: Why did you choose that strategy?

Tell your partner: The strategy I used to find the answer was . . .

Explore one way to understand subtracting four-digit numbers.

> Mr. Diaz travels 4,002 miles for work in April. He travels 2,153 miles in May. How many more miles does Mr. Diaz travel in April than in May? Use any strategy to subtract.

MODEL IT

You can use place value to find 4,002 − 2,153.

You cannot subtract 3 from 2. So, you need to regroup.

Write 4,002 in a place-value chart.

There are zeros in the tens and hundreds places. So you cannot regroup the tens or hundreds yet.

Start by regrouping the thousands place.

Keep regrouping until you can subtract.

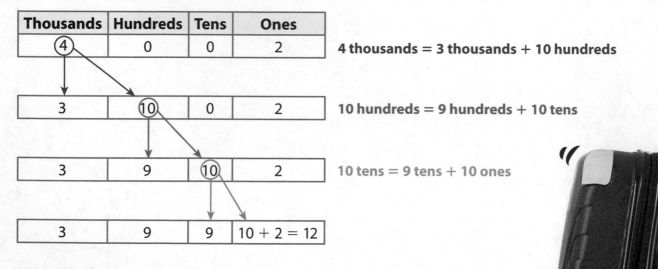

Thousands	Hundreds	Tens	Ones
④	0	0	2

4 thousands = 3 thousands + 10 hundreds

Thousands	Hundreds	Tens	Ones
3	⑩	0	2

10 hundreds = 9 hundreds + 10 tens

Thousands	Hundreds	Tens	Ones
3	9	⑩	2

10 tens = 9 tens + 10 ones

Thousands	Hundreds	Tens	Ones
3	9	9	10 + 2 = 12

Now you can subtract.

	Thousands	Hundreds	Tens	Ones
	3	9	9	12
−	2	1	5	3
	1	8	4	9

CONNECT IT

Now you will use the problem from the previous page to help you understand how to use the standard algorithm for subtraction to show regrouping.

$$4{,}002 \qquad \overset{3\ \ 10}{\cancel{4}{,}\cancel{0}02} \qquad \overset{\ \ \ 9}{\underset{}{\overset{3\ \cancel{10}10}{\cancel{4}{,}\cancel{0}\cancel{0}2}}} \qquad \overset{\ \ 9\ 9}{\overset{3\ \cancel{10}\cancel{10}12}{\cancel{4}{,}\cancel{0}\cancel{0}\cancel{2}}}$$
$$-\ 2{,}153 \qquad -\ 2{,}153 \qquad -\ 2{,}153 \qquad \underline{-\ 2{,}153}$$
$$\phantom{-\ 2{,}153} \qquad \phantom{-\ 2{,}153} \qquad \phantom{-\ 2{,}153} \qquad 1{,}849$$

1 How is regrouping thousands shown in the problem above?

2 Why is the **10** crossed out in the hundreds column?

3 Explain the regrouping shown in the tens column.

4 Why are **12 ones** shown in the ones column?

5 Explain how to subtract two four-digit numbers if you need to regroup in all places.

6 **REFLECT**

Look back at your **Try It**, strategies by classmates, **Model It**, and the subtraction problem in **Connect It** on this page. Which models or strategies do you like best for subtracting four-digit numbers? Explain.

....

....

....

Lesson 5 Subtract Whole Numbers **77**

APPLY IT

Use what you just learned to solve these problems.

7 Find the difference 8,091 − 3,467. Show your work.

Solution ....

8 There are 11,408 fans at the hockey game and 9,617 fans at the basketball game. How many more fans are at the hockey game than are at the basketball game? Show your work.

Solution ....

9 What is the missing digit that makes the subtraction problem correct?

```
  7 0, 0 9 6
−    2, □ 1 5
───────────
  6 7, 3 8 1
```

Ⓐ 3

Ⓑ 6

Ⓒ 7

Ⓓ 8

Practice Using Strategies to Subtract

Study the Example showing two ways to subtract multi-digit numbers.
Then solve problems 1–6.

EXAMPLE

Pete takes 7,192 steps in one day. Joe takes 5,210 steps.
How many more steps does Pete take than Joe?

Use a place-value chart.

First, regroup.

Thousands	Hundreds	Tens	Ones
⑦	1	9	2

6	10 + 1 = 11	9	2

Then subtract.

	Thousands	Hundreds	Tens	Ones
	6	11	9	2
−	5	2	1	0
	1	9	8	2

Pete takes 1,982 more steps than Joe.

Use the standard algorithm.

$$
\begin{array}{r}
{\scriptstyle 6\,11} \\
\cancel{7},\cancel{1}92 \\
-\ 5{,}210 \\
\hline
1{,}982
\end{array}
$$

1 Subtract.

3,008
− 1,265

2 Find the difference.

16,407
− 9,524

3 The table shows the number of seats in two basketball arenas. How many more seats are in Arthur Arena than are in Griffin Fieldhouse? Show your work.

Number of Seats	
Griffin Fieldhouse	22,826
Arthur Arena	44,750

Solution ....

4 A city has a population of 29,000 people. Ten years ago, the population was 9,500 people. How many more people does the city have now? Show your work.

Solution ....

5 Use the tiles below to find a number that makes each subtraction problem true. You may use a tile more than once.

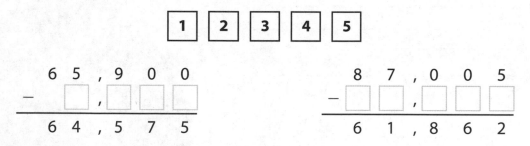

$$\begin{array}{r} 6\ 5\ ,\ 9\ 0\ 0 \\ -\ \square\ ,\ \square\ \square\ \square \\ \hline 6\ 4\ ,\ 5\ 7\ 5 \end{array} \qquad \begin{array}{r} 8\ 7\ ,\ 0\ 0\ 5 \\ -\ \square\ \square\ ,\ \square\ \square\ \square \\ \hline 6\ 1\ ,\ 8\ 6\ 2 \end{array}$$

6 Peter listed his car for sale at $21,550. He dropped the sale price by $1,650 after a week. Before he sold the car, he dropped the sale price again. This time he dropped the price by $1,955. What was the final sale price of the car? Show your work.

Solution ....

Develop Using the Standard Algorithm to Subtract Greater Numbers

Read and try to solve the problem below.

> **Find the difference 68,408 – 41,923. Use the standard algorithm to subtract. Then use addition to check whether your answer is correct.**

TRY IT

 **Math Toolkit**
• grid paper

DISCUSS IT

Ask your partner: Can you explain that again?

Tell your partner: I started by . . .

Explore how to use the subtraction algorithm to subtract and how to check your answer.

> **Find the difference 68,408 – 41,923. Use the standard algorithm to subtract. Then use addition to check whether your answer is correct.**

MODEL IT

You can use the standard algorithm for subtraction to subtract.

Line up the numbers. Subtract from right to left.

Subtract the **ones**.

Regroup if you need to.

There are not enough **tens** to subtract.

Write the regrouped **4 hundreds** as **3 hundreds** and **10 tens** above the problem.

Now subtract the tens.

You will finish solving the problem on the next page.

$$
\begin{array}{r}
{\scriptstyle 3\ 10} \\
6\ 8,\cancel{4}\,\cancel{0}\ 8 \\
-\ 4\ 1,9\ 2\ 3 \\
\hline
\square\square,\square\ 8\ 5
\end{array}
$$

MODEL IT

You can use the relationship between addition and subtraction to check your answer.

Add the difference to the number being subtracted. Check whether the sum is the same as the initial number in the subtraction problem.

You will finish the problem on the next page.

$$
\begin{array}{r}
\square\square,\square\ 8\ 5 \\
+\ 4\ 1,9\ 2\ 3 \\
\hline
\end{array}
$$

CONNECT IT

Now you will use the problem from the previous page to understand how to use the subtraction algorithm and how to use addition to check your answer.

1 Finish solving the problem by subtracting the hundreds, thousands, and ten thousands. Write your answers in the boxes shown.

2 Why did you need to regroup a second time?

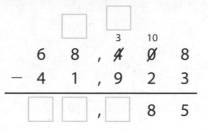

3 Look at the second **Model It**. Write your answer from problem 1 in the boxes shown for the top number. Add to finish solving the problem. Regroup when you need to.

4 Is your sum in problem 3 the same as the number you subtracted from in problem 1? .... Is your answer to problem 1 correct? ....

5 How is using addition to check an answer to a subtraction problem different than using estimation?

6 REFLECT

Look back at your **Try It**, think about your discussion with classmates, and look back at the first **Model It** and **Connect It** problem 1. Describe what you like or do not like about using the standard algorithm compared to other strategies you have seen in this lesson or used in the past to solve subtraction problems.

....

....

....

APPLY IT

Use what you just learned to solve these problems.

7 Find the difference 13,390 – 11,567. Show your work.

Solution ....

8 What is the difference of 129,027 and 98,918?

Ⓐ 20,109

Ⓑ 30,102

Ⓒ 30,109

Ⓓ 227,945

9 Find the difference 80,508 – 31,632. Use addition or estimation to check your answer. Show your work.

Solution ....

Practice Subtracting Whole Numbers

Study the Example showing how to use the subtraction algorithm to subtract five-digit numbers. Then solve problems 1–5.

EXAMPLE

Use the subtraction algorithm to find the difference 93,600 − 51,429.
Then estimate to check whether your answer is reasonable.

$$
\begin{array}{r}
\overset{9}{}\,\overset{5\ 10\ 10}{}\\
93,\cancel{600}\\
-\ 51,429\\
\hline
42,171
\end{array}
$$

Step 1: Line up the numbers by place value.

Step 2: Subtract the ones digits. Regroup if needed.

Step 3: Repeat **Step 2** for all other place values.

Estimate to check: Round 93,600 to 94,000.
                     Round 51,429 to 51,000.

$$
\begin{array}{r}
94,000\\
-\ 51,000\\
\hline
43,000
\end{array}
$$

43,000 is close to 42,171.
The answer is reasonable.

The difference of 93,600 and 51,429 is 42,171.

1 Subtract.

$$
\begin{array}{r}
58,904\\
-\ 31,782\\
\hline
\end{array}
$$

2 Find the difference.

$$
\begin{array}{r}
75,099\\
-\ 28,315\\
\hline
\end{array}
$$

3 Find the difference 88,003 – 17,516. Then use addition to check your answer. Show your work.

4 Use the tiles below to find a number that makes each subtraction problem true. Use a digit on each tile only once.

$$\boxed{0}\ \boxed{1}\ \boxed{2}\ \boxed{3}\ \boxed{4}\ \boxed{5}\ \boxed{6}\ \boxed{7}\ \boxed{8}\ \boxed{9}$$

```
  □ □ , 0  0  0              □ 5  2 , 6  8  1
-   4 2 , □ □ □          -    □ 4 , □  □  □
  2 6 , 4  5  3            1 1 7 , 8  6  1
```

5 There is a mistake in the subtraction shown. Explain how the mistake was made. Then find the correct difference.

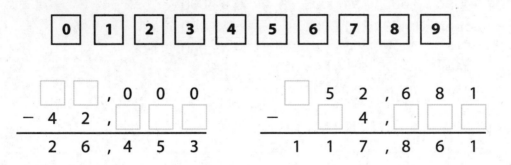

```
   3 13    1 10
   4̸3̸8,6̸2̸0̸
 − 3 5 9,4 1 9
     8 1,2 0 1
```

Refine Subtracting Whole Numbers

Complete the Example below. Then solve problems 1–9.

EXAMPLE

Last year, a museum had 224,313 visitors. This year, the museum had 300,506 visitors. How many more visitors did the museum have this year than last year?

Look at how you could show your work using the standard algorithm for subtraction.

$$\begin{array}{r} \overset{9}{\cancel{3}}\overset{2\;10\;10}{\cancel{0}\cancel{0}}\overset{4\;10}{\cancel{5}}\cancel{0}6 \\ -\;224{,}313 \\ \hline 76{,}193 \end{array}$$

Solution ....

The student regrouped in each place except for the ones place.

PAIR/SHARE
How can you check that your answer is reasonable?

APPLY IT

1 What is the difference of 484,392 and 53,674? Show your work.

How can you line up the numbers to solve this problem?

PAIR/SHARE
In which place values did you regroup?

Solution ....

2 Find the difference 840,000 – 671,600. Show your work.

Which place value do you need to regroup first?

Solution ....

3 Antonio tracks the number of steps he takes each day. He takes 158,516 steps in the month of July. He takes 136,720 steps in the month of August. How many more steps does he take in July than in August?

Ⓐ 21,786

Ⓑ 21,796

Ⓒ 22,216

Ⓓ 22,796

Jamie chose Ⓓ as the correct answer. How did she get that answer?

Do you need to regroup to solve this problem?

PAIR/SHARE
How can you check that your answer is correct?

PAIR/SHARE
How can you check your answer?

4 Which equation can help you estimate the difference of 63,412 and 31,500?

Ⓐ 6,300 − 3,200 = 3,100

Ⓑ 60,000 − 3,000 = 57,000

Ⓒ 60,000 − 40,000 = 20,000

Ⓓ 63,000 − 32,000 = 31,000

5 Prince Edward Island in Canada is made up of three counties: Kings, Prince, and Queens. There were 17,990 people in Kings County and 44,348 people in Prince County one year. The total number of people on Prince Edward Island that year was 140,204. How many people were in Queens County?

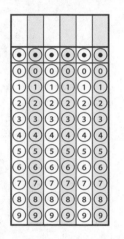

6 Tell whether each equation is *True* or *False*.

	True	False
8,902 − 3,407 = 5,405	Ⓐ	Ⓑ
16,234 − 5,235 = 9,999	Ⓒ	Ⓓ
97,000 − 65,881 = 31,119	Ⓔ	Ⓕ
420,508 − 130,274 = 290,234	Ⓖ	Ⓗ

7 Find 806,289 − 784,976. Then estimate or use addition to check your answer. Show your work.

Solution ....

8 A school raised $13,809 during its fall fundraiser and $20,786 during its winter fundraiser. The total fundraising goal for the school year is $50,000. How much more money does the school need to raise during the spring fundraiser to reach its goal? Show your work.

The school needs to raise .... during the spring fundraiser.

9 MATH JOURNAL

Write your own subtraction problem in which you need to regroup at least once. Each number in your problem must have at least 4 digits. Solve the problem. Explain how you know how many times you need to regroup.

☑ SELF CHECK Go back to the Unit 1 Opener and see what you can check off.

Self Reflection

In this unit you learned to . . .

Skill	Lesson
Read and write numbers using number names, for example: 495 is *four hundred ninety-five.*	1
Read and write numbers using expanded form, for example: 352 = 300 + 50 + 2.	1
Compare two multi-digit whole numbers, for example: 6,131 > 6,113.	2
Round multi-digit whole numbers, for example: 3,528 rounded to the nearest hundred is 3,500.	3
Add multi-digit whole numbers, for example: 3,966 + 7,550 = 11,516.	4
Subtract multi-digit whole numbers, for example: 25,082 − 11,919 = 13,163.	5

Think about what you learned.

Use words, numbers, and drawings.

1 Two things I learned in math are . . .

2 Something I know well is . . .

3 One thing I could do better is . . .

Work with Whole Numbers

Study an Example Problem and Solution

SMP 1 Make sense of problems and persevere in solving them.

Read this problem about adding whole numbers. Then look at Max's solution to this problem.

Blog Site Visitors

Max posts the number of visitors to his gaming blog.

Max's Video Game Blog Visitors

▶ **January Visitors**
30,000 + 2,000 + 50 + 1

➤ **February Visitors**
28,486

▶ **March Visitors**
thirty thousand eighteen

In his April blog, Max will post hints about a popular new computer game. He sets some goals for the number of visitors he hopes to get in April.

• Get more than the total of two of the months combined.

• Get between 999 and 9,999 more visitors than the two combined months.

What is a number of visitors that would meet Max's goal? Tell why your number works.

Read the sample solution on the next page. Then look at the checklist below. Find and mark parts of the solution that match the checklist.

☑ PROBLEM-SOLVING CHECKLIST

☐ Tell what is known.

☐ Tell what the problem is asking.

☐ Show all your work.

☐ Show that the solution works.

a. Circle something that is known.

b. Underline something that you need to find.

c. Draw a box around what you do to solve the problem.

d. Put a checkmark next to the part that shows the solution works.

MAX'S SOLUTION

Hi, I'm Max. Here's how I solved this problem.

- **I need to find the total visitors for two months combined.**
  I know that I can pick any two months. I'll use February and March.

- **Next, I write the number for March in standard form.**
  thirty thousand eighteen = 30,018

- **Then, I add the numbers for February and March.**

$$
\begin{array}{r}
28,486 \\
+\ 30,018 \\
\hline
14 \\
90 \\
400 \\
8,000 \\
50,000 \\
\hline
58,504
\end{array}
$$

- **For April I want between 999 and 9,999 more visitors than 58,504 visitors.**
  I can round 999 to 1,000 and 9,999 to 10,000.

  I had to choose a number that met the goal.

- **5,000 is about halfway between 1,000 and 10,000.**

- **Last, I add to find the goal.**

  Two-month total: $\overset{1}{58,504}$
  Number used to set goal: $+\ 5,000$
  ────────
                            $63,504$

  I added 5,000 to the total for February and March.

- **My goal for April is 63,504 visitors.**
  The number of visitors for both February and March is about 30,000. I want an extra 5,000 visitors.

  $$30,000 + 30,000 + 5,000 = 65,000.$$

  My goal of 63,504 makes sense.

  I rounded to check that my answer makes sense.

Try Another Approach

There are many ways to solve problems. Think about how you might solve the Blog Site Visitors problem in a different way.

Blog Site Visitors

Max posts the number of visitors to his gaming blog.

Max's Video Game Blog Visitors

▶ **January Visitors**
30,000 + 2,000 + 50 + 1

▶ **February Visitors**
28,486

▶ **March Visitors**
thirty thousand eighteen

In his April blog, Max will post hints about a popular new computer game. He sets some goals for the number of visitors he hopes to get in April.

- Get more than the total of two of the months combined.

- Get between 999 and 9,999 more visitors than the two months combined.

What is a number of visitors that would meet Max's goal? Tell why your number works.

PLAN IT

Answer these questions to help you start thinking about a plan.

A. What are all the possible pairs of months? Which pairs are different than the ones used in Max's Solution?

B. What steps will you take to set a goal for April?

SOLVE IT

Find a different solution for the Blog Site Visitors problem. Show all your work on a separate sheet of paper.

You may want to use the Problem-Solving Tips to get started.

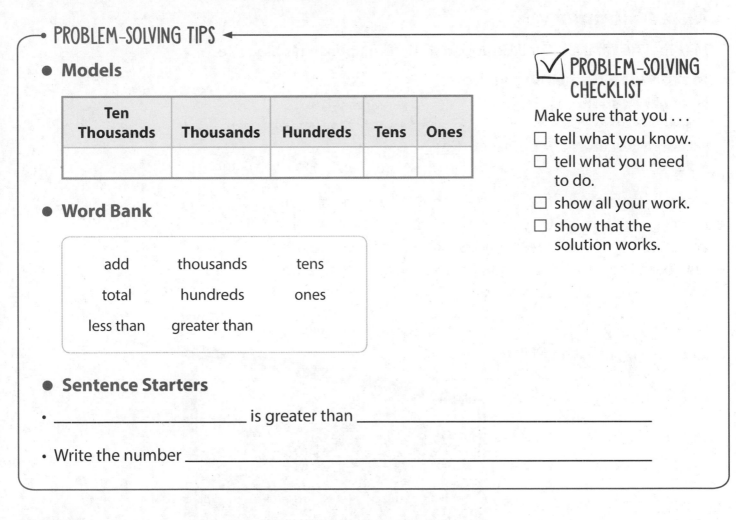

PROBLEM-SOLVING TIPS

● **Models**

Ten Thousands	Thousands	Hundreds	Tens	Ones

● **Word Bank**

add	thousands	tens
total	hundreds	ones
less than	greater than	

● **Sentence Starters**

• _____ is greater than _____

• Write the number _____

✓ **PROBLEM-SOLVING CHECKLIST**

Make sure that you . . .
- ☐ tell what you know.
- ☐ tell what you need to do.
- ☐ show all your work.
- ☐ show that the solution works.

REFLECT

Use Mathematical Practices As you work through the problem, discuss these questions with a partner.

• **Use Structure** How can your understanding of place value help you find a number that is between two given numbers?

• **Use a Model** How can you use a place-value chart to help you think about the numbers?

Discuss Models and Strategies

Read the problem. Write a solution on a separate sheet of paper. Remember, there are lots of ways to solve a problem!

Max's Summary

Max met his goal for April! He added the information to his blog site.

Max's Video Game Blog Visitors

▶ **January Visitors**
30,000 + 2,000 + 50 + 1

▶ **February Visitors**
28,486

▶ **March Visitors**
thirty thousand eighteen

▶ **April Visitors**
50,000 + 9,000 + 600 + 30 + 2

Max wants you to write a summary about the number of visitors to his blog site from January to April. He wants the summary to tell about how many visitors he had. So, he doesn't want to use exact numbers. Then Max needs help setting a goal for the number of visitors he hopes to get in May.

What should your summary say and what number of visitors should Max set for his May goal?

PLAN IT AND SOLVE IT

Find a solution to the Max's Summary problem.

Write a detailed plan and support your answer. Be sure to include:

- a sentence about your estimate that Max could put in his summary.
- a goal for the number of visitors he hopes to get in May.
- how you decided on the goal for May.

You may want to use the Problem-Solving Tips to get started.

PROBLEM-SOLVING TIPS

- **Questions**
  - Will I round to the nearest hundred? Nearest thousand?
  - Will I round the numbers first or add first?

- **Word Bank**

round	close to	less than
estimate	greater than	just under
about	a little more than	

- **Sentence Starters**
  - From January to April there were about _____
  - The goal for the number of visitors in May _____

☑ PROBLEM-SOLVING CHECKLIST

Make sure that you . . .
- ☐ tell what you know.
- ☐ tell what you need to do.
- ☐ show all your work.
- ☐ show that the solution works.

REFLECT

Use Mathematical Practices As you work through the problem, discuss these questions with a partner.

- **Be Precise** Why is an estimate appropriate for the situation in the problem?
- **Make Sense of Problems** What is your first step in solving the problem? Why?

Persevere On Your Own

Read the problems. Write a solution on a separate sheet of paper.

Yearly Blog Visits

Max's blog site now shows the monthly visitors through June. He asks you to write a report about the number of visitors he had during this time. He also wants you to estimate numbers for the whole year.

Max's Video Game Blog Visitors

▶ **January Visitors**
30,000 + 2,000 + 50 + 1

▶ **February Visitors**
28,486

▶ **March Visitors**
thirty thousand eighteen

▶ **April Visitors**
50,000 + 9,000 + 600 + 30 + 2

▶ **May Visitors**
62,187

▶ **June Visitors**
sixty-three thousand nine hundred two

How many visitors should Max expect to get on his blog site in one year?

SOLVE IT

Write a report for Max about visitors to his blog site.

Use rounding and estimation to help you write a report. Include:

• the approximate number of visitors each month and a 6-month total.

• a prediction of the total number of visitors there will be for the whole year.

• an explanation of how you made the one-year prediction.

REFLECT

Use Mathematical Practices After you complete the task, choose one of these questions to discuss with a partner.

• **Look for Structure** What number patterns helped you make a prediction?

• **Make an Argument** Why is your prediction a reasonable estimate?

Blog Topics

Max recorded the number of visitors to his blog site for the rest of the year. This time he listed the major topics that he reported on each month.

Which of Max's major blog topics are the most and least popular?

Month	Number of Visitors	Blog Topics
July	49,467	art reviews, characters
August	65,118	strategies, walkthroughs
September	60,096	story/narrative
October	68,734	strategies
November	70,643	walkthroughs
December	48,942	characters, reviews

SOLVE IT

Help Max decide which blog topics are the most popular and which topics are the least popular.

Compare the actual numbers of monthly visitors to Max's blog site.

- List the months in order, either from the greatest to least number of visitors or from the least to greatest number of visitors.

- Find the difference between the least and greatest number of visitors.

- Tell which topics seem to be the most popular and which seem to be the least popular. Explain your reasoning.

REFLECT

Use Mathematical Practices After you complete the task, choose one of these questions to discuss with a partner.

- **Make an Argument** How did you use the monthly numbers to explain which topic is the most popular?

- **Be Precise** Why did you use actual numbers for this problem and not rounded numbers?

1 How does the value of the 3 in 34,560 compare to the value of the 3 in 345,600?

....

....

....

....

2 A recent survey reported that 713,298 people visited the local science museum last year. How can 713,298 be written in word form?

Ⓐ seventy-one thousand, three hundred twenty-nine

Ⓑ seven hundred thirteen thousand, two hundred ninety-eight

Ⓒ seven hundred thirteen, two ninety-eight

Ⓓ seven hundred thirty thousand, two hundred ninety-eight

3 Decide if > or < completes a true comparison for each pair of numbers.

Choose > or < for each pair of numbers.

	>	<
2,634 ☐ 2,643	Ⓐ	Ⓑ
62,800 ☐ 62,799	Ⓒ	Ⓓ
7,314 ☐ 7,414	Ⓔ	Ⓕ
14,924 ☐ 4,925	Ⓖ	Ⓗ

4 What is the sum of 7,447 and 1,027? Record your answer on the grid. Then fill in the bubbles.

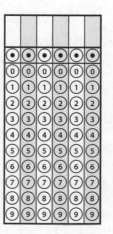

5 Look at the place-value chart below.

Hundred Thousands	Ten Thousands	Thousands	Hundreds	Tens	Ones
	4	2	3	0	4

How can you write the number shown in the place-value chart?

Choose all the correct answers.

Ⓐ forty-two thousand, three hundred four

Ⓑ 40,000 + 2,000 + 300 + 40

Ⓒ four hundred twenty thousand, three hundred four

Ⓓ 42,304

Ⓔ 40,000 + 2,000 + 300 + 4

6 What is the difference? Write your answer in the blank.

235,207 − 67,034 = ...

7 Kangchenjunga is a mountain with a height of 28,169 feet. Lhotse is a mountain with a height of 27,940 feet.

Part A Use >, <, or = to write a comparison of the heights of Kangchenjunga and Lhotse. Which mountain is higher? Show your work.

Kangchenjunga: .... feet

Lhotse: .... feet

Part B To the nearest thousand feet, how tall is each mountain? Show your work.

Kangchenjunga: .... feet

Lhotse: .... feet

Performance Task

Answer the questions and show all your work on separate paper.

The students at Water Street Elementary School have been given a "Half-Million Minute Reading Challenge." Students record the number of minutes that they read each day, and their teachers find the total for each grade. The table below shows the number of minutes students read in the first four months of the challenge.

Checklist

Did you . . .
☐ show the original data and all calculations?
☐ explain how you made your estimate?
☐ write a complete letter?

	First Grade	Second Grade	Third Grade	Fourth Grade	Fifth Grade
Number of Minutes	18,050	30,451	55,870	80,689	67,270

The principal of Water Street Elementary School wants a report on the school's progress. She wants to know the total for each grade to the nearest thousand and about how close the school is to reaching the goal of 500,000 minutes. Write a letter to the principal describing how close students are to the goal and estimating how much more time they need to reach the goal. In the letter, you should show your work and explain your reasoning.

REFLECT

Use Mathematical Practices After you complete the task, choose one of the following questions to answer.

- **Persevere** Which information given in this problem helped you decide how to begin?

- **Reason Mathematically** How does rounding help you to solve this problem?

Draw or write to show examples for each term. Then draw or write to show other math words in the unit.

algorithm a set of routine steps used to solve problems.

My Example

estimate (verb) to give an approximate number or answer based on mathematical thinking.

My Example

expanded form a way a number is written to show the place value of each digit. For example, $249 = 200 + 40 + 9$.

My Example

period a group of three places in a number, usually separated by commas. The first three periods are the ones period, the thousands period, and the millions period.

My Example

reasonable something that makes sense when given facts are taken into account.

My Example

regroup to compose or decompose ones, tens, hundreds, thousands, and so forth. For example, 10 ones can be regrouped as 1 ten, or 1 hundred can be regrouped as 10 tens.

My Example

standard form the way a number is written with numerals.

My Example

word form the way a number is written with words or said aloud.

My Example

My Word: _____

_____

_____

My Example

My Word: _____

_____

_____

My Example

My Word: _____

_____

_____

My Example

My Word: _____

_____

_____

My Example

☑ SELF CHECK

Before starting this unit, check off the skills you know below. As you complete each lesson, see how many more skills you can check off!

I can . . .	Before	After
Multiply and divide to solve comparison problems, for example: 28 is 4 times as many as 7.	☐	☐
Identify factor pairs for a number, for example: 4 and 5 are a factor pair for 20.	☐	☐
Identify multiples of a number, for example: 42 is a multiple of 6.	☐	☐
Identify prime or composite numbers, for example: 16 is composite.	☐	☐
Describe rules in number and shape patterns, for example: the pattern "3, 10, 17, 24, . . . " has the rule "add 7" and the numbers go back and forth between odd and even.	☐	☐
Model and solve multi-step word problems using equations, for example: $(6 \times 3) - 11 + 2 = 9$.	☐	☐

Build Your Vocabulary

Math Vocabulary

Label each item with a review word. Then work with your partner to clarify.

1 $4 \times (4 \times 10)$
$(4 \times 4) \times 10$

2

2×3 3×2

....

3 $3 \times 4 = 12$

4 ↓
$3 \times 4 = 12$

....

Academic Vocabulary

Put a check next to the academic words you know. Then use the words to complete the sentences.

☐ identify   ☐ opinion   ☐ confirm   ☐ refer

1 You should check your work to .... the answer is correct.

2 An .... is something that may or may not be true.

3 If you do not know the meaning of a word, you can .... to the glossary to learn the definition.

4 Knowing what math symbols represent helps you .... the operations to use.

Understand Multiplication as a Comparison

Dear Family,

This week your child is exploring multiplication as a comparison.

Your child is learning about multiplication as a way to compare two numbers.

This model shows that
12 is 3 times as many as 4.
You can write the comparison as
a multiplication equation:
$$12 = 3 \times 4$$

This model shows that
12 is 4 times as many as 3.
You can write the comparison as
a multiplication equation:
$$12 = 4 \times 3$$

Your child is also learning how to use bar models to help understand multiplication as a comparison.

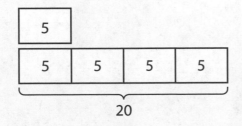

This bar model shows that 20 is 4 times as many as 5: $20 = 4 \times 5$.

Invite your child to share what he or she knows about multiplication as a comparison by doing the following activity together.

ACTIVITY MULTIPLICATION AS A COMPARISON

Do this activity with your child to explore multiplication as a comparison.

Materials 20 pennies or other identical small objects

- With your child, arrange 10 pennies to show that 10 is 2 times as many as 5. The pennies should look like this:

- Now ask your child to arrange 10 pennies to show that 10 is 5 times as many as 2. (The pennies should be arranged in 5 rows with 2 pennies in each row.)

- Repeat the activity, asking your child to arrange pennies to show other multiplication comparisons.
    Examples:
    14 is 7 times as many as 2.
    14 is 2 times as many as 7.
    18 is 6 times as many as 3.
    18 is 3 times as many as 6.

Look for real-life opportunities to explore multiplication as a comparison of two numbers with your child.

Explore Multiplication as a Comparison

What are some ways to think about multiplication?

MODEL IT
Complete the problems below.

1 You can think about multiplication as joining equal groups.

a. Draw 3 groups of 5 stars.

b. Write a multiplication equation to find the total number of stars.

.... × .... = ...

2 You can also think about multiplication as a way to compare two numbers.

a. Draw a group of 5 stars in the box on the left. Draw three times as many stars in the boxes on the right.

    5 stars   **3 times as many**

b. Use the model to complete the sentence and the multiplication equation.

.... is 3 times as many as 5.

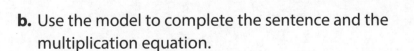

.... = ... × ....

MODEL IT

Complete the problems below.

3 When you multiply, the order of the factors does not matter.

a. Draw a group of 3 stars in the first box. Draw five times as many stars in the boxes to the right.

3 stars   **5 times as many**

b. Use the model to complete the sentence and multiplication equation.

.... is 5 times as many as 3.

.... = ... × ....

4 You can also show **multiplicative comparisons** as connected bars in a model. Complete the descriptions and equations for each model.

DISCUSS IT

• How are the equations you write in problem 4 alike and different?

• I think models and equations can help you understand multiplication as a comparison because . . .

a.   **5 stars** ★ ★ ★ ★ ★

.... **times as many** ★ ★ ★ ★ ★ | ★ ★ ★ ★ ★ | ★ ★ ★ ★ ★

.... is .... times as many as 5.

.... = ... × 5

b.   **3 stars** ★ ★ ★

.... **times as many** ★ ★ ★ | ★ ★ ★ | ★ ★ ★ | ★ ★ ★ | ★ ★ ★ | ★ ★ ★

.... is .... times as many as 3.

.... = ... × 3

5 REFLECT

Explain how finding *3 times as many as 5* is different from finding *3 more than 5*.

....

....

Prepare for Multiplication as a Comparison

1 Think about what you know about multiplication. Fill in each box. Use words, numbers, and pictures. Show as many ideas as you can.

What Is It?	What I Know About It

multiplication

Examples	Examples	Examples

2 Draw 5 groups of 4 squares. Write a multiplication equation to find the total number of squares.

Solve.

3 **a.** Draw a group of 2 circles in the first box. Draw six times as many circles in the boxes to the right.

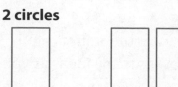

2 circles   **6 times as many**

b. Use the model to complete the sentence and multiplication equation.

.... is 6 times as many as 2.

.... = ... × 2

4 Complete the descriptions and equations for each model.

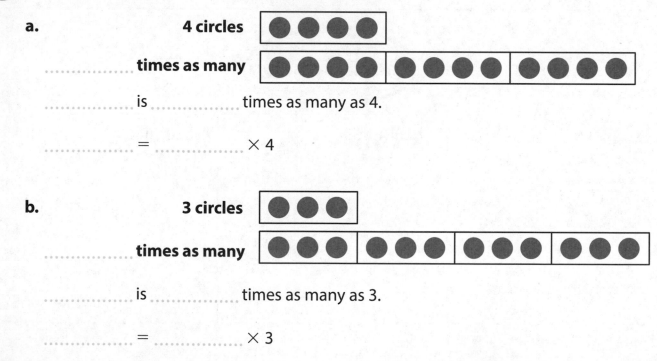

a.   **4 circles**

.... **times as many**

.... is .... times as many as 4.

.... = ... × 4

b.   **3 circles**

.... **times as many**

.... is .... times as many as 3.

.... = ... × 3

5 How are the multiplication equations you wrote in problem 4 alike? How are they different?

Develop Understanding of Multiplication as a Comparison

MODEL IT: BAR MODELS AND EQUATIONS

Try these two problems.

1 Complete the bar model below to show the comparison
36 is 4 times as many as 9. Then write a multiplication equation.

9

Equation ....

2 Draw and label a bar model to show a number that is 6 times
as many as 9. Then write a multiplication equation.

Equation ....

DISCUSS IT

- How do you and your partner think that a bar model shows how to compare two numbers?

- I think a bar model helps me understand multiplication as a comparison because . . .

MODEL IT: WORDS AND EQUATIONS

Use words to describe multiplication equations as comparisons.

3 Complete the sentence to interpret $7 \times 5 = 35$ as a comparison.

.... times as many as .... is ....

4 Write a comparison word problem that could be modeled by the equation $4 \times 6 = 24$.

> ### DISCUSS IT
>
> • How do you use words to interpret a multiplication equation as a comparison?
>
> • I think using words helps me understand a multiplication equation as a comparison because . . .

CONNECT IT

Complete the problems below.

5 Think about $7 \times 9 = 63$. How could you use a bar model and words to represent this multiplication equation as a comparison?

6 Yao blew up 8 balloons. Flora blew up 2 times as many balloons as Yao. Choose any model to show the number of balloons Flora blew up. Show your work.

Solution ....

Practice Multiplication as a Comparison

Study how the Example shows using a bar model to show multiplication as a comparison. Then solve problems 1–7.

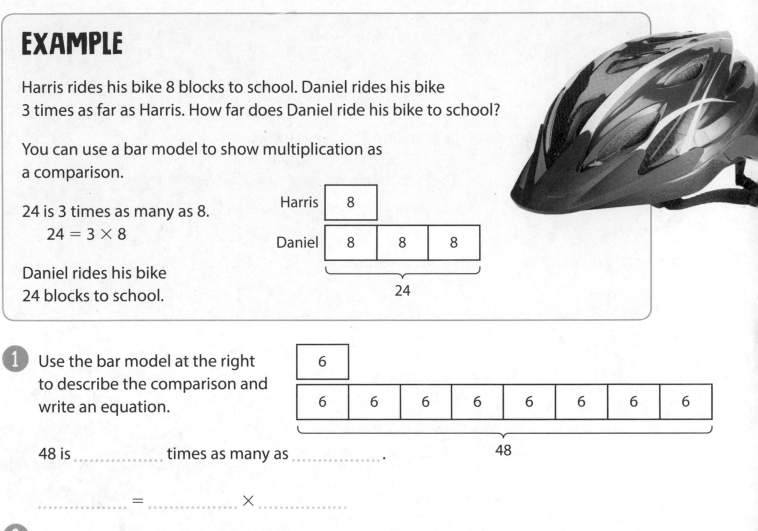

EXAMPLE

Harris rides his bike 8 blocks to school. Daniel rides his bike 3 times as far as Harris. How far does Daniel ride his bike to school?

You can use a bar model to show multiplication as a comparison.

24 is 3 times as many as 8.

$24 = 3 \times 8$

Daniel rides his bike 24 blocks to school.

Harris [8]

Daniel [8 | 8 | 8]

24

1 Use the bar model at the right to describe the comparison and write an equation.

6

6 | 6 | 6 | 6 | 6 | 6 | 6 | 6

48

48 is .... times as many as ....

.... = ... × ....

2 Draw and label a bar model to show a number that is 5 times as many as 7.

3 Write a word problem that the bar model in problem 2 could represent.

4 Tara scores 6 times as many soccer goals as Leah during one season. Leah scores 3 goals. Draw a bar model and write an equation that represents the number of goals Tara scores.

5 What two comparisons does the equation $4 \times 2 = 8$ show?

a. .... is .... times as many as ....

b. .... is .... times as many as ....

6 Draw two different bar models to represent $2 \times 4 = 8$.

7 A pet caretaker walks dogs 9 times a day. He walks dogs 5 days a week from Monday to Friday. Draw and label a bar model to show the total number of times the caretaker walks dogs in a week.

Refine Ideas About Multiplication as a Comparison

APPLY IT

Complete these problems on your own.

1 EXPLAIN

Mia plants 8 seeds. Her sister plants 6 times as many seeds as Mia. How could you find the number of seeds Mia's sister plants?

2 COMPARE

How is 4 times as many as 7 related to 7 times as many as 4? Explain your reasoning.

3 ANALYZE

Sergio found 4 pennies on the ground. His sister said she found 2 times as many pennies. Sergio figured out that his sister found 6 pennies. What did Sergio do wrong?

PAIR/SHARE
Discuss your solutions for these three problems with a partner.

Use what you have learned to complete problem 4.

4 Paige and Ben each babysit one week. Paige babysits for 3 times as many hours as Ben. Ben babysits for 7 hours.

Part A Draw a bar model to represent the situation.

Part B Look at your model. Now write a different word problem that could also be represented by the model. Then write an equation that the model represents.

Equation ....

5 MATH JOURNAL

Show two ways you can think about $5 \times 8 = 40$ as a comparison.

Multiplication and Division in Word Problems

Dear Family,

This week your child is learning about multiplication and division in word problems.

Your child will be solving problems like the one below.

A card store sells bags of 7 markers. Mark needs 3 times that amount. How many markers does Mark need?

You can use a bar model to help understand the problem.

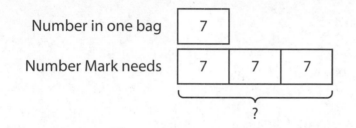

Number in one bag | 7 |

Number Mark needs | 7 | 7 | 7 |

?

Then you can use the bar model to write an equation to help understand the problem.

3 × number of markers in one bag = total markers needed

3 × 7 = ?

Then you can solve the equation.

3 × 7 = 21

So, Mark needs 21 markers.

Invite your child to share what he or she knows about multiplication and division in word problems by doing the following activity together.

ACTIVITY MULTIPLICATION AND DIVISION IN WORD PROBLEMS

Do this activity with your child to explore using multiplication and division in word problems.

Materials number cube, 45 counters, such as pennies, beans, shells, or paper clips

- Have your child roll the number cube first. Your child takes that number of counters and records the number.
    Example: Your child rolls a 4 and takes 4 counters.

- Then you roll the number cube. This number tells you how many times the number of your child's counters you take.
    Example: You roll a 3. You take 3 times as many counters as your child.
        You take 12 counters.

- Have your child count to check the number of counters you get in all. Then have your child tell or write a comparison multiplication equation.
    Example: $3 \times 4 = 12$

- Finally, write a real-world story to match the multiplication equation.
    Example: Tess has 4 seashells. I have 3 times as many seashells as Tess.
        I have 12 seashells.

- Repeat at least 6 times.

Explore Multiplication and Division in Word Problems

Previously, you thought about equations that compare numbers using multiplication. In this lesson, you will solve problems by comparing numbers. Use what you know to try to solve the problem below.

> **Hannah scored 3 goals last season. She scores 4 times as many goals this season. How many goals does Hannah score this season?**

Learning Target

- Multiply or divide to solve word problems involving multiplicative comparison, e.g., by using drawings and equations with a symbol for the unknown number to represent the problem, distinguishing multiplicative comparison from additive comparison.

SMP 1, 2, 3, 4, 5, 6, 7

TRY IT

🧰 Math Toolkit

- counters and cups
- number lines 🖱
- multiplication models 🖱
- grid paper
- sticky notes

DISCUSS IT

Ask your partner: Do you agree with me? Why or why not?

Tell your partner: I agree with you about . . . because . . .

CONNECT IT

① LOOK BACK

Explain how you could find how many goals Hannah scores this season.

② LOOK AHEAD

You often need to find an unknown number in comparison problems.
Suppose you want to solve the problem below.

Hannah's team won 5 games last season and 4 times as many games this
season. How many games did the team win this season?

One way to show a comparison such as this is to use a bar model.

a. Fill in the boxes to complete the bar model that shows the problem.

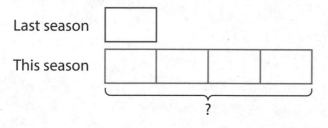

b. Complete the equation that shows the problem and matches the bar model.

how many times as many		number of games won last season		unknown
....	×	....	=	?

c. You can use a question mark, ?, as a **symbol** to stand for the **unknown**.
What is the unknown number in the problem? Explain how this number
answers the question.

③ REFLECT

How does the bar model in problem 2 show *4 times as many*?

....

....

Prepare for Multiplication and Division in Word Problems

1 Think about what you know about unknowns in equations. Fill in each box. Use words, numbers, and pictures. Show as many ideas as you can.

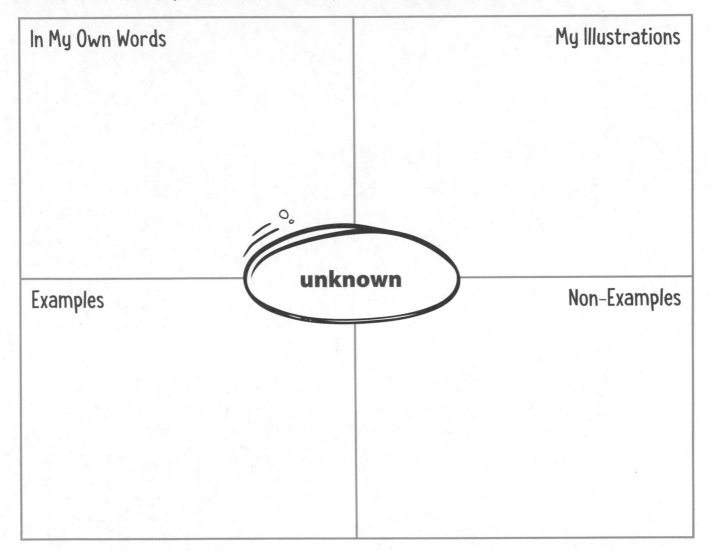

In My Own Words	My Illustrations
Examples	Non-Examples

unknown

2 How does the bar model at the right show *5 times as many?* Write an equation with an unknown to match the bar model.

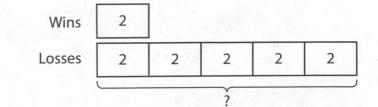

Wins	2

Losses	2	2	2	2	2

?

3 Solve the problem. Show your work.

Joseph picked 6 flowers today. He picked 3 times as many flowers yesterday. How many flowers did Joseph pick yesterday?

Solution ....

4 Check your answer. Show your work.

Develop Multiplication in Word Problems

Read and try to solve the problem below.

> Janelle's Market sells bags of 8 oranges. Simone needs 5 times that amount. Write and solve an equation to find the number of oranges that Simone needs.

TRY IT

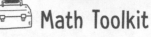 **Math Toolkit**
- counters and cups
- number lines
- multiplication models
- grid paper
- sticky notes

DISCUSS IT

Ask your partner: How did you get started?

Tell your partner: I knew . . . so I . . .

Explore different ways to understand multiplication in word problems.

> **Janelle's Market sells bags of 8 oranges. Simone needs 5 times that amount. Write and solve an equation to find the number of oranges that Simone needs.**

MODEL IT

You can use a bar model to help understand the problem.

Number in one bag	8

Number Simone needs

8	8	8	8	8

?

Skip-count to find the total Simone needs: 8, 16, 24, 32, 40.

MODEL IT

You can use the bar model to make an equation to help understand the problem.

5 × oranges in one bag = total oranges needed

The number of oranges in one bag is known (**8**). The total number of oranges needed is unknown.

$5 \times 8 = \square$

CONNECT IT
Now you will use the problem from the previous page to help you understand how to use multiplication in word problems.

 You do not know how many oranges Simone needs. What symbol on the bar model shows how many she needs?

 How does the bar model show how many oranges are in one bag?

3 How does the bar model show how many oranges Simone needs?

 How can you find *5 times as many* as 8?

5 Write an equation using numbers to show how many oranges Simone needs.

Simone needs .... oranges.

6 Explain how you can write a multiplication equation from a bar model.

 REFLECT

Look back at your **Try It**, strategies by classmates, and **Model Its**. Which models or strategies do you like best for showing a comparison between the numbers to solve the word problem? Explain.

....

....

....

APPLY IT

Use what you just learned to solve these problems.

8 Neil and Vincent collect cans. Neil collects 10 cans. Vincent collects 3 times as many cans as Neil. Write an equation with an unknown to find the number of cans Vincent collects. Then solve the equation. Show your work.

Solution ....

9 Mimi eats 6 times as many raisins as Mary. Mary eats 9 raisins. Write an equation with an unknown to find the number of raisins Mimi eats. Then solve the equation. Show your work.

Solution ....

10 Tyler runs 4 laps around the track. Jorge runs 8 times as many laps as Tyler. How many laps does Jorge run? Which equation can help you answer the question?

Ⓐ $8 + 4 = ?$

Ⓑ $8 - 4 = ?$

Ⓒ $8 \times 4 = ?$

Ⓓ $8 \div 4 = ?$

Practice Multiplication in Word Problems

Study the Example showing one way to use multiplication to solve a word problem. Then solve problems 1–5.

EXAMPLE

Sue swims 4 laps in a pool. Andy swims 5 times as many laps as Sue. How many laps does Andy swim?

Number of laps Sue swims	4

Number of laps Andy swims

4	4	4	4	4

?

$5 \times 4 = \square$
$5 \times 4 = 20$

Andy swims 20 laps.

1 Adam has 9 pennies. Ryan has 3 times as many pennies as Adam. How many pennies does Ryan have?

Label the bar model.

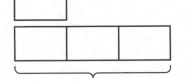

Write an equation.
Use $\square$ for the unknown. .... $\times$ .... = ...

Solve the equation. ....

Write the answer.　　Ryan has .... pennies.

Vocabulary

unknown the value you need to find to solve a problem.

2 Jade picks 5 pounds of berries. She needs 3 times that amount to make jam. How many pounds of berries does Jade need to make jam?

Skip-count to find the amount Jade needs: 5, ..., ...

Jade needs ....

3 Look at how a student solved the problem below.

A cook uses 6 eggs at lunch. He used 3 times as many eggs at breakfast. How many eggs did the cook use at breakfast?

> Skip-count: 6, 12, 18, 24
> The cook used 24 eggs at breakfast.

What did the student do wrong?

4 Look at problem 3. Draw a bar model. Use the model to write and solve an equation to find the correct answer.

The cook used .... at breakfast.

5 Which problems can be solved using the equation $8 \times 2 = m$?

Ⓐ Ali reads 8 books in June. She reads half as many books in July. How many books does Ali read in July?

Ⓑ Cal is twice as old as his sister. His sister is 8 years old. How old is Cal?

Ⓒ A muffin costs $2. Dylan buys 8 muffins. How much does Dylan spend on muffins?

Ⓓ Jordan has 8 apples and 2 oranges. How many pieces of fruit does she have altogether?

Ⓔ Lee buys 8 muffins. He gives 2 muffins to a friend. How many muffins does Lee have now?

Develop Division in Word Problems

Read and try to solve the problem below.

> Juan finds 3 times as many shells at the beach as Jeremy finds. Juan finds 24 shells. Write and solve an equation to find the number of shells Jeremy finds.

TRY IT

Math Toolkit
- counters and cups
- number lines
- multiplication models
- grid paper
- sticky notes

DISCUSS IT

Ask your partner: Can you explain that again?

Tell your partner: At first, I thought . . .

Explore different ways to understand division in word problems.

> Juan finds 3 times as many shells at the beach as Jeremy finds.
> Juan finds 24 shells. Write and solve an equation to find the
> number of shells Jeremy finds.

MODEL IT

You can use a bar model to help understand the problem.

Jeremy finds one group of shells.
Juan finds 3 times as many shells as Jeremy.

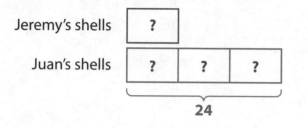

Divide 24 by 3 to find the number of shells in each group.

MODEL IT

**You can use the bar model to make an equation to help understand
the problem.**

3 × Jeremy's shells = Juan's shells

The number of shells Juan finds is known (24).
The number of shells Jeremy finds is not known (*s*).

3 × *s* = 24

CONNECT IT

Now you will use the problem from the previous page to help you understand how to use division in word problems.

 You do not know the number of shells Jeremy finds. What part of the bar model shows the number of shells Jeremy finds?

 How does the bar model show how many shells Juan finds?

3 How does the bar model show that 24 is 3 times another number?

4 How can you find what number times 3 is 24?

5 Write a division equation using numbers to show how many shells Jeremy finds.

Jeremy finds .... shells.

6 Explain how you can write a division equation from a model.

 REFLECT

Look back at your **Try It**, strategies by classmates, and **Model Its**. Which models or strategies do you like best for solving the *times as many* word problem? Explain.

....

....

....

....

APPLY IT

Use what you just learned to solve these problems.

8 Monique and Wint read the same book. Monique reads 63 pages one weekend. She reads 7 times as many pages as Wint. Write an equation with an unknown to find the number of pages Wint reads. Then solve the equation. Show your work.

Solution ....

9 The winning baseball team scores 4 times as many runs as its opponent. The winning team scores 8 runs. Write an equation with an unknown to find the number of runs its opponent scores. Then solve the equation. Show your work.

Solution ....

10 Kianna sells 40 tickets to the school play. She sells 2 times as many tickets as Reese. How many tickets, t, does Reese sell? Which equation can help you find the value of t?

Ⓐ $40 + 2 = t$

Ⓑ $40 - 2 = t$

Ⓒ $40 \times 2 = t$

Ⓓ $40 \div 2 = t$

Practice Division in Word Problems

Study the Example showing a way to use division to solve a word problem.
Then solve problems 1–5.

EXAMPLE

The Tigers score 36 points. They score 4 times as many points
as the Lions. How many points do the Lions score?

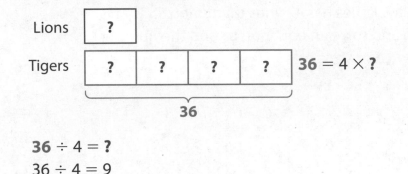

Lions | ?

Tigers | ? | ? | ? | ? $36 = 4 \times ?$

36

$36 \div 4 = ?$
$36 \div 4 = 9$

The Lions score 9 points.

1　Charlie and Gabe collect cans to recycle. Charlie collects
5 times as many cans as Gabe. Charlie collects 50 cans.
Draw a bar model to compare the number of cans each
boy collects.

2　Look at the model you drew in problem 1. Write
and solve an equation to show how many cans Gabe
collects. Show your work.

Vocabulary

divide to separate into equal
groups and find the number
in each group or the number
of groups.

division an operation used
to separate a number of items
into equal-sized groups.

Solution ....

3 Tell whether each equation is solved correctly.

	Yes	No
$6 = 2 \times ?$ $? = 12$	Ⓐ	Ⓑ
$7 \times h = 28$ $h = 4$	Ⓒ	Ⓓ
$2 = p \div 5$ $p = 10$	Ⓔ	Ⓕ

4 James and Chris are in the school play. James has 42 lines to memorize. That is 6 times as many lines as Chris. Write and solve an equation to find the number of lines Chris has to memorize. Show your work.

Solution ....

5 Choose numbers from the tiles below to fill in the bar model. Use the model to write an equation with an unknown. Then solve the equation.

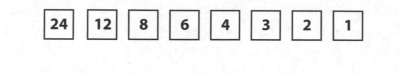

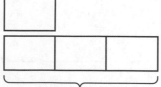

Equation ....

Solution ....

Refine Multiplication and Division in Word Problems

Complete the Example below. Then solve problems 1–9.

EXAMPLE

Karina is 6 feet tall. Her cousin is 3 feet tall. How many times as tall as her cousin is Karina?

Look at how you could show your work using a bar model.

Cousin's height | 3 |

Karina's height | 3 | 3 |
                      6

$\square \times 3 = 6; \square = 2$

Solution ....

> There are twice as many boxes in the model for Karina's height as there are for her cousin's height.

PAIR/SHARE
How else could you solve this problem?

APPLY IT

1 A small shrimp taco has 5 shrimp. There are 3 times as many shrimp in a large taco. How many shrimp are in a large taco? Write and solve an equation to find the answer. Show your work.

> What does it mean when the problem says *3 times as many?*

Solution ....

PAIR/SHARE
Did you and your partner write the same or different equations?

2 Christina reads 7 pages in a magazine. She reads 5 times as many pages in a book. How many pages does Christina read altogether? Show your work.

I think this problem has more than one step.

PAIR/SHARE
How can you check your answer?

Solution

3 Aida swims 7 laps in a pool. Kaya swims 28 laps. How many times the number of laps Aida swims does Kaya swim?

Ⓐ 4

Ⓑ 21

Ⓒ 35

Ⓓ 196

Jae Ho chose Ⓓ as the correct answer. How did he get that answer?

I can use multiplication or division to solve this problem.

PAIR/SHARE
How did you and your partner know what operation to use?

4 Kyle sells 20 boxes of fruit for a fundraiser. Omar sells 2 times as many boxes of fruit as Kyle sells. What is the total number of boxes that Kyle and Omar sell?

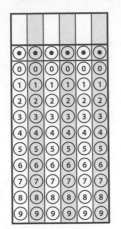

5 Raoul bikes 7 miles one week. Jackson bikes 28 miles the same week. How many times as many miles as Raoul bikes does Jackson bike? Which equation can help you answer the question?

Ⓐ $28 - 7 = \square$

Ⓑ $28 \div 7 = \square$

Ⓒ $7 \times 28 = \square$

Ⓓ $7 + 28 = \square$

6 Which problems can be solved using the equation $3 \times 9 = a$?

Ⓐ Pam is 9 years old. She is 3 times as old as Kate. How old is Kate?

Ⓑ Marco makes 9 apple tortes. He uses 3 apples for each torte. How many apples does he use?

Ⓒ Three groups of actors perform in plays at a festival. There are 9 actors in each group. How many actors perform in plays?

Ⓓ An art class meets 3 times a week for 9 weeks. How many times does the art class meet?

Ⓔ Judy finds 3 acorns. Aaron finds 3 times as many acorns as Judy. How many acorns does Aaron find?

7 Maria has 32 postcards. Henry has *h* postcards. Maria has 4 times as many postcards as Henry. Select all the correct statements.

Ⓐ The number of postcards Henry has can be represented by the expression $32 \div 4$.

Ⓑ Henry has 6 postcards.

Ⓒ The number of postcards Henry has can be found by solving the equation $32 = 4 \times h$.

Ⓓ Henry has 8 postcards.

Ⓔ The number of postcards Henry has can be represented by the expression 32×4.

8 Viet learns 25 new spelling words. That is 5 times as many words as Max learns. How many words does Max learn? Draw a bar model to find the number of words Max learns. Show your work.

Max learns .... new spelling words.

9 **MATH JOURNAL**

Sarah writes 4 songs. Ronnie writes 6 more songs than Sarah. Paul writes 2 times as many songs as Sarah.

Find the number of songs Ronnie and Paul each write. Can you use multiplication as a comparison to find the number of songs each boy writes? Explain.

☑ **SELF CHECK** Go back to the Unit 2 Opener and see what you can check off.

Multiples and Factors

LESSON 8

Dear Family,

This week your child is learning about multiples and factors.

Your child will be using factor pairs, multiples, and composite numbers to solve problems like the one below.

Monica is pasting 18 stars in rows on the wall. She wants to put the same number of stars in each row. Find all the ways she can arrange the stars.

- One way to paste the stars is 3 rows of 6. Another way is 6 rows of 3.
  3 and 6 are a **factor pair** of 18 because $3 \times 6 = 18$.

- Other ways to paste the stars are:
  2 rows of 9 or 9 rows of 2
  1 row of 18 or 18 rows of 1
- 18 is a **composite number.** It has factor pairs besides 1 and 18.
  Factor pairs of 18 are 3 and 6, 2 and 9, 1 and 18.
- 18 is a **multiple** of 1, 2, 3, 6, 9, and 18.
- There are 6 ways Monica can arrange the stars.

Invite your child to share what he or she knows about multiples and factors by doing the following activity together.

ACTIVITY FACTORS

Do this activity with your child to explore factors.

Materials 2 number cubes

- One player rolls both number cubes and uses the numbers on the cubes to make a two-digit number. Roll again if both numbers are the same.

- The other player reverses the order of the digits to make another two-digit number.

    Example:

Player 1: 21
Player 2: 12

- Each player finds all the factor pairs of his or her number.

    Example:

    Player 1: Factor pairs of 21 are 1 and 21, 3 and 7.
    Player 2: Factor pairs of 12 are 1 and 12, 2 and 6, 3 and 4.

- The player with the most factor pairs is the winner of the round.

    Example:

    Player 2 wins the round because the number 12 has 3 factor pairs. Player 1's number, 21, has only 2 factor pairs.

- Play 5 rounds.

Explore Multiples and Factors

In previous lessons, you multiplied and divided numbers. Now you can use multiplication and division to find factors and multiples and learn a way to classify a number by how many factors it has. Use what you know to try to solve the problem below.

A garden has several rows of pumpkin plants. Each row has 10 plants. How many pumpkin plants could be in the garden?

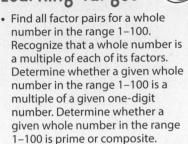

Learning Target

- Find all factor pairs for a whole number in the range 1–100. Recognize that a whole number is a multiple of each of its factors. Determine whether a given whole number in the range 1–100 is a multiple of a given one-digit number. Determine whether a given whole number in the range 1–100 is prime or composite.

SMP 1, 2, 3, 4, 5, 6, 7, 8

TRY IT

Math Toolkit

- counters
- number lines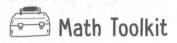
- index cards
- sticky notes
- multiplication models

DISCUSS IT

Ask your partner: Do you agree with me? Why or why not?

Tell your partner: I disagree with this part because . . .

CONNECT IT

 LOOK BACK

How can you describe how many pumpkin plants there could be?

 LOOK AHEAD

You can extend your thinking about multiplication by looking at **factors of a number**, factor pairs, multiples, prime numbers, and composite numbers.

a. A **factor pair** is two numbers that are multiplied to give a product.

Since $1 \times 20 = 20$, a factor pair of 20 is .... and ....

b. Fill in the multiplication equations to show the other factor pairs of 20.

.... $\times$ .... $= 20$ .... $\times$ .... $= 20$

Factor pair: .... and ....   Factor pair: .... and ....

c. What are the six different factors of 20? ....

d. A **multiple** is the product of a given number and any other whole number. When you multiply numbers, the product is a multiple of each factor. So, 20 is a multiple of each of its six factors.

The number 20 is a multiple of .... , ... , ... , ... , ... , and ....

e. A number with more than one factor pair is called a **composite number**. A **prime number** has only one factor pair: the number itself and 1. The number 1 is neither prime nor composite.

There is only one way to put 11 pumpkins in equal rows.

Is 11 a *prime* or *composite* number? ....

③ REFLECT

How is 20 a multiple of 5? Explain using multiplication and skip-counting.

....

....

Prepare for Multiples and Factors

1 Think about what you know about multiplication. Fill in each box. Use words, numbers, and pictures. Show as many ideas as you can.

Word	In My Own Words	Example
factor pair		
multiple		
prime number		
composite number		

2 Is 9 a prime or composite number? Explain.

Solve the problem. Show your work.

**A park has several rows of trees. Each row has 5 trees.
How many trees could be in the park?**

Solution ....

④ Check your answer. Show your work.

Develop Multiples

Read and try to solve the problem below.

Leona has 5 cups of oats. She needs 2 cups of oats for one full batch of oatmeal muffins. Can she use all of her oats by making multiple full batches of muffins?

TRY IT

Math Toolkit
- counters
- cups
- number lines
- index cards
- sticky notes
- multiplication models

DISCUSS IT

Ask your partner: Can you explain that again?

Tell your partner: I knew . . . so I . . .

Explore different ways to understand multiples.

> Leona has 5 cups of oats. She needs 2 cups of oats for one full batch of oatmeal muffins. Can she use all of her oats by making multiple full batches of muffins?

PICTURE IT

You can use a picture to help understand the problem.

The picture shows the oats Leona has, divided into 2-cup measuring cups.

MODEL IT

You can also use a number line to help understand the problem.

The number line shows multiples of 2 circled. To find the multiples of 2, you can start at 0 and skip-count by 2s. You can see that the **multiples of 2** are even numbers.

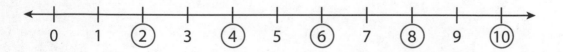

CONNECT IT

Now you will use the problem from the previous page to help you understand how to use multiples to solve a problem.

 Why does the picture use measuring cups that hold 2 cups of oats?

2 How can you tell from the measuring-cup picture that Leona cannot use all 5 cups of oats in 2-cup batches?

3 What do the circled numbers on the number line represent?

4 How can you tell from the number line that 5 is not a multiple of 2?

5 How many cups of oats would Leona use in 3 batches of muffins?

6 Explain how you can find out whether a number, such as 5, is a multiple of 2.

 REFLECT

Look back at your **Try It**, strategies by classmates, and **Picture It** and **Model It**. Which models or strategies do you like best for using multiples to solve a problem? Explain.

APPLY IT

Use what you just learned to solve these problems.

8 There are 4 bottles of water in a pack. Patrick needs 20 bottles of water for his soccer team. Can he buy exactly 20 bottles in packs of 4? Show your work.

Solution

9 What are the first five multiples of the number 3? Show your work.

Solution

10 How can you tell if 24 is a multiple of a given number?

Practice Multiples

**Study the Example showing how to use multiples to solve a word problem.
Then solve problems 1–6.**

EXAMPLE

Markers come in boxes of 5. Paul needs 40 markers for students in the art club. Can Paul buy exactly 40 markers in boxes of 5? How many boxes does he need to buy?

Find multiples of 5.

$5 \times 1 = 5$ $5 \times 4 = 20$ $5 \times 7 = 35$
$5 \times 2 = 10$ $5 \times 5 = 25$ $\boxed{5 \times 8 = 40}$
$5 \times 3 = 15$ $5 \times 6 = 30$ $5 \times 9 = 45$

40 is a multiple of 5.
Paul can buy exactly 40 markers in boxes of 5.
Paul needs to buy 8 boxes.

1 Skip-count by 4s to find multiples of 4. Circle the multiples on the number line.

```
←——+——+——+——+——+——+——+——+——+——+——+——→
    0   2  (4)  6   8  10  12  14  16  18  20
```

2 Complete the multiplication facts to find more multiples of 4.

$4 \times 6 =$ .... $4 \times$ .... $=$ ....

$4 \times$ .... $=$ .... $4 \times$ .... $=$ ....

$4 \times$ .... $=$ .... $4 \times$ .... $=$ ....

3 Look at problems 1 and 2. Are these the only multiples of 4? Use words and numbers to explain.

> **Vocabulary**
>
> **multiple** the product of a given number and any other whole number.

4 Amare orders 72 mugs. Mugs are packed 8 to a box.
   How many boxes of mugs does Amare order?

   Tell whether each equation or statement could be
   used to solve the problem.

	Yes	No
$72 = 8 \times b$	Ⓐ	Ⓑ
$72 \div 8 = b$	Ⓒ	Ⓓ
List multiples of 8: 8, 16, 24, 32, 40, . . .	Ⓔ	Ⓕ
$b = 72 + 8$	Ⓖ	Ⓗ

5 A box of cupcakes has 6 cupcakes. Abby wants to
   buy only full boxes of cupcakes. Find two possible
   numbers of cupcakes Abby can buy. Show your work.

   Abby can buy .... cupcakes or .... cupcakes.

6 Strawberries come in 1-pound, 2-pound, and 5-pound boxes. Stacy wants to
   buy exactly 10 pounds of strawberries. What are two ways that Stacy can buy
   exactly 10 pounds of strawberries? Tell which sizes of boxes she can buy and
   how many of each size box. Show your work.

   Solution ....

   ....

Develop Factors and Factor Pairs

Read and try to solve the problem below.

> Alfred is arranging 40 model cars into rows. He wants to put the same number of cars in each row. Find all the ways he can arrange the cars.

TRY IT

Math Toolkit
- counters
- unit tiles
- grid paper
- sticky notes

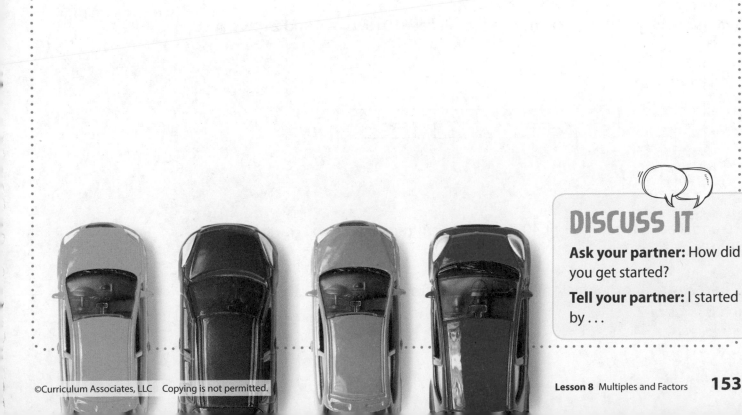

DISCUSS IT

Ask your partner: How did you get started?

Tell your partner: I started by . . .

Explore different ways to understand factors and factor pairs.

> **Alfred is arranging 40 model cars into rows. He wants to put the same number of cars in each row. Find all the ways he can arrange the cars.**

MODEL IT

You can use arrays to help understand the problem.

One way Alfred can arrange his cars is in 5 rows of 8.

5 and 8 are a factor pair of 40. This means Alfred could also arrange the cars in 8 rows of 5.

MODEL IT

You can also use area models to help understand the problem.

Two more ways Alfred can arrange the cars are 10 rows of 4 and 2 rows of 20.

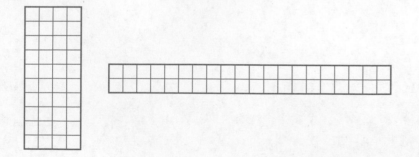

10 and 4 are a factor pair of 40. This means Alfred could also arrange the cars in 4 rows of 10.

2 and 20 are another factor pair of 40. So Alfred could also arrange the cars in 20 rows of 2.

CONNECT IT

Now you will use the problem from the previous page to help you understand how to find factors and factor pairs.

 List all of the factor pairs of 40.

 Each number in a factor pair is a factor. How many factors does 40 have?

....

 Why might it be helpful to always start with the number 1 and work up when finding factors of a number?

 Explain how to use arrays or area models to find factor pairs.

⑤ **REFLECT**

Look back at your **Try It**, strategies by classmates, and **Model Its**. Which models or strategies do you like best for finding all of the factors of a number? Explain.

....

....

....

....

APPLY IT

Use what you just learned to solve these problems.

 Brad has 18 blocks. He wants to make an array with the same number of blocks in each row. What are all the different ways Brad can arrange the blocks? Show your work.

Solution ....

 What are the factors of the number 27? Show your work.

Solution ....

8 Heidi arranges 12 photos on pages in her photo album. She puts the same number of photos on each page. Which list shows all of the possible numbers of photos that Heidi can put on each page?

Ⓐ 2, 3, 4, 6

Ⓑ 1, 3, 4, 12

Ⓒ 1, 2, 3, 4, 6, 12

Ⓓ 1, 2, 3, 4, 6, 8, 12

Practice Factors and Factor Pairs

Study the Example about factors and factor pairs.
Then solve problems 1–6.

EXAMPLE

Mr. Kennedy arranges the 16 chairs in his classroom
for a presentation. He wants to put the chairs in rows
with an equal number of chairs in each row.
Find all the ways he can arrange the chairs.

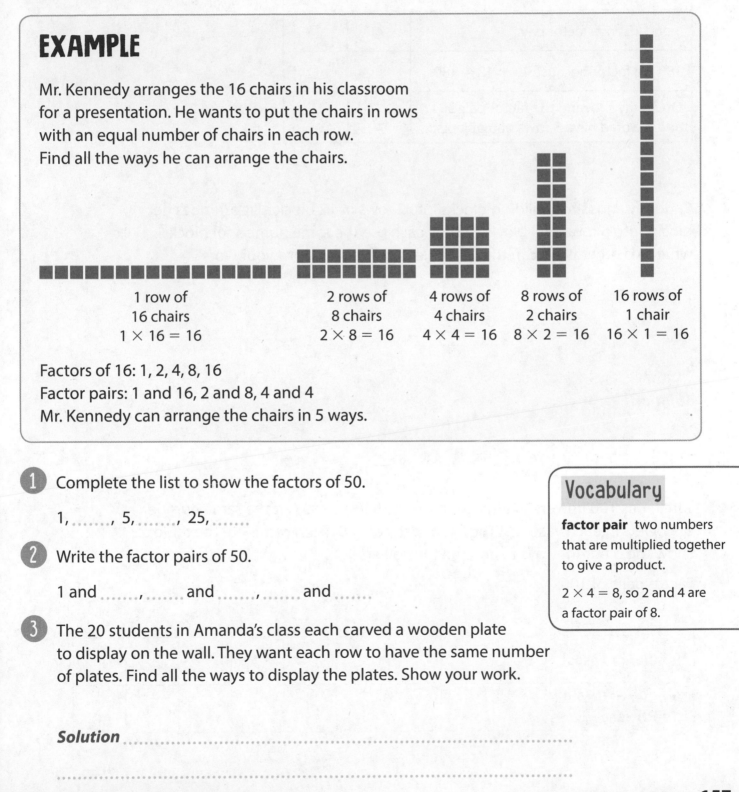

| 1 row of
16 chairs
$1 \times 16 = 16$ | 2 rows of
8 chairs
$2 \times 8 = 16$ | 4 rows of
4 chairs
$4 \times 4 = 16$ | 8 rows of
2 chairs
$8 \times 2 = 16$ | 16 rows of
1 chair
$16 \times 1 = 16$ |

Factors of 16: 1, 2, 4, 8, 16
Factor pairs: 1 and 16, 2 and 8, 4 and 4
Mr. Kennedy can arrange the chairs in 5 ways.

1 Complete the list to show the factors of 50.

1, ..., 5, ..., 25, ...

2 Write the factor pairs of 50.

1 and ...., ... and ...., ... and ....

3 The 20 students in Amanda's class each carved a wooden plate
to display on the wall. They want each row to have the same number
of plates. Find all the ways to display the plates. Show your work.

Solution ....

....

> ### Vocabulary
>
> **factor pair** two numbers
> that are multiplied together
> to give a product.
>
> $2 \times 4 = 8$, so 2 and 4 are
> a factor pair of 8.

4 Tell whether each statement about the factors of 18 is *True* or *False*.

	True	False
All the factors of 18 are 2, 3, 6, 9, and 18.	Ⓐ	Ⓑ
1 and 18 are a factor pair.	Ⓒ	Ⓓ
180 is a factor because 10 × 18 = 180.	Ⓔ	Ⓕ
One array showing the factor pair of 3 and 6 would have 3 rows of 6 objects.	Ⓖ	Ⓗ

5 Carlos arranges his building blocks into 2 rows of 12 blocks. Liz arranges her blocks into 6 rows of 4 blocks. If they each use the same number of blocks, what two other ways can they arrange their blocks? Show your work.

Solution ....

....

6 Jonah has 100 flowers to arrange in vases. He wants to put the same number of flowers in each vase. List the factor pairs of 100. Then complete the table to show the different ways to arrange the flowers.

Factor pairs of 100: ....

Number of vases								
Number of flowers in each vase								

Develop Prime and Composite Numbers

Read and try to solve the problem below.

> Janae has 36 pennies. Nate has 23 pennies. Are these numbers prime or composite?

TRY IT

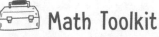 **Math Toolkit**
- pennies
- counters
- unit tiles
- grid paper

DISCUSS IT

Ask your partner: Why did you choose that strategy?

Tell your partner: The strategy I used to find the answer was . . .

Explore different ways to understand prime and composite numbers.

> **Janae has 36 pennies. Nate has 23 pennies. Are these numbers prime or composite?**

PICTURE IT

You can use pictures to help understand the problem.

Janae

36 pennies can be divided
into 3 equal stacks of 12.

Nate

23 pennies cannot
be divided into equal stacks.

MODEL IT

You can also use area models to help understand the problem.

With composite numbers, you can make area models that have more than one equal-sized row.

Janae

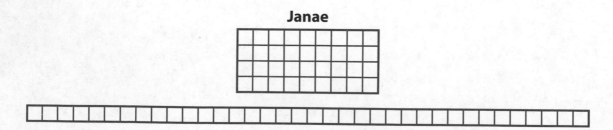

With prime numbers, you can only make one area model that has one equal-sized row.

Nate

CONNECT IT

Now you will use the problem from the previous page to help you understand how to identify prime and composite numbers.

 What factor pair is shown by Janae's stacks of pennies?

 Is 36 a prime or composite number?

How do you know?

 Is 23 a prime or composite number?

How do you know?

 Explain how you can use models to decide if a number is prime or composite.

 REFLECT

Look back at your **Try It**, strategies by classmates, and **Picture It** and **Model It**. Which models or strategies do you like best for deciding if a number is *prime* or *composite*? Explain.

....

....

....

....

APPLY IT

Use what you just learned to solve these problems.

6 Mrs. Reynaldo picks up 17 playground balls after recess. She wants to put the same number of balls into each ball bin. What different ways can she put the balls into bins? Show your work.

Solution ....

7 Is 17 a *prime number* or a *composite number*? Show your work.

Solution ....

8 Tell whether 18 and 19 are *prime* or *composite*. Explain how knowing the factors of the numbers help you decide whether they are prime or composite.

Practice Prime and Composite Numbers

Study the Example showing how to identify prime and composite numbers. Then solve problems 1–6.

EXAMPLE

Ms. Morris teaches a morning class with 13 students and an afternoon class with 14 students. Which class has a prime number of students?

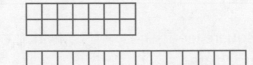

13 has one factor pair: **1** and **13**.   **14** has more than one factor pair: **2** and **7**, **1** and **14**.
13 is a prime number.   14 is a composite number.

The morning class has a prime number of students.

---

1 Is the number 2 prime or composite? Explain.

2 Kevin runs 23 laps around the track. Is the number 23 prime or composite? Explain.

3 Mae has more than 3 bracelets. She has an even number of bracelets. Is the number of bracelets that Mae has a prime number or a composite number? Explain.

Vocabulary

prime number a whole number greater than 1 whose only factors are 1 and itself.

5 is a prime number; its factors are 5 and 1.

composite number a number that has more than one pair of factors.

8 is a composite number; it has the factors 1, 2, 4, and 8.

4 Tell whether each statement is *True* or *False*.

	True	False
The number 9 is prime.	Ⓐ	Ⓑ
2 is the only even prime number.	Ⓒ	Ⓓ
All the odd numbers between 1 and 10 are prime.	Ⓔ	Ⓕ
Some composite numbers have only two factors.	Ⓖ	Ⓗ

5 The area of a garden is 5 square feet. The dimensions of the garden are 1 foot and 5 feet. 1 and 5 are factors of the number 5.

1 foot

5 feet

a. Is the number 5 a prime number? ....

b. Suppose another rectangular garden has an area of 11 square feet. What could be the dimensions of the garden?

6 Jordan and Mitchell plan a graduation party with 45 guests. They want to seat an equal number of guests at each table. They want each table to have more than one guest. Answer the questions below.

a. List the different ways the guests and tables can be arranged. Tell how many tables are needed for each group of guests.

b. Jordan and Mitchell forgot to include themselves in the seating. They still want to have an equal number of guests at each table. List the ways the guests and tables can be arranged now.

Refine Multiples and Factors

Complete the Example below. Then solve problems 1–9.

EXAMPLE

School pictures have 9 pictures on a sheet. Hallie needs 45 pictures for her family and classmates. Can she get exactly 45 pictures in sheets of 9? If so, how many sheets does she need?

Look at how you could show your work using a picture.

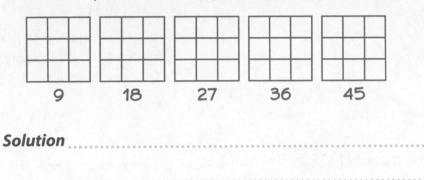

9   18   27   36   45

Solution ....

....

Any number that has 0 or 5 in the ones place is a multiple of 5!

PAIR/SHARE
How else could you solve this problem without using models?

APPLY IT

1 There are 12 levels in Liang's new video game. Suppose he plays the same number of levels each day. What are all the possibilities for the number of days Liang could play the game without repeating a level? Show your work.

I notice that 2 is a factor of every even number!

PAIR/SHARE
Why do you need to find the factors of 12 to solve this problem?

Solution ....

2 A basketball team scores 37 points in one quarter. Is the number 37 prime or composite? Show your work.

Starting with 1 is a good way to find factors!

PAIR/SHARE
Why do you need to find the factors of 37 to solve this problem?

Solution ....

3 Grant walks 2 miles every day. Which could NOT be the number of miles that Grant has walked after some number of days?

Ⓐ 2

Ⓑ 3

Ⓒ 10

Ⓓ 18

Noelle chose Ⓑ as the correct answer. How did she get that answer?

What do you know about multiples of 2?

PAIR/SHARE
Discuss why answer Ⓐ is incorrect.

4 Simon arranges his 36 toy cars into equal-sized piles. Which list shows all of the possible numbers of cars that could be in each pile?

Ⓐ 2, 3, 4, 6

Ⓑ 1, 2, 3, 4, 6

Ⓒ 2, 3, 4, 6, 9, 12, 18

Ⓓ 1, 2, 3, 4, 6, 9, 12, 18, 36

5 Reggie eats 31 raisins. Which correctly describes 31 as a prime number or a composite number and tells the number of factor pairs 31 has?

Ⓐ 31 is a prime number because it has 0 factor pairs.

Ⓑ 31 is a prime number because it has 1 factor pair.

Ⓒ 31 is a composite number because it has 1 factor pair.

Ⓓ 31 is a composite number because it has 2 factor pairs.

6 Sara is playing a memory card game with 24 cards. She wants to arrange the cards in equal rows. Shade in 24 boxes below to show one way that Sara could arrange the cards.

7 Tell whether each sentence is *True* or *False*.

	True	False
The number 96 is a multiple of 8. That means all of the factors of 8 are also factors of 96.	Ⓐ	Ⓑ
The number 1 is prime.	Ⓒ	Ⓓ
The number 1 is composite.	Ⓔ	Ⓕ
The number 2 is prime.	Ⓖ	Ⓗ
The number 9 has four factors.	Ⓘ	Ⓙ

8 Draw and label models to show all the factors of 15. Then tell if 15 is a prime or composite number. Show your work.

15 is a .... number.

9 MATH JOURNAL

Write a multiple of 4. Explain how you know it is a multiple. List all the factor pairs of the number. Explain whether the number is prime or composite.

☑ SELF CHECK Go back to the Unit 2 Opener and see what you can check off.

Number and Shape Patterns

Dear Family,

This week your child is learning about number and shape patterns.

Your child might see a number pattern like the one below. He or she is learning how to find the next numbers in the pattern.

3, 6, 9, 12, _____ , _____

The **rule** in the number pattern is "add 3." So, the next numbers in the pattern are 15, 18.

Another way to describe the pattern is to say that the numbers alternate in an odd/even pattern. The first number is odd, the second number is even, the third number is odd, and so on.

Your child is also learning about shape patterns such as the one below.

⬠ ◻ △ ⬠ ◻ △ ⬠ ◻ △ _____ _____

The pattern of shapes is:
pentagon, square, triangle, pentagon, square, triangle, pentagon, square, triangle

So, the next two shapes in the pattern are pentagon, square.

Another way to describe the shape pattern is to say that the pattern has shapes with:
5 sides, 4 sides, 3 sides, 5 sides, 4 sides, 3 sides, and so on.

Invite your child to share what he or she knows about patterns by doing the following activity together.

ACTIVITY NUMBER PATTERNS

Do this activity with your child to find patterns in numbers.

- Look at the number pattern below with your child.

> 11, 22, 33, 44, 55, 66, 77, 88, 99, . . .

- Work together to identify the rule for the pattern.

- Talk about other patterns you notice in the numbers.

  For example:

  - *The numbers alternate between odd and even: the first number is odd, the second number is even, and so on.*

  - *The tens and ones digits are the same in each number.*

  - *The tens and ones digits each go up by 1 in the next number in the pattern.*

- Next, look at another number pattern and work together to identify the rule for the pattern.

> 12, 23, 34, 45, 56, 67, 78, 89, . . .

- Talk about other patterns you notice in the numbers. Discuss how this pattern and the first pattern are alike and different.

- Challenge your child to think about the kind of number pattern you would get using the rule "subtract 11."

Explore Number and Shape Patterns

You have used rules to describe patterns in numbers. In this lesson, you will explore patterns further. Use what you know to try to solve the problem below.

Learning Target

- Generate a number or shape pattern that follows a given rule. Identify apparent features of the pattern that were not explicit in the rule itself.

SMP 1, 2, 3, 4, 5, 6, 7, 8

What are the next two numbers in the pattern below?

5, 10, 15, 20, 25, _____ , _____

TRY IT

 **Math Toolkit**

- counters
- unit tiles
- hundred charts
- number lines
- index cards

 **DISCUSS IT**

Ask your partner: How did you get started?

Tell your partner: I knew . . . so I . . .

CONNECT IT

1 LOOK BACK

Explain how you found the next two numbers in the pattern.

2 LOOK AHEAD

Sometimes there are other patterns you can find. Look at the number and dot model patterns below.

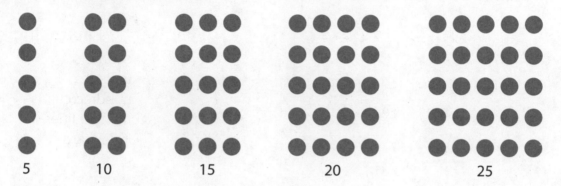

a. What pattern do you see in the digits in the ones places of the numbers?

b. Is there an even and odd pattern in the numbers and dots? If so, what is it?

c. Look at the number patterns 5, 10, 15, 20, 25 and 17, 22, 27, 32, 37, 42. How are they the same? How are they different?

3 REFLECT

Describe a pattern that you have noticed in the real world.

....

....

Prepare for Number and Shape Patterns

1 Think about what you know about patterns. Fill in each box. Use words, numbers, and pictures. Show as many ideas as you can.

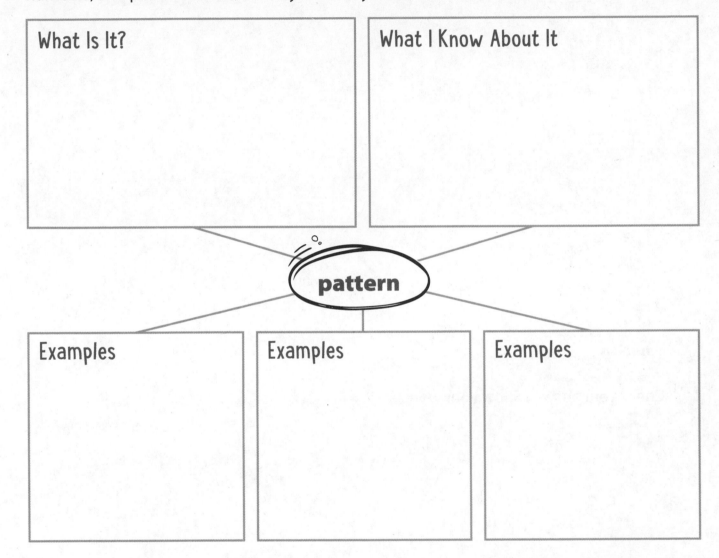

What Is It?

What I Know About It

pattern

Examples

Examples

Examples

2 What patterns can you find in the number pattern below?

10, 25, 40, 55, 70

Solve the problem. Show your work.

What are the next two numbers in the pattern below?

1, 7, 13, 19, 25, ____ , ____

Solution ....

 Check your answer. Show your work.

Develop Number Patterns

Read and try to solve the problem below.

> Orlando swims laps in a pool every day. This week he swims 4 more laps each day than the day before. He swims 20 laps on Monday. Find how many laps Orlando swims each weekday this week.

TRY IT

🧰 **Math Toolkit**
- counters
- unit tiles
- hundred charts
- number lines
- index cards

DISCUSS IT

Ask your partner: Do you agree with me? Why or why not?

Tell your partner: I disagree with this part because . . .

Explore different ways to identify and use number patterns.

> Orlando swims laps in a pool every day. This week he swims 4 more laps each day than the day before. He swims 20 laps on Monday. Find how many laps Orlando swims each weekday this week.

PICTURE IT

You can use a table to help understand the problem.

Day	Monday	Tuesday	Wednesday	Thursday	Friday
Number of Laps	20				

+4   +4   +4   +4

MODEL IT

You can also use a number line to help understand the problem.

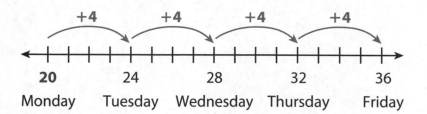

20	24	28	32	36
Monday	Tuesday	Wednesday	Thursday	Friday

Start at 20, which is the number of laps Orlando swims on Monday.
Then count on 4 more for each weekday.

CONNECT IT

Now you will use the problem from the previous page to help you understand how to identify and use number patterns.

 How many laps does Orlando swim each day?

Monday: .... Tuesday: .... Wednesday: .... Thursday: .... Friday: ....

 What is the **rule** you follow to get from one number to the next in the pattern?

....

3 What does the pattern show you about what happens when you start with an even number and add an even number?

4 Describe another pattern you see in this set of numbers.

5 Explain how you found the additional pattern(s).

 REFLECT

Look back at your **Try It**, strategies by classmates, and **Picture It** and **Model It**. Which models or strategies do you like best for solving a problem about a number pattern? Explain.

....

....

....

....

APPLY IT

Use what you just learned to solve these problems.

7 The first time Lori plays a new game, she scores 100 points. Each of the next 3 times she plays the game, she doubles her previous score. What are Lori's scores for the first 4 times she plays the game? Show your work.

Solution ....

8 What is another pattern in Lori's scores?

Solution ....

....

9 Start with the number 16. Use the rule "divide by 2." Write the next three numbers in the pattern. Show your work.

Solution ....

Practice Number Patterns

Study the Example showing how to use a pattern on a number line to solve a word problem. Then solve problems 1–8.

EXAMPLE

Riley saves $10 from her weekly babysitting job for 4 weeks. She starts with $50 in savings. How much does Riley have in savings at the end of 4 weeks?

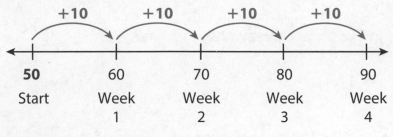

50	60	70	80	90
Start	Week 1	Week 2	Week 3	Week 4

Rule: add 10
Pattern: 50, 60, 70, 80, 90
Riley has $90 in savings at the end of 4 weeks.

Eduardo practices the flute each weekday. His music teacher wants him to practice 5 minutes longer each day this week. Eduardo practices for 20 minutes on Monday. How many minutes does Eduardo practice on Friday?

1 Complete the table to show how many minutes Eduardo practices each day this week.

Day	Monday	Tuesday	Wednesday	Thursday	Friday
Number of Minutes	20				

2 Complete the sentence.

Eduardo practices for .... on Friday.

3 Eric starts with $18 in savings. Then he saves $15 each month. Use the table below to answer the questions.

Month	0	1	2	3	4
Eric's Savings	$18	$33	$48	$63	$78

a. What will Eric's total savings be at the end of Month 5 and Month 6? Show your work.

b. What are two different patterns in Eric's monthly savings amounts?

Eve's soccer team has 48 water bottles in the locker room. Each of the 12 players takes a water bottle before a game.

4 Complete the table to show how many water bottles are left in the locker room at the end of each of the first three games.

Game		1	2	3
Number of Bottles	48			

5 Use words and numbers to explain how to find the number of water bottles left after Game 1.

6 What is the rule for the pattern?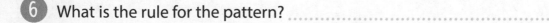

7 What number would come after 12 in the pattern? ....

8 What does this number mean?

Develop Shape Patterns

Read and try to solve the problem below.

> Camille made a shape pattern with pattern blocks that goes back and forth between a triangle and a square. Show the pattern that Camille made.

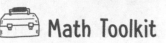

TRY IT

🧰 **Math Toolkit**
- pattern blocks
- pattern block templates
- rulers
- sticky notes

DISCUSS IT

Ask your partner: Can you explain that again?

Tell your partner: At first, I thought . . .

Explore different ways to understand and model patterns with shapes.

> **Camille made a shape pattern with pattern blocks that goes back and forth between a triangle and a square. Show the pattern that Camille made.**

PICTURE IT
You can use drawings to show the pattern.

Start by describing the pattern with words.
Repeat the pattern at least three times.

     triangle   square   triangle   square   triangle   square

Now draw the shapes in the order you named them.

△ ☐ △ ☐ △ ☐

MODEL IT
You can also use pattern blocks to show the pattern.

Use pattern blocks in the shapes Camille used to make her pattern.
Use numbers to describe each shape.
Count the number of sides each shape has to label the shapes.

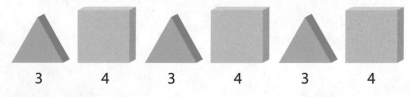

    3   4   3   4   3   4

CONNECT IT

Now you will use the problem from the previous page to help you understand and further explore shape patterns.

 How many sides does a triangle have? ....

 How many sides does a square have? ....

3 How could you describe the pattern using the number of sides the shapes have?

4 What would the 10th shape in the pattern be, and how many sides would

it have? ....

5 Explain how you can figure out what the 85th shape in the pattern would be and how many sides it would have without drawing all 85 shapes.

 REFLECT

Look back at your **Try It**, strategies by classmates, and **Picture It** and **Model It**. Which models or strategies do you like best for exploring shape patterns? Explain.

....

....

....

....

APPLY IT

Use what you just learned to solve these problems.

7 The pattern below follows the rule "add a row of two circles each time." Describe how the total number of circles in each figure of the pattern is related to the number of the figure.

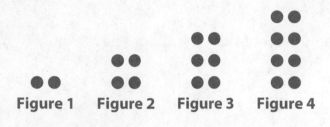

Figure 1   Figure 2   Figure 3   Figure 4

Solution ....

....

8 Draw a shape pattern that goes back and forth between a 5-sided shape and a 6-sided shape. Then describe the shape pattern in another way.

Solution ....

....

9 The shapes in Sarah's pattern go back and forth between having an even number of sides and an odd number of sides. Which pattern is Sarah's pattern?

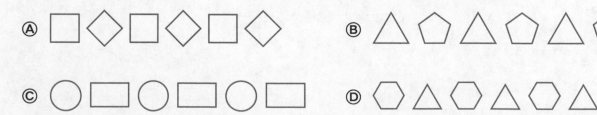

Practice Shape Patterns

**Study the Example showing ways to describe a shape pattern.
Then solve problems 1–6.**

EXAMPLE

A banner has the shape pattern below. What will the next shape in the pattern be?

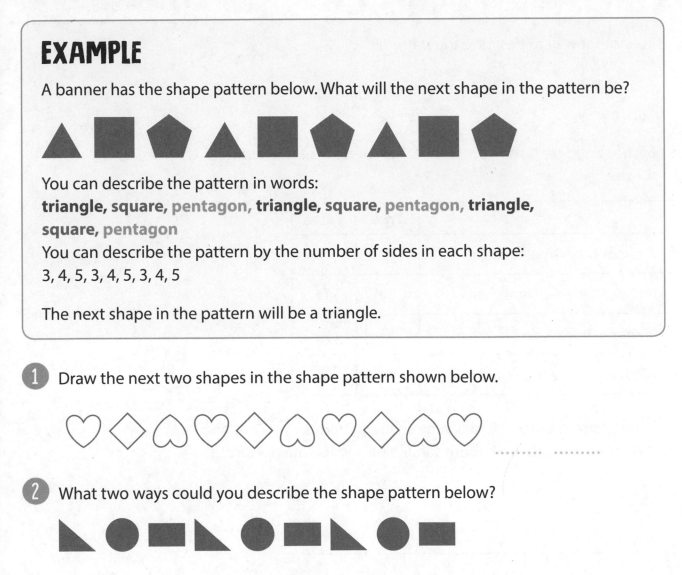

You can describe the pattern in words:
triangle, square, pentagon, triangle, square, pentagon, triangle, square, pentagon
You can describe the pattern by the number of sides in each shape:
3, 4, 5, 3, 4, 5, 3, 4, 5

The next shape in the pattern will be a triangle.

---

1 Draw the next two shapes in the shape pattern shown below.

2 What two ways could you describe the shape pattern below?

3 Look at problem 2. The 3rd, 6th, and 9th shapes are the same. Explain how to figure out what the 27th shape will be without drawing all 27 shapes.

④ Sasha draws a shape pattern that goes back and forth between a 5-pointed star and 4-pointed star.

What is another way to describe the pattern?

⑤ Look at the shape pattern in problem 4. Tell whether each statement is *True* or *False*.

	True	False
The 7th spot has a 4-pointed star.	Ⓐ	Ⓑ
The 8th spot has a 5-pointed star.	Ⓒ	Ⓓ
The 99th spot has a 5-pointed star.	Ⓔ	Ⓕ
The 100th spot has a 4-pointed star.	Ⓖ	Ⓗ

⑥ Jamel used pattern blocks to make the shape pattern shown below. Tell whether each statement about Jamel's pattern is *True* or *False*.

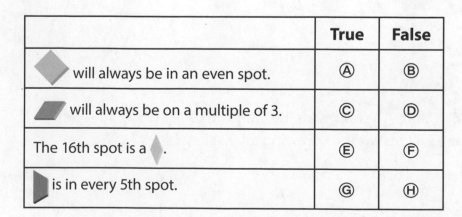

	True	False
◇ will always be in an even spot.	Ⓐ	Ⓑ
▱ will always be on a multiple of 3.	Ⓒ	Ⓓ
The 16th spot is a ◊.	Ⓔ	Ⓕ
▮ is in every 5th spot.	Ⓖ	Ⓗ

Refine Number and Shape Patterns

Complete the Example below. Then solve problems 1–9.

EXAMPLE

Hungry Heath's sells four different sizes of sandwiches: small, medium, large, and jumbo. The small sandwich costs $3. Each size after that costs $2 more than the next smaller size. How much does each sandwich cost?

Look at how you could show your work using a picture.

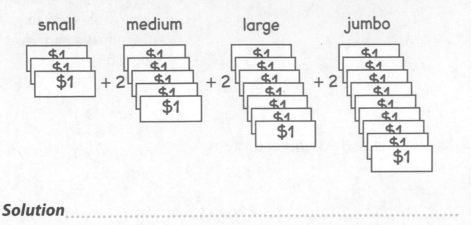

Solution ....

The student used the rule "add 2" because each sandwich costs $2 more than the next smaller size.

PAIR/SHARE
Are there any other patterns in this set of numbers?

APPLY IT

1 Write a rule for the pattern below. Draw the next figure in the pattern. How many circles will the next figure in the pattern have?

 ....

Solution ....

What shape do the circles form in each of the group of circles after the first group?

PAIR/SHARE
Is your rule the same as your partner's?

2 Eva drew a shape pattern that goes back and forth between rectangles and ovals.

There are several ways to describe a pattern!

What are two other ways you can describe this set of shapes?

Solution

....

....

....

....

....

3 Lana used the rule "multiply by 2" to write the number pattern shown below.

10, 20, 40, 80

If the pattern continues, what would be the next number in the pattern?

Ⓐ 82

Ⓑ 90

Ⓒ 160

Ⓓ 180

How can you check your answer?

Diego chose Ⓐ as the correct answer. How did he get that answer?

4 The rule for the pattern shown below is "add 10." What would be the 99th number in the pattern?

10, 20, 30, 40, 50

Ⓐ 99

Ⓑ 900

Ⓒ 909

Ⓓ 990

5 Khadija drew the shape pattern shown below.

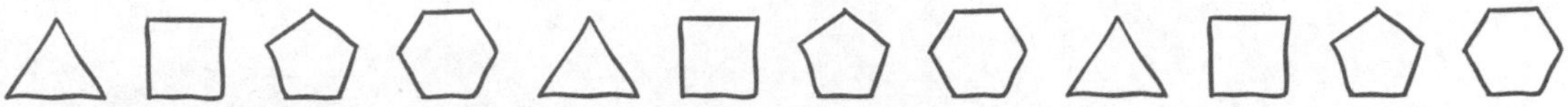

Select all the statements that correctly describe the pattern.

Ⓐ Each shape has one more side than the shape before it.

Ⓑ The shapes in the odd-numbered spots have an odd number of sides.

Ⓒ The shapes in the even-numbered spots have an even number of sides.

Ⓓ The hexagon only appears in spots that are multiples of 4.

Ⓔ A square appears in all the spots that are multiples of 2.

6 Tell whether each pattern follows the rule "add 7."

	Yes	No
7, 17, 27, 37	Ⓐ	Ⓑ
1, 7, 49, 343	Ⓒ	Ⓓ
3, 10, 17, 24	Ⓔ	Ⓕ
9, 17, 25, 33	Ⓖ	Ⓗ
7, 14, 21, 28	Ⓘ	Ⓙ

7 Draw a shape pattern that follows the rule that the shapes go back and forth between four sides and five sides. Show your work.

Solution ....

8 Write a number pattern that follows the rule "subtract 6" and also has all odd numbers. Show your work.

Solution ....

9 MATH JOURNAL

Rich says that a number pattern with the rule "add 2" always has even numbers. Is Rich correct? Explain.

☑ SELF CHECK Go back to the Unit 2 Opener and see what you can check off.

©Curriculum Associates LLC   Copying is not permitted.

Model and Solve Multi-Step Problems

Dear Family,

This week your child is learning to model and solve multi-step problems.

Your child might see a problem like the one below.

> *Jana is making apple tarts. Each tart uses 3 apples. Jana has 5 red apples and 9 green apples. Write and solve an equation to find out how many apple tarts she can make.*

Your child is learning to use a number line to help understand the problem and write an equation.

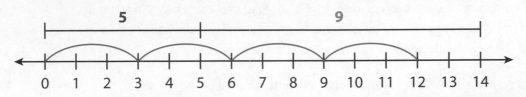

The number line shows the **5 red apples** and the **9 green apples** that Jana has. The curves above the number line show jumps of 3 because **3 apples** are needed to make each apple tart. Looking at the number line can help your child write an equation such as the one shown below.

$$(5 + 9) \div 3 = t$$

Your child can solve the equation for *t*, the number of apple tarts that Jana can make.

$$14 \div 3 = 4\,R\,2$$

The answer to the problem is that Jana can make 4 apple tarts with 2 apples left over.

Invite your child to share what he or she knows about solving multi-step problems by doing the following activity together.

ACTIVITY MODELING AND SOLVING MULTI-STEP PROBLEMS

Do this activity with your child to model and solve multi-step problems.

- Work together with your child to look around the house or think about family activities that involve more than one of an item. Examples might be buying 6-packs of sports drinks or ordering an 8-slice pizza.

- Take turns. One person says a sentence about the item that includes the number of the item (for example, 6 bottles of sports drink or 8 slices of pizza). The second person asks a question about the item that uses a one-digit number.

  For example: *There are 8 slices of pizza in a pizza pie.*
  How many slices are in 2 pizzas?

- Work together with your child to answer the question. Then the first person asks how many of each item (sports drinks, slices of pizza, etc.) each person in your family would get if you divided the items among the number of people in your family. Would there be any items left over?

- Work together with your child to solve the problem. Encourage your child to write an equation that shows the information in the problem. Then work together to solve the equation.

Look for real-life opportunities to model and solve multi-step problems with your child.

Explore Modeling and Solving Multi-Step Problems

You know how to solve two-step problems. Now you will write equations in order to solve problems that have multiple steps. Use what you know to try to solve the problem below.

> **On a test, Lola scores 6 points on each of the first three questions and 4 points on each of the other two questions. How many points does Lola score on all five questions?**

Learning Target

- Solve multistep word problems posed with whole numbers and having whole-number answers using the four operations, including problems in which remainders must be interpreted. Represent these problems using equations with a letter standing for the unknown quantity. Assess the reasonableness of answers using mental computation and estimation strategies including rounding.

SMP 1, 2, 3, 4, 5, 6

TRY IT

Math Toolkit

- counters
- cups
- paper plates
- number lines
- index cards
- base-ten blocks
- multiplication models

DISCUSS IT

Ask your partner: How did you get started?

Tell your partner: I knew . . . so I . . .

CONNECT IT

 LOOK BACK

Explain how you found the number of points Lola scores on all five questions.

 LOOK AHEAD

You can model and solve problems in different ways.

a. You can use a bar model to model the problem. Complete the bar model to show the points Lola scores on all five questions.

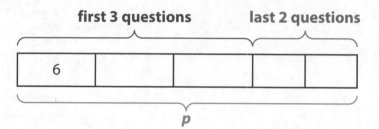

b. You can also model the problem with an equation. In an equation, you can use a letter, such as **p** in the bar model above, to represent the unknown. The unknown in this problem is the total number of points Lola scores.

Complete one way to write an equation.

$$(\underline{\hspace{2cm}} \times \underline{\hspace{2cm}}) + (\underline{\hspace{2cm}} \times \underline{\hspace{2cm}}) = p$$

points on first 3 questions   **points on last 2 questions**

c. How many points does Lola score in all? **p =** ....

 REFLECT

You can model problems in different ways. Look at the bar model in problem 2a and your equation in problem 2b. What different equation could you write to represent this problem?

....

Prepare for Modeling and Solving Multi-Step Problems

1 Think about what you know about bar models. Fill in each box. Use words, numbers, and pictures. Show as many ideas as you can.

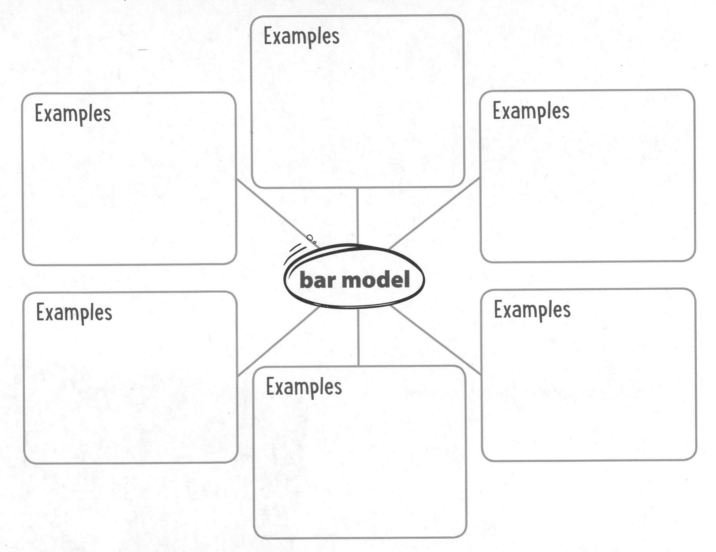

Examples

Examples

Examples

Examples

Examples

Examples

bar model

2 Fill in the bar model below to represent the equation $5 + 5 + 4 + 4 + 4 = p$. Then find the value of p.

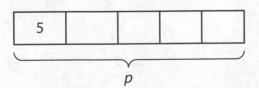

5				

p

3   Solve the problem. Show your work.

In a video game, Adrien earns 5 bonus spins on each of the first three levels and 2 bonus spins on each of the next three levels. How many bonus spins does Adrien earn on all six levels?

Solution ....

4   Check your answer. Show your work.

Develop Modeling Multi-Step Problems

Read and try to solve the problem below.

> Garrett is paid $4 for each hour he babysits. Mrs. Becker pays him for 5 hours of babysitting. On the way home, Garrett spends $9 on a book and $6 on a puzzle. Write an equation to find how much money Garrett has left from the money Mrs. Becker pays him.

TRY IT

**Math Toolkit**
- play money
- counters
- paper plates
- number lines
- index cards
- base-ten blocks
- multiplication models

DISCUSS IT

Ask your partner: Why did you choose that strategy?

Tell your partner: A model I used was . . . It helped me . . .

Explore different ways to understand modeling multi-step problems.

> **Garrett is paid $4 for each hour he babysits. Mrs. Becker pays him for 5 hours of babysitting. On the way home, Garrett spends $9 on a book and $6 on a puzzle. Write an equation to find how much money Garrett has left from the money Mrs. Becker pays him.**

MODEL IT

You can use a bar model to help understand the problem.

$4	$4	$4	$4	$4

$9	$6	?

The top bar of the model shows the amount Garrett is paid for each hour and the number of hours he babysits.

The bottom bar of the model shows the total amount he spends. You do not know how much money Garrett has left.

MODEL IT

You can use the bar model to write equations for the problem.

Let **b** equal the amount Mrs. Becker pays Garrett.

$$b = 5 \times 4$$

He spends $9 on a book and $6 on a puzzle, so represent the amount he spends with the **expression 9 + 6**.

Let **g** be the amount Garrett has left after he spends money on a book and a puzzle.

$$g = b - (9 + 6)$$

CONNECT IT

Now you will use the problem from the previous page to help you understand how to model multi-step problems.

 Look at the second **Model It**. What is represented by $\times\, 4$ in the equation $b = 5 \times 4$?

2 Why are the two amounts that Garrett spends in parentheses in the equation $g = b - (9 + 6)$?

3 Alissa combines the two equations into one equation: $g = 20 - (9 + 6)$. What does the 20 in her equation represent?

4 Ben uses the equation $g = (4 \times 5) - 9 - 6$. Is his equation correct? Explain.

5 Explain how it is possible for two equations to look different but still represent the same problem.

 REFLECT

Look back at your **Try It**, strategies by classmates, and **Model Its**. Which models or strategies do you like best for modeling a multi-step problem using an equation? Explain.

....

....

....

....

APPLY IT

Use what you just learned to solve these problems.

7 There are 4 vans and 2 cars going to a museum. Each van carries 9 people. Each car carries 3 people.

Write an equation to represent the number of people who travel in a van, *v*. Then write an equation to represent the total number of people who go to the museum, *t*. Show your work.

Solution ....

8 Miguel has 28 markers. His sister has 33 markers. They buy 3 more boxes of markers. Each box has 8 markers. Write an equation to represent the total number of markers Miguel and his sister have. Show your work.

Solution ....

9 Mrs. Barker buys tickets to the school play. She buys 2 adult tickets for $8 each and 3 child tickets for $5 each. She uses a coupon for $2 off the total amount. Write an equation to represent the total amount Mrs. Barker pays for tickets. Show your work.

Solution ....

Practice Modeling Multi-Step Problems

Study the Example showing how to model a multi-step problem and write an equation. Then solve problems 1–4.

EXAMPLE

The table shows Eli's after-school activities. Write an equation to show how many hours a week Eli spends doing activities, *a*.

Activity	How long?	How often?
Volunteer at the library	2 hours	2 times a week
Work at the skate shop	2 hours	4 times a week
Swim practice	1 hour	5 times a week

Library Skate shop Swim

2	2	2	2	2	2	1	1	1	1	1

(2 × 2) (4 × 2) (5 × 1)

$a = (2 \times 2) + (4 \times 2) + (5 \times 1)$

Mia volunteers at the animal shelter on 7 weekends. On Saturdays, she volunteers for 3 hours. On Sundays, she volunteers for 2 hours.

 Write an equation to find how many hours Mia volunteers.

a. Complete the bar model.

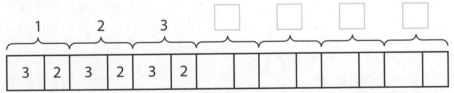

1   2   3   ☐   ☐   ☐   ☐

3	2	3	2	3	2								

b. What do the numbers above the bar represent?

c. What do the numbers in each part of the bar represent?

d. Write an equation.

2 A bike rental is $3 for an hour. The rental for a day is
   6 times as much. Caroline rents a bike for 1 day and
   2 hours. Which equations could you use to find how
   much money, *m*, Caroline spends on a bike rental?

   Ⓐ $m = (6 \times 3) + (2 \times 3)$

   Ⓑ $m = (6 \times 1) + (2 \times 3)$

   Ⓒ $m = (6 \times 2) \times (3 \times 3)$

   Ⓓ $m = (3 \times 6) + (3 \times 2)$

   Ⓔ $m = (1 \times 6) + (3 \times 2)$

3 Zara goes to the book fair and buys 3 comic
   books for $5 each, 2 chapter books for $9 each,
   4 posters for $2 each, and 1 picture book for $7.
   Write an equation that can be used to find how
   much Zara spends at the book fair. Show your work.

Solution ....

4 The table below shows clothing sales at a school fair.
   Use the information in the table to write an
   expression that equals *t*, the total amount of money
   spent on clothing at the school fair.

Item	Price	Number Sold
T-shirts	$12	100
Sweatshirts	$20	50

$t =$ ....

Vocabulary

equation a mathematical
statement that uses an
equal sign ($=$) to show that
two expressions have the
same value. For example,
$r = (6 \times 3) + 4$.

expression a group of one
or more numbers,
unknowns, and/or operation
symbols that represents a
quantity. For example, 3×4
or $5 \times h$.

Develop Solving Multi-Step Problems

Read and try to solve the problem below.

> Ms. Dennison packs up the books in her classroom for the summer. Each box holds 9 books. She has 24 math books and 27 science books to pack in boxes. Write and solve an equation to find how many boxes Ms. Dennison needs for the books.

TRY IT

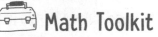 **Math Toolkit**
- counters
- cups
- paper plates
- number lines
- index cards
- base-ten blocks
- multiplication models

DISCUSS IT

Ask your partner: Can you explain that again?

Tell your partner: I am not sure how to find the answer because . . .

Explore different ways to understand using equations to model and solve multi-step problems.

> Ms. Dennison packs up the books in her classroom for the summer. Each box holds 9 books. She has 24 math books and 27 science books to pack in boxes. Write and solve an equation to find how many boxes Ms. Dennison needs for the books.

MODEL IT

You can use a number line to help understand the problem and write an equation.

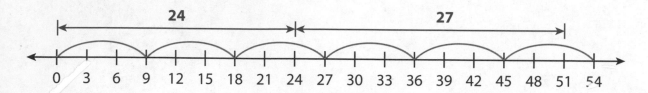

The total number of books is shown above the number line (24 + 27). The number line shows jumps of 9 because each box holds 9 books.

Let x equal the number of boxes needed. Remember to use parentheses to show what to do first.

$$x = (24 + 27) \div 9$$

SOLVE IT

You can solve the equation that represents the problem.

This is one way to represent the problem with equations.

$$x = (24 + 27) \div 9$$

$$x = 51 \div 9$$

When a number does not divide another number a whole number of times, you have some left over. The amount left over is called a **remainder**, shown with an R.

$$51 \div 9 \longrightarrow 5 \, R \, 6$$

CONNECT IT

Now you will use the problem from the previous page to help you understand how to solve multi-step problems.

1 What does the 5 in the solution 5 R 6 mean?

What does the R 6 mean?

2 How many books are left over that do not make a full box? ....

Is another box needed to hold the 6 leftover books? ....

3 How many boxes does Ms. Dennison need? ....

4 Check the solution to the equation:

.... boxes × .... books per box + ... books = 51 total books

5 How could you estimate to make sure your answer is reasonable?

6 Explain why the solution to an equation is not always the answer to a problem when there is a remainder.

7 REFLECT

Look back at your **Try It,** strategies by classmates, and **Model It** and **Solve It**. Which models or strategies do you like best for solving a multi-step problem? Explain.

....

....

....

....

APPLY IT

Use what you just learned to solve these problems.

8 Cadence shops for hiking gear. She picks out a $95 tent, a pair of boots for $54, and a $38 backpack. She has $200 to spend on gear. Write and solve an equation to find out if she has enough money for the hiking gear. Estimate to check that your answer is reasonable. Show your work.

Solution ....

....

....

....

9 Look at your answer to problem 8. Does Cadence get any change back from her $200? Explain how you know.

Solution ....

....

10 Adam wants to buy the same number of puppets for 4 of his friends. He has $53, and each puppet costs $2.

a. Write and solve an equation to find how many puppets Adam can buy for each friend. Show your work.

Solution ....

b. Explain what the remainder in your equation represents.

Practice Solving Multi-Step Problems

**Study the Example showing how to solve a multi-step problem
with a remainder. Then solve problems 1–5.**

EXAMPLE

Mrs. Murray has 12 students in one science class and 14 students in another.
She wants to combine both classes to do group work. Each table in the science
room can seat 4 students. How many tables does Mrs. Murray need?

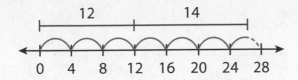

Let t equal the number of tables needed.

$t = (12 + 14) \div 4$

$t = 26 \div 4$

$26 \div 4 = 6\,R\,2$

Mrs. Murray needs 7 tables.

> 6 R 2 means:
> - 6 tables with 4 students each
> - 2 more students need another table

---

1 Check the solution to the equation in the Example.

.... tables × .... students per table + ... students = ... total students

2 Leticia earns $8 each time she rakes the yard. She
has earned $24 so far. Write and solve an equation
to show how many more times Leticia needs to rake
the yard to earn enough to buy a music player that
costs $45. Show your work.

Vocabulary

remainder the amount left
over when one number
does not divide another
number a whole number
of times.

$26 \div 4 = 6\,R\,2$

Solution ....

3. Meghan found 15 pieces of sea glass on the beach. The next day she found 4 more pieces than she found the day before. Write and solve an equation to find how many pieces of sea glass she found altogether. Estimate to check that your answer is reasonable. Show your work.

Solution

4. The table shows ticket prices at a movie theater. Ticket sales to an afternoon show were $106. There were 10 child tickets sold. Write and solve an equation to find how many adult tickets were sold. Show your work.

	Child	Adult
Ticket price	$5	$7

Solution

5. Ticket prices for 3-D movies are $10 for a child and $15 for an adult. One adult spends $55 to take a group of children to the movies. Write and solve an equation to find how many children go to the movies. Show your work.

Solution

Refine Modeling and Solving Multi-Step Problems

Complete the Example below. Then solve problems 1–8.

EXAMPLE

Myron and Suzanne make banana bread. Each batch uses 3 bananas. Myron has 5 bananas, and Suzanne has 8 bananas. Write and solve an equation to find how many batches of banana bread they make. Do they have bananas left over?

Look at how you could show your work using a model.

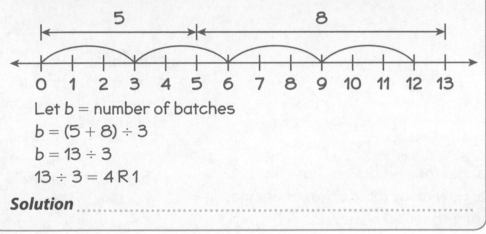

Let b = number of batches
$b = (5 + 8) \div 3$
$b = 13 \div 3$
$13 \div 3 = 4 \, R \, 1$

Solution ....

PAIR/SHARE
Discuss the reasonableness of the answer.

APPLY IT

1 A pet store has 18 rabbits. That is 3 times the number of cats the store has. Write and solve an equation to find how many rabbits and cats the store has altogether. Check the reasonableness of your answer. Show your work.

How many cats does the store have?

Solution ....
....

PAIR/SHARE
Do you get the same answer if you write the equation a different way?

2 Taylor earns $5 each time she walks her neighbor's dog. She has already earned $25. Write and solve an equation to find out how many more times Taylor needs to walk the dog to earn enough to buy a bike that costs $83. Check the reasonableness of your answer. Show your work.

What does the remainder tell you?

Solution ....

....

....

....

PAIR/SHARE
What would happen if Taylor did not think about the remainder?

3 Tiana sells 47 boxes of oranges for a fundraiser. Tim sells 12 fewer boxes than Tiana. How many more boxes of oranges does Tim need to sell in order to sell 60 boxes?

Ⓐ 1

Ⓑ 25

Ⓒ 35

Ⓓ 48

Shonda chose Ⓐ as the correct answer. How did she get that answer?

A picture can help make sense of all the numbers!

PAIR/SHARE
Compare the strategies you both used to solve the problem.

4 Franklin uses 3 eggs to make a large omelet and 2 eggs to make a small omelet. How many eggs does he need to make 5 large omelets and 4 small omelets?

Ⓐ 14 eggs

Ⓑ 22 eggs

Ⓒ 23 eggs

Ⓓ 26 eggs

5 Petra walks 9 miles the first week of this month, twice that far the second week, and 6 miles the third week. Which equations can you use to find how many miles Petra walks altogether this month?

Ⓐ $m = 9 + 9 + (3 \times 6)$

Ⓑ $m = 9 + 9 + 9 + 6$

Ⓒ $m = (2 \times 9) + (3 \times 6)$

Ⓓ $m = 9 + 18 + 6$

Ⓔ $m = 9 + (2 \times 9) + 6$

6 Ms. Ruiz plants 14 flowers in three pots. She plants 4 flowers in the one blue pot and splits the rest of the flowers equally between the two red pots.

Write and solve an equation to find the number of flowers Ms. Ruiz plants in each of the two red pots. Show your work.

Solution ....

7 Gabriel owns 27 fiction books and 23 nonfiction books. Each shelf can hold 8 books. How many shelves does Gabriel need for all of his books?

Solve the problem and explain how the remainder affects your answer. Show your work.

Solution ....

....

....

8 MATH JOURNAL

Write your own numbers in the boxes to complete the word problem. Use different numbers in each box. Do not use the numbers 0 or 1. Write and solve an equation to find the number of robots the toy store has to sell.

A toy store had ☐ robots on its shelves. The store ordered ☐ more boxes of robots to sell. Each box has ☐ robots. How many robots does the store have to sell now?

✓ SELF CHECK Go back to the Unit 2 Opener and see what you can check off.

Self Reflection

In this unit you learned to . . .

Skill	Lesson
Multiply and divide to solve comparison problems, for example: 28 is 4 times as many as 7.	6, 7
Identify factor pairs for a number, for example: 4 and 5 are a factor pair for 20.	8
Identify multiples of a number, for example: 42 is a multiple of 6.	8
Identify prime or composite numbers, for example: 16 is composite.	8
Describe rules in number and shape patterns, for example: the pattern "3, 10, 17, 24, . . . " has the rule "add 7" and the numbers go back and forth between odd and even.	9
Model and solve multi-step word problems using equations, for example: $(6 \times 3) - 11 + 2 = 9$.	10

Think about what you learned.

Use words, numbers, and drawings.

1 I am proud that I can . . .

2 I would like to learn more about how to . . .

3 A question I still have is . . .

Solve Multiplication Problems

Study an Example Problem and Solution

SMP 1 Make sense of problems and persevere in solving them.

Read this problem about comparing numbers. Then look at G.O.'s solution to this problem.

Pine Cones and Needles

G.O. is with his friend Azul at a wildlife park. A worker at the nature center is arranging pine cones and pine needles in pairs for a display. Here are the rules.

Rules for Pairing Objects

- One length is a multiple of another length.
- The longer length is no more than 5 times the shorter length.
- A pair can have two needles, two cones, or one needle and one cone.

Kind of Tree	Sugar Pine	Jack Pine	Ponderosa Pine	Longleaf Pine
Cone Length	50 cm	5 cm	8 cm	24 cm
Needle Length	10 cm	4 cm	15 cm	40 cm

Use a cone or needle only once. Cones and needles do not need to be from the same tree. Find three possible pairs that fit the rules. Tell why these pairs work.

Read the sample solution on the next page. Then look at the checklist below. Find and mark parts of the solution that match the checklist.

✓ PROBLEM-SOLVING CHECKLIST

- ☐ Tell what is known.
- ☐ Tell what the problem is asking.
- ☐ Show all your work.
- ☐ Show that the solution works.

a. **Circle** something that is known.

b. **Underline** something that you need to find.

c. **Draw a box around** what you do to solve the problem.

d. **Put a checkmark** next to the part that shows the solution works.

G.O.'S SOLUTION

- **I already know** that the length of one object in the pair has to be a multiple of the length of the other object. So one length is multiplied by a factor to get the other length as the product.

- **I can think about any two numbers in the table.**
  I need to find pairs in which one number is a multiple of the other. I'll make a chart showing some multiples of the lengths.

Shorter Length	× Number	Longer Length
10 cm	× 5	50 cm
5 cm	× 2	10 cm
5 cm	× 3	15 cm
8 cm	× 3	24 cm
4 cm	× 6	24 cm

Hi, I'm G.O. Here's how I solved this problem.

I made a table to organize my thinking.

The longer length is no more than 5 times the shorter length. These pairs all work.

24 is 6 times 4, and 6 times is more than 5 times. This doesn't work.

- **Now I can pick three pairs that work and name the objects and lengths.**

Here's my final answer.

Pair 1:
  sugar pine needle (10 cm)
  sugar pine cone (50 cm)

Pair 2:
  jack pine cone (5 cm)
  ponderosa pine needle (15 cm)

Pair 3:
  ponderosa pine cone (8 cm)
  longleaf pine cone (24 cm)

Try Another Approach

There are many ways to solve problems. Think about how you might solve the Pine Cones and Needles problem in a different way.

Pine Cones and Needles

G.O. is with his friend Azul at a wildlife park. A worker at the nature center is arranging pine cones and pine needles in pairs for a display. Here are the rules.

Rules for Pairing Objects

- One length is a multiple of another length.
- The longer length is no more than 5 times the shorter length.
- A pair can have two needles, two cones, or one needle and one cone.

Kind of Tree	Sugar Pine	Jack Pine	Ponderosa Pine	Longleaf Pine
Cone Length	50 cm	5 cm	8 cm	24 cm
Needle Length	10 cm	4 cm	15 cm	40 cm

Use a cone or needle only once. Cones and needles do not need to be from the same tree. Find three possible pairs that fit the rules. Tell why these pairs work.

PLAN IT

Answer these questions to help you start thinking about a plan.

A. Look at G.O.'s Solution. What are some other factors of the numbers in the *Longer Length* column?

B. Can you pair the cone of each kind of tree with its needle? Why or why not?

SOLVE IT

**Find a different solution for the Pine Cones and Needles problem.
Show all your work on a separate sheet of paper.**

You may want to use the Problem-Solving Tips to get started.

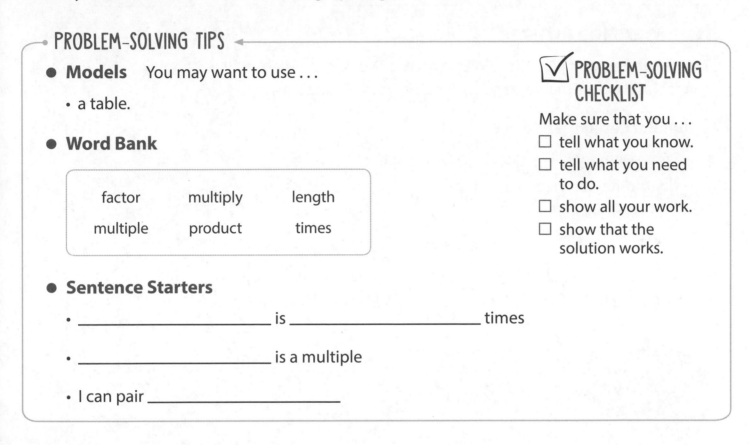

PROBLEM-SOLVING TIPS

- **Models**   You may want to use . . .
  - a table.

- **Word Bank**

factor	multiply	length
multiple	product	times

- **Sentence Starters**

  - _____ is _____ times

  - _____ is a multiple

  - I can pair _____

☑ PROBLEM-SOLVING CHECKLIST

Make sure that you . . .
- ☐ tell what you know.
- ☐ tell what you need to do.
- ☐ show all your work.
- ☐ show that the solution works.

REFLECT

Use Mathematical Practices As you work through the problem, discuss these questions with a partner.

- **Use Reasoning** How is your partner's reasoning different than your own?

- **Make Sense of Quantities** Look at the lengths in the pairs you made. How do you know how many times as many one number is than the other?

Discuss Models and Strategies

Read the problem. Write a solution on a separate sheet of paper.
Remember, there are lots of ways to solve a problem!

Numbers in Nature

The nature center is planning a display called "Numbers in Nature." It will show animals and plants that represent different types of numbers.

Number Categories

- Prime Numbers
- Composite Numbers
- Even Numbers
- Odd Numbers

One part of the display shows the number of petals that flowers have.
G.O. is sorting these flowers into the number categories listed above.

How can G.O. arrange these flowers?

PLAN IT AND SOLVE IT

Find a solution to the Numbers in Nature problem.

Help G.O. sort the flowers. Be sure to . . .

• find the number of petals each flower has.

• identify all the categories that each number fits in.

• study all the numbers and categories. Tell what you notice about how even and odd numbers relate to prime and composite numbers.

You may want to use the Problem-Solving Tips to get started.

PROBLEM-SOLVING TIPS

● **Questions**

• Do some numbers fit in more than one category?

• Are there any numbers that fit in only one category?

● **Word Bank**

prime	odd	divide
composite	factor	add
even	factor pair	

● **Sentence Starters**

• The flower has _____

• This number belongs to _____

✓ **PROBLEM-SOLVING CHECKLIST**

Make sure that you . . .

☐ tell what you know.

☐ tell what you need to do.

☐ show all your work.

☐ show that the solution works.

REFLECT

Use Mathematical Practices As you work through the problem, discuss these questions with a partner.

• **Use a Model** How can you make a model that will help you see the relationship between the different types of numbers?

• **Make an Argument** How can you justify the relationships that you describe?

Persevere On Your Own

Read the problems. Write a solution on a separate sheet of paper.

G.O.'s Planting Project

By the 1950s, almost all American chestnut trees in the country had been destroyed by a fungus. Now a conservation group plants groves of chestnut trees in suitable places. They hope the trees will make a strong comeback.

G.O. volunteers for a planting project at the park. Below is G.O.'s plan.

My Planting Plan

- Plant 48 chestnut trees.
- Plant the trees in rows.
- Include an equal number of trees in each row.
- Plant a tree every 10 feet in the row.
- Leave 20 feet of space between rows.

How many rows of trees will G.O.'s plan make? How many trees are in each row?

SOLVE IT

Describe a way to plant the 48 trees that works with the plan.

- Draw and label a diagram.
- Tell how many rows there are and how many trees are in each row.
- Tell the length and width of the rectangular area you need for your plan.
- Explain why your plan works.

REFLECT

Use Mathematical Practices After you complete the task, choose one of these questions to discuss with a partner.

- **Make Sense of Problems** What was your first step in solving the problem? Why?
- **Use Tools** What tools did you use to help you find the length and width of the rectangular area?

Plant Sale

G.O. has $100 to spend on plants for the community center.
He sees a plant sale in the park and checks out the prices.

Plants in 3-inch Pots
2 plants........$10
5 plants........$25
10 plants $50

Plants in 5-inch Pots
2 plants $16
5 plants $40
10 plants $80

What plants should G.O. buy for the community center?

SOLVE IT

Help G.O. decide which plants he should buy.

• Find the price of one plant of each size.

• Tell how many of each size plant G.O. should buy.

• Show that the total amount is within the money that G.O. has to spend.

• Explain why you chose these sizes and amounts.

REFLECT

Use Mathematical Practices After you complete the task, choose
one of these questions to discuss with a partner.

• **Make Sense of Problems** How did you find the price of one plant
of each size?

• **Check Your Answer** What did you do to make sure your answer
works and makes sense?

Unit 2 Math in Action Solve Multiplication Problems

1 Which comparisons describe the equation $5 \times 4 = 20$?
Choose all the correct answers.

Ⓐ 20 is 4 times as many as 5.

Ⓑ 4 is 5 times as many as 20.

Ⓒ 4 times as many as 20 is 5.

Ⓓ 20 is 5 times as many as 4.

Ⓔ 5 is 4 times as many as 20.

Ⓕ 5 times as many as 4 is 20.

2 Sal rides his bike 24 miles on Sunday. That is 3 times as many miles as he rode his bike on Saturday. What is the total number of miles Sal has ridden his bike on Saturday and Sunday? Record your answer on the grid. Then fill in the bubbles.

3 Start with the number 8. Use the rule "add 12".
Write the next three numbers in the pattern.
Show your work.

Solution ....

4 What do all of the numbers below have in common?

6, 12, 18, 24, 30

Choose all the correct answers.

Ⓐ They have 4 as a factor.

Ⓑ They have 6 as a factor.

Ⓒ They are factors of 6.

Ⓓ They are multiples of 4.

Ⓔ They are multiples of 6.

5 A group of 23 students go on a canoe trip. Three teachers and 2 parents also go on the trip. Each canoe can hold 3 people. How many canoes do they need?

Part A Write and solve an equation to determine the number of canoes, *c*, they need. Show your work.

Solution ....

Part B Explain how you use the remainder in your answer.

....

....

6 Sondra draws the shape pattern below. Which statement describes the shape pattern?

Ⓐ The thirtieth spot will have a square.

Ⓑ The twenty-first spot will have a square.

Ⓒ The square only appears in even-numbered spots.

Ⓓ The circle appears in both odd and even-numbered spots.

7 Sharon and Dani make invitations for a party. Sharon makes 27 invitations. That is 3 times as many as Dani makes. Write and solve an equation to find the number of invitations Dani makes. Show your work.

Solution ....

Performance Task

Answer the questions and show all your work on separate paper.

Melanie is in charge of setting up chairs for the Student Jazz Concert. She has 96 chairs to arrange into rows in a large classroom. She wants each row to have an equal number of chairs.

Find at least six different ways that Melanie can arrange the chairs. Choose one arrangement and explain why it does not make sense to use that arrangement.

Then choose the arrangement that you think works best. Draw a picture that shows how the chairs should be set up and explain why you chose this arrangement.

Checklist

Did you . . .

☐ make a list?

☐ draw a diagram?

☐ explain your reasoning?

REFLECT

Use Mathematical Practices After you complete the task, choose one of the following questions to answer.

- **Persevere** Did you have a plan to help you find at least six different ways to arrange the chairs? Explain.

- **Reason Mathematically** How did you decide which arrangements work well?

Vocabulary

Draw or write to show examples for each term. Then draw or write to show other math words in the unit.

composite number a number that has more than one pair of factors.

My Example

expression a group of one or more numbers, unknowns, and/or operation symbols that represents a quantity. For example, 3×4.

My Example

factor pair two numbers that are multiplied together to give a product.

My Example

factors of a number whole numbers that multiply together to get the given number.

My Example

multiple the product of a given number and any other whole number.

My Example

multiplicative comparison a comparison that tells how many times as many. For example, $7 \times 3 = 21$ tells that 21 is 3 times as many as 7, and that 21 is 7 times as many as 3.

My Example

prime number   a whole number greater than 1 whose only factors are 1 and itself.

My Example

remainder   the amount left over when one number does not divide another number a whole number of times.

My Example

rule   a procedure that is followed to go from one number or shape to the next in a pattern.

My Example

symbol   a character, such as a letter or question mark, that can be used to stand for an unknown number in an equation.

My Example

unknown   the value you need to find to solve a problem.

My Example

My Word: _____

_____

_____

My Example

Multi-Digit Operations and Measurement

Multiplication, Division, Perimeter, and Area

☑ SELF CHECK

Before starting this unit, check off the skills you know below. As you complete each lesson, see how many more skills you can check off!

I can . . .	Before	After
Multiply a four-digit number by a one-digit number, for example: 2,810 × 3 = 8,430.	☐	☐
Multiply a two-digit number by a two-digit number, for example: 62 × 33 = 2,046.	☐	☐
Use multiplication to convert measurements.	☐	☐
Divide a three-digit number by a one-digit number, for example: 348 ÷ 6 = 58.	☐	☐
Divide a four-digit number by a one-digit number, for example: 6,328 ÷ 4 = 1,582.	☐	☐
Use the perimeter formula for rectangles, for example: $P = (2 \times 12) + (2 \times 5)$ for a rectangle with length of 12 feet and width of 5 feet.	☐	☐
Use the area formula for rectangles, for example: $A = 9 \times 3$ for a rectangle with length of 9 feet and width of 3 feet.	☐	☐

Build Your Vocabulary

Math Vocabulary

Label the multiplication equation using review words.

4   ×   8   =   32

....

Write a multiplication equation. Then describe it to your partner using review words.

.... × .... = ...

Label each red number with a review word. Then discuss the difference between the two words with your partner.

20 ÷ 5 = **4**   4 × 5 = **20**

....

Academic Vocabulary

Put a check next to the academic words you know. Then use the words to complete the sentences.

☐ label   ☐ process   ☐ develop   ☐ likely

1 When you .... the parts of a diagram, you describe what each part is called.

2 You should always follow the same .... during a fire drill. Knowing the steps to take will help you exit safely.

3 Reading helps you .... your vocabulary.

4 The storm clouds and wind mean it is .... it will rain.

Multiply by One-Digit Numbers

LESSON 11

Dear Family,

This week your child is learning to multiply two-, three-, and four-digit numbers by one-digit numbers.

Your child is learning to multiply a greater number by a one-digit number, such as 324 × 9.

One way to multiply is to use **partial products**. With this strategy, you multiply each digit in 324 by 9, taking into account the place value of each digit.

The first step is to write the multiplication vertically. Next, find the individual partial products. Then add the partial products together to find the total product of the multiplication.

$$
\begin{array}{r}
324 \\
\times \quad 9 \\
\hline
36 \\
180 \\
+\ 2,700 \\
\hline
2,916
\end{array}
$$

$36 \longrightarrow 9 \times 4$ ones
$180 \longrightarrow 9 \times 2$ tens
$2,700 \longrightarrow 9 \times 3$ hundreds

So, 324 × 9 = 2,916.

Invite your child to share what he or she knows about multiplying by one-digit numbers by doing the following activity together.

ACTIVITY MULTIPLYING BY ONE-DIGIT NUMBERS

Do this activity with your child to multiply a three-digit number by a one-digit number.

An adult elephant can eat between 200 and 600 pounds of food each day. Multiplication is a good way to find how much an elephant can eat over several days.

- Have your child choose a number between 200 and 600. Suppose this number is the number of pounds of food an elephant eats in one day. For example, your child might choose 532.

- Have your child use this number to find out how much the elephant eats in a week (7 days).

- Have your child multiply to find the answer.

$$
\begin{array}{r}
532 \\
\times \quad 7 \\
\hline
14 \\
210 \\
+ \, 3{,}500 \\
\hline
3{,}724
\end{array}
$$

$\quad 14 \longrightarrow 7 \times 2$
$\quad 210 \longrightarrow 7 \times 30$
$\quad +\,3{,}500 \longrightarrow 7 \times 500$

So, the elephant eats 3,724 pounds of food in one week!

- Switch roles and repeat the activity.

Look for real-life opportunities to multiply two-, three-, and four-digit numbers by one-digit numbers with your child.

Explore Multiplying by One-Digit Numbers

You have learned how to break apart numbers to multiply and how to multiply one-digit numbers by multiples of ten. Use what you know to try to solve the problem below.

What is the product of 3 and 57?

TRY IT

 **Math Toolkit**
• base-ten blocks
• counters
• bowls
• grid paper
• sticky notes
• number lines
• multiplication models

DISCUSS IT

Ask your partner: How did you get started?

Tell your partner: I started by . . .

CONNECT IT

 LOOK BACK

Explain how you found the product of 3 and 57.

2 LOOK AHEAD

You can use arrays, area models, and **partial products** to break apart numbers to help you multiply. The array at the right uses base-ten blocks to show 3 × 157.

100   +   50   +   7

a. Write 157 in expanded form. ....

b. Fill in the blanks below to show how to find 3 × 157.

3 × 157 = (3 × ....) + (3 × ....) + (3 × ....)

= .... + ... + ...

= ....

3 {

c. What do you notice about the number of zeros in the product of 3 and 50 and in the product of 3 and 100? How many zeros would be in the product of 3 × 1,000? Explain.

3 REFLECT

How does breaking apart the multiplication problem above by place value help you solve the problem?

....

....

....

Prepare for Multiplying by One-Digit Numbers

1 Think about what you know about multiplication. Fill in each box. Use words, numbers, and pictures. Show as many ideas as you can.

What Is It?	What I Know About It

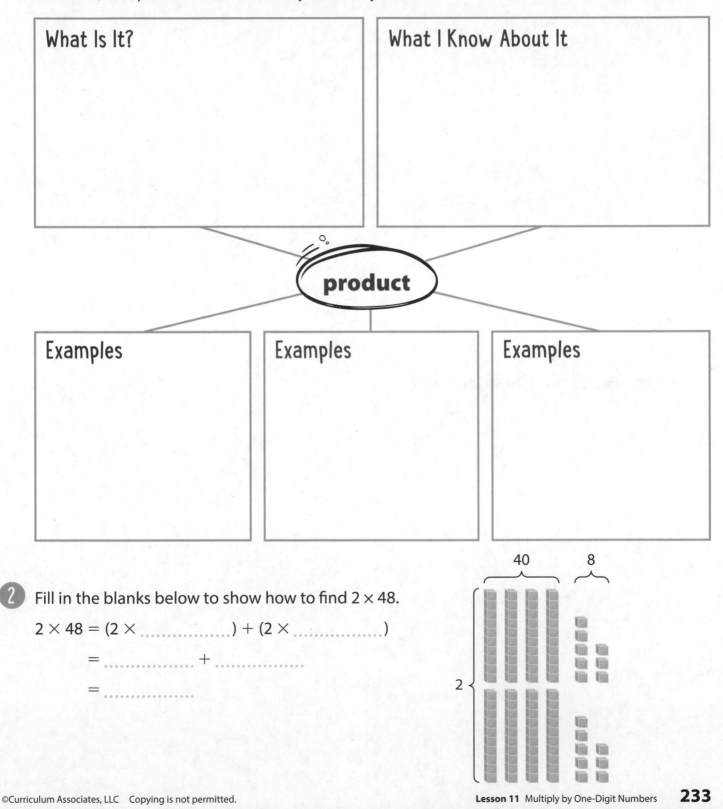

product

Examples	Examples	Examples

2 Fill in the blanks below to show how to find 2×48.

$2 \times 48 = (2 \times \underline{\hspace{2cm}}) + (2 \times \underline{\hspace{2cm}})$

$= \underline{\hspace{2cm}} + \underline{\hspace{2cm}}$

$= \underline{\hspace{2cm}}$

Solve the problem. Show your work.

What is the product of 4 and 62?

Solution ....

 Check your answer. Show your work.

Develop Multiplying a Three-Digit Number by a One-Digit Number

Read and try to solve the problem below.

What is the product of 3 and 254?

TRY IT

Math Toolkit
- base-ten blocks
- grid paper
- index cards
- sticky notes
- number lines
- multiplication models

DISCUSS IT

Ask your partner: Can you explain that again?

Tell your partner: I agree with you about . . . because . . .

Explore different ways to understand multiplying a three-digit number by a one-digit number.

What is the product of 3 and 254?

MODEL IT

You can use an array of base-ten blocks to help you multiply.

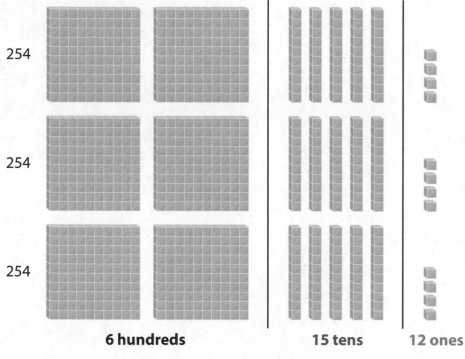

254

254

254

6 hundreds   **15 tens**   **12 ones**

$3 \times 254 = \mathbf{600} + \mathbf{150} + \mathbf{12}$

MODEL IT

You can also multiply using partial products.

$$
\begin{array}{r}
254 \\
\times \quad 3 \\
\hline
\mathbf{12} \longrightarrow 3 \times 4 \text{ ones} \\
\mathbf{150} \longrightarrow 3 \times 5 \text{ tens} \\
+\ \mathbf{600} \longrightarrow 3 \times 2 \text{ hundreds} \\
\hline
?
\end{array}
$$

The partial products are **12**, **150**, and **600**.

The product is the sum of the partial products: **12** + **150** + **600**.

CONNECT IT

Now you will use the problem from the previous page to help you understand how to multiply three-digit numbers by one-digit numbers.

 In the first Model It, what do the numbers 600, 150, and 12 in the equation below the array represent?

 How can you find the product of 3 and 254 in the first Model It?

 Where do you see the 6 hundreds, 15 tens, and 12 ones in the second Model It?

④ What is the sum of the partial products in the second Model It? ....

⑤ How can you use estimation to check that your answer is reasonable?

 How do both Model Its show breaking apart a factor to multiply?

⑦ **REFLECT**

Look back at your Try It, strategies by classmates, and Model Its. Which models or strategies do you like best for multiplying a three-digit number by a one-digit number? Explain.

....

....

....

....

APPLY IT

Use what you just learned to solve these problems.

 $2 \times 163 = ?$

Show your work.

Solution ....

 Find the product of 5 and 738. Estimate to check that your answer is reasonable. Show your work.

Solution ....
....

10 What is the product of 859 and 7? Show your work.

Solution ....

Practice Multiplying a Three-Digit Number by a One-Digit Number

Study the Example showing one way to multiply a three-digit number by a one-digit number. Then solve problems 1–5.

EXAMPLE

Find the product of 2 and 546.

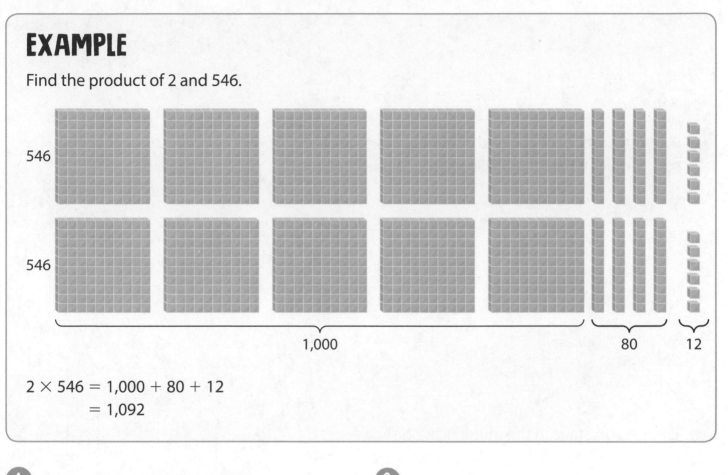

546

546

1,000   80   12

$2 \times 546 = 1,000 + 80 + 12$
$\quad\quad\quad = 1,092$

① Look at the multiplication above. Use partial products to find 2×546. Fill in the boxes.

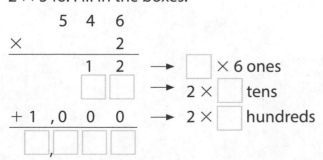

$\boxed{} \times 6$ ones

$2 \times \boxed{}$ tens

$2 \times \boxed{}$ hundreds

② $3 \times 132 = ?$

Show your work.

Solution ....

Find 6 × 915. Show your work.

Solution ....

4 Find the product of 483 and 7. Estimate to check that your answer is reasonable. Show your work.

Solution ....

5 There is a mistake in the multiplication shown. Explain what mistake is made. Then find the correct product.

$$
\begin{array}{r}
607 \\
\times \quad 4 \\
\hline
28 \\
+ \ 240 \\
\hline
268
\end{array}
$$

Solution ....

Develop Multiplying a Four-Digit Number by a One-Digit Number

Read and try to solve the problem below.

> Ezekiel has 3 building sets. Each set includes 1,125 pieces. How many pieces are in all 3 sets?

TRY IT

Math Toolkit
- base-ten blocks
- grid paper
- index cards
- sticky notes
- number lines
- multiplication models

DISCUSS IT

Ask your partner: Do you agree with me? Why or why not?

Tell your partner: I disagree with this part because …

Explore different ways to understand multiplying a four-digit number by a one-digit number.

> **Ezekiel has 3 building sets. Each set includes 1,125 pieces.
> How many pieces are in all 3 sets?**

PICTURE IT

You can use an area model to help understand the problem.

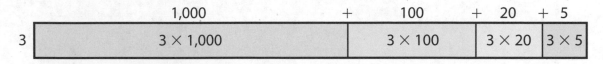

	1,000	+	100	+ 20	+ 5
3	3 × 1,000		3 × 100	3 × 20	3 × 5

$$3 \times 1{,}125 = (3 \times 1{,}000) + (3 \times 100) + (3 \times 20) + (3 \times 5)$$
$$= 3{,}000 + 300 + 60 + 15$$

MODEL IT

You can also multiply the numbers using partial products.

$$
\begin{array}{r}
1{,}125 \\
\times \quad 3 \\
\hline
15 \\
60 \\
300 \\
+ \ 3{,}000 \\
\hline
? \\
\end{array}
$$

15 → 3 × 5 ones
60 → 3 × 2 tens
300 → 3 × 1 hundred
3,000 → 3 × 1 thousand

The partial products are **15**, **60**, **300**, and **3,000**.

The product is the sum of the partial products.

CONNECT IT

Now you will use the problem from the previous page to help you understand how to multiply four-digit numbers by one-digit numbers.

1 What is the expanded form of 1,125? .... + ... + ... + ...

2 How is the expanded form used in the equation in **Picture It**?

3 What is the sum of the numbers in the equation in **Picture It** and the sum of the partial products in **Model It**? ....

4 The partial products in **Model It** shows first multiplying the 3 by the value of the digit in the ones column. Would the product change if you first multiplied the 3 by the value of the digit in the thousands column? Explain.

5 Describe how the factor 3 is used with the factor 1,125 to find the product.

6 Explain how you multiply a four-digit number by a one-digit number.

7 **REFLECT**

Look back at your **Try It**, strategies by classmates, and **Picture It** and **Model It**. Which models or strategies do you like best for multiplying a four-digit number by a one-digit number? Explain.

....

....

....

....

....

APPLY IT

Use what you just learned to solve these problems.

8 5,342 × 4 = ? Show your work.

Solution ....

9 Find the product of 7 and 3,928. Estimate to check that your answer is reasonable. Show your work.

Solution ....

10 2,041 × 6 = ? Show your work.

Solution ....

Practice Multiplying a Four-Digit Number by a One-Digit Number

Study the Example showing one way to multiply a four-digit number by a one-digit number. Then solve problems 1–5.

EXAMPLE

Jesse's family has 4 music players. Each music player can hold 8,352 songs. What is the total number of songs all 4 music players can hold?

Use an area model.

	8,000	+	300	+ 50	+ 2
4	4 × 8,000		4 × 300	4 × 50	4 × 2

$$4 \times 8,352 = (4 \times 8,000) + (4 \times 300) + (4 \times 50) + (4 \times 2)$$
$$= 32,000 + 1,200 + 200 + 8$$
$$= 33,408$$

All 4 music players can hold a total of 33,408 songs.

1 Complete the multiplication to use partial products to find 4 × 8,352.

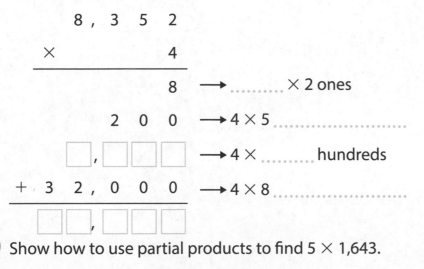

```
      8 , 3  5  2
   ×            4
   ──────────────
              8  ⟶ ·········· × 2 ones
        2  0  0  ⟶ 4 × 5 ······················
   ☐ , ☐ ☐ ☐   ⟶ 4 × ·········· hundreds
 + 3 2 , 0  0  0  ⟶ 4 × 8 ······················
   ☐ ☐ , ☐ ☐ ☐
```

2 Show how to use partial products to find 5 × 1,643.

3. Write $4 \times 3{,}569$ in expanded form to show the place value of each digit. Then find the product.

4. Lee earns $1,075 each month. How much does he earn in 6 months? Estimate to check that your answer is reasonable. Show your work.

Solution

5. Look at Callie's work for finding $3 \times 9{,}423$.

   a. Explain what Callie did wrong.

   $$
   \begin{array}{r}
   9{,}423 \\
   \times \quad 3 \\
   \hline
   9 \\
   60 \\
   120 \\
   + \, 2{,}700 \\
   \hline
   2{,}889
   \end{array}
   $$

   b. How can using estimation show that Callie's answer is wrong?

   c. What is the correct answer?

Refine Multiplying by One-Digit Numbers

Complete the Example below. Then solve problems 1–9.

EXAMPLE

An aquarium has 6 female sea turtles. Each turtle lays up to 1,785 eggs a year. Suppose each turtle lays 1,785 eggs this year. How many eggs do the turtles lay in all this year?

Look at how you could show your work using an area model.

	1,000 +	700 +	80 +	5
6	6 × 1,000	6 × 700	6 × 80	6 × 5

$6 \times 1{,}785 = (6 \times 1{,}000) + (6 \times 700) + (6 \times 80) + (6 \times 5)$
$= 6{,}000 + 4{,}200 + 480 + 30$

Solution ....

The student multiplied 6 by the value of the digit in each place in 1,785.

PAIR/SHARE
How else could you solve this problem?

APPLY IT

1 Find 435 × 2. Show your work.

Could you use an array to help you solve this problem?

PAIR/SHARE
How can you check that your answer is reasonable?

Solution ....

2 Find 4 × 6,309. Estimate to check that your answer is reasonable. Show your work.

How could partial products help you solve this problem?

Solution ....

PAIR/SHARE
Is your estimate close to your answer?

3 A hardware store has 147 containers of paint. Each container holds 5 gallons of paint. How many gallons of paint does the store have?

Ⓐ 235

Ⓑ 505

Ⓒ 735

Ⓓ 905

Dale chose Ⓐ as the correct answer. How did he get that answer?

Multiply 5 by the value of the digit in each place in 147.

PAIR/SHARE
Does Dale's answer make sense?

4 Select all the expressions that have a product of 810.

Ⓐ 90 × 9

Ⓑ 405 × 2

Ⓒ (3 × 20) + (3 × 70)

Ⓓ (2 × 400) × (2 × 5)

Ⓔ (5 × 100) + (5 × 60) + (5 × 2)

5 Mr. Larson is planning a pizza party for 273 people. He plans on 3 slices of pizza for each person. How many slices of pizza is this in all?

Ⓐ 276

Ⓑ 546

Ⓒ 619

Ⓓ 819

6 Find 2,906 × 2.

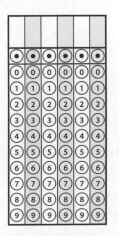

7 Lara says, "When you multiply a three-digit number by a one-digit number, the product is always a four-digit number." Lara writes an equation to support her statement. Greg writes an equation to show that Lara's statement is false.

Complete the equations below to show a possible equation each person could have written.

Lara's equation: 328 × .... = ...

Greg's equation: 328 × .... = ...

8 Fourth-grade students hold a recycling drive. In one week, they collect 1,238 water bottles each day. How many water bottles do the fourth graders collect that week? Estimate to check that your answer is reasonable. Show your work. [*Hint*: There are 7 days in one week.]

Solution ....

....

9 MATH JOURNAL

Explain what strategy you would use to find 357 × 8. Then use that strategy to find the product.

☑ SELF CHECK Go back to the Unit 3 Opener and see what you can check off.

Multiply by Two-Digit Numbers

Dear Family,

This week your child is learning to multiply two-digit numbers by two-digit numbers.

Your child is learning to multiply a two-digit number by another two-digit number, such as 17×38.

One way to multiply two-digit numbers is to use an area model. With this strategy, you multiply using the place value of each digit.

The area model below shows the number **17** as **10 + 7** at the left of the rectangle as its width and the number **38** as **30 + 8** along the top of the rectangle as its length. First, find the individual products that represent each individual area. Then add the products together to find the total area. The total area is the product of 17 and 38.

	30	**+**	**8**
10	10×30 1 ten $\times$ 3 tens = 3 hundreds **300**		10×8 1 ten $\times$ 8 = 8 tens **80**
+			
7	7×30 7×3 tens = 21 tens **210**		$7 \times 8 = 56$

$300 + 210 + 80 + 56 = 646$

$17 \times 38 = 646$

Invite your child to share what he or she knows about multiplying by two-digit numbers by doing the following activity together.

ACTIVITY MULTIPLYING BY TWO-DIGIT NUMBERS

Do this activity with your child to multiply two-digit numbers.

Materials timer or watch with a second hand

- Together with your child, think of things that can be counted in one minute, such as the number of times you clap your hands or the number of steps you walk.

- Choose one idea. Have one person do the activity while the other person uses a timer or watch to time the activity for one minute.

- The person doing the activity counts how many. Count carefully.
  Stop counting when the person with the timer says "Stop!"
  For example, you might clap your hands for one minute and count 92 claps.

- Have your child use that number to figure out how many could be counted in 15 minutes.
  For example, to find out the number of times you might clap your hands in 15 minutes, your child would find: 15×92.

- Have your child multiply to find the answer.

- Switch roles and repeat the activity.

Look for other real-life opportunities to multiply two-digit numbers with your child.

Explore Multiplying by Two-Digit Numbers

You have learned how to multiply two-digit numbers by one-digit numbers, how to multiply one-digit numbers by multiples of 10, and how to break apart numbers by place value to multiply. Use what you know to try to solve the problem below.

▼ **What is the product of 14 and 13?**

TRY IT

🧰 Math Toolkit
• base-ten blocks
• counters
• cups
• paper plates
• grid paper
• multiplication models

DISCUSS IT

Ask your partner: Can you explain that again?

Tell your partner: I am not sure how to find the answer because . . .

CONNECT IT

LOOK BACK

Explain how you found the product of 14 and 13.

LOOK AHEAD

To multiply a two-digit number by another two-digit number, you need to understand how to multiply by multiples of 10.

a. Fill in the blanks to show how to multiply by multiples of 10.

Expression	Think of it as . . .	Think of it as . . .	Product
3 × 2	3 × 2 ones	6 ones	....
3 × 20	3 × 2 tens	.... tens	60
30 × 20	3 tens × 2 tens	.... hundreds	600
	3 × 10 × 2 × 10		
	3 × 2 × 10 × 10		
	6 ×		

b. Complete the area model. Then add the four partial products to find 25 × 32.

	30 +	2
20	20 × 30 =	20 × 2 =
+ 5	5 × 30 =	5 × 2 =

.... + ... + ... + ... = ...

3 REFLECT

Suppose you want to find 30 × 30. How can you use a basic fact and breaking apart numbers to find the product of these multiples of 10?

....

....

Prepare for Multiplying by Two-Digit Numbers

1 Think about what you know about multiplication. Fill in each box. Use words, numbers, and pictures. Show as many ideas as you can.

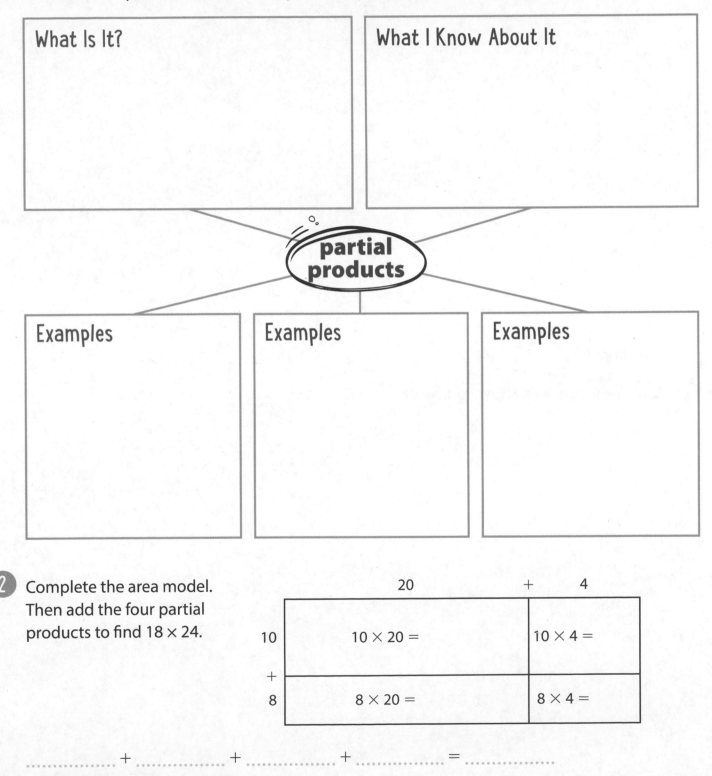

What Is It?

What I Know About It

partial products

Examples

Examples

Examples

2 Complete the area model. Then add the four partial products to find 18 × 24.

	20	+	4
10	10 × 20 =		10 × 4 =
+ 8	8 × 20 =		8 × 4 =

.... + ... + ... + ... = ...

Solve the problem. Show your work.

What is the product of 16 and 12?

Solution ....

 Check your answer. Show your work.

Develop Multiplying by Two-Digit Numbers

Read and try to solve the problem below.

> **Folding chairs are set up in a school auditorium for a play. There are 16 rows of chairs. Each row has 28 chairs. How many folding chairs are set up for the play?**

TRY IT

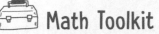 **Math Toolkit**
- base-ten blocks
- grid paper
- multiplication models

DISCUSS IT

Ask your partner: Why did you choose that strategy?

Tell your partner: A model I used was … It helped me …

Explore different ways to understand multiplying a two-digit number by a two-digit number.

> **Folding chairs are set up in a school auditorium for a play. There are 16 rows of chairs. Each row has 28 chairs. How many folding chairs are set up for the play?**

PICTURE IT

You can use an area model to multiply two-digit numbers.

To solve this problem, multiply 28 by 16.

	20	+	8
10	$10 \times 20 = 200$		$10 \times 8 = 80$
+			
6	$6 \times 20 = 120$		$6 \times 8 = 48$

$$200 + 80 + 120 + 48 = ?$$

MODEL IT

You can also multiply two-digit numbers using partial products.

$$
\begin{array}{r}
28 \\
\times\ 16 \\
\hline
48 \\
120 \\
80 \\
+\ 200 \\
\hline
? \\
\end{array}
$$

$48 \longrightarrow$ 6 ones $\times$ 8 ones
$120 \longrightarrow$ 6 ones $\times$ 2 tens
$80 \longrightarrow$ 1 ten $\times$ 8 ones
$200 \longrightarrow$ 1 ten $\times$ 2 tens

CONNECT IT

Now you will use the problem from the previous page to help you understand how to multiply a two-digit number by a two-digit number.

 Why is the area model divided into four sections?

 How do the four steps in the multiplication using partial products in **Model It** relate to the four sections in the area model in **Picture It**?

3 What is the sum of the partial products and also the product of 28 and 16?

4 Would the product change if 20 + 8 on the top of the area model were changed to 10 + 10 + 8? Explain.

5 How could you estimate to check the reasonableness of your answer to 28 × 16 by multiplying with easier numbers?

6 REFLECT

Look back at your **Try It**, strategies by classmates, and **Picture It** and **Model It**. Which models or strategies do you like best for multiplying a two-digit number by a two-digit number? Explain.

APPLY IT

Use what you just learned to solve these problems.

7 Complete the area model below. Then add the partial products to find the product of 27 and 21. Show your work.

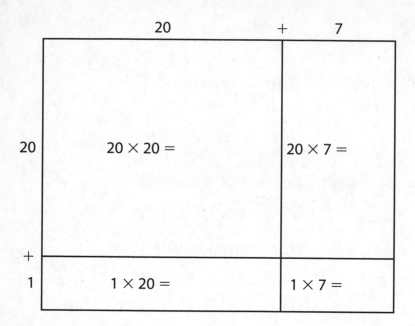

Solution

8 Find 37×23. Show your work.

Solution

9 Select all the expressions that have a product of 640.

Ⓐ 10×64

Ⓑ 60×40

Ⓒ 80×80

Ⓓ $(30 + 2) \times 20$

Ⓔ $(40 \times 10) + (40 \times 6)$

Practice Multiplying by Two-Digit Numbers

Study the Example showing how to multiply a two-digit number by a two-digit number to solve a word problem. Then solve problems 1–6.

EXAMPLE

Aaron spends 35 minutes at each guitar lesson. He has 12 guitar lessons. How many minutes does Aaron spend at his guitar lessons?

Use an area model to multiply 35 by 12.

	30	+	5
10	10 × 30 1 ten × 3 tens = 3 hundreds **300**		10 × 5 1 ten × 5 = 5 tens **50**
+ 2	2 × 30 2 × 3 tens = 6 tens **60**		2 × 5 = **10**

$300 + 50 + 60 + 10 = 420$

Aaron spends 420 minutes at his guitar lessons.

1 Look at the Example above. Use partial products to multiply 35 by 12. Fill in the blanks.

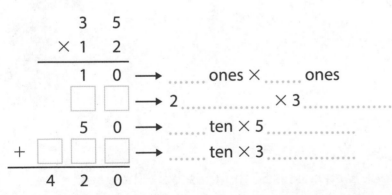

```
      3   5
  ×   1   2
  ─────────
      1   0   ⟶  ........ ones × ........ ones
    □   □     ⟶  2 .............. × 3 ..............
      5   0   ⟶  ........ ten × 5 ..............
+ □  □  □     ⟶  ........ ten × 3 ..............
  ─────────
    4   2   0
```

2 Show how to use an area model to multiply 71 by 48.

$71 \times 48 =$ .... + ... + ... + ... = ...

③ Show how to use partial products to multiply 48 by 71.

$48 \times 71 =$ ....

④ Tell whether each equation is *True* or *False*.

	True	False
$18 \times 42 = (10 \times 40) + (10 \times 2) + (8 \times 40) + (8 \times 2)$	Ⓐ	Ⓑ
$60 \times 15 = (6 \times 10) + (6 \times 5)$	Ⓒ	Ⓓ
$37 \times 22 = (30 \times 20) + (30 \times 20) + (7 \times 20) + (7 \times 20)$	Ⓔ	Ⓕ
$99 \times 11 = (1 \times 9) + (1 \times 90) + (10 \times 9) + (10 \times 90)$	Ⓖ	Ⓗ

⑤ Mr. Greene prepares 28 bags of glass tiles for his art class. He puts 40 glass tiles in each bag. How many glass tiles does Mr. Greene use? Estimate to check that your answer is reasonable. Show your work.

Solution ....

⑥ Stephanie has 6 classes a day at school. Each class is 52 minutes long. She goes to school 5 days a week. How much time does she spend in class each week? Show two different ways to solve this problem. Show your work.

Solution ....

Refine Multiplying by Two-Digit Numbers

Complete the Example below. Then solve problems 1–9.

EXAMPLE

What is the product of 73 and 58?

Look at how you could show your work using partial products.

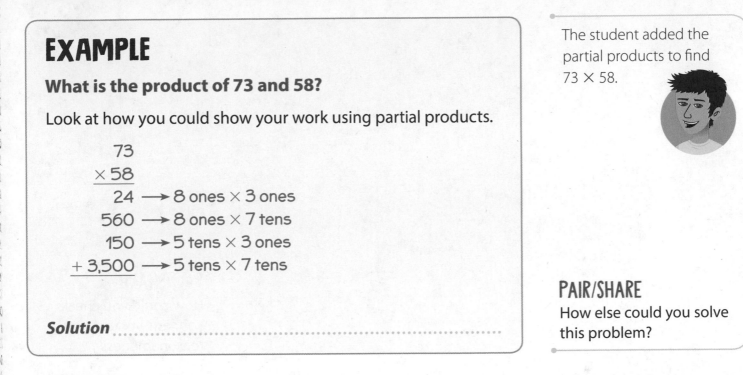

```
      73
    × 58
      24  ──→ 8 ones × 3 ones
     560  ──→ 8 ones × 7 tens
     150  ──→ 5 tens × 3 ones
  + 3,500 ──→ 5 tens × 7 tens
```

Solution ....

The student added the partial products to find 73 × 58.

PAIR/SHARE
How else could you solve this problem?

APPLY IT

1 Find the product of 15 and 24. Show your work.

Should you multiply 15 × 24 or 24 × 15?

PAIR/SHARE
How did you decide which method to use to help you solve the problem?

Solution ....

2 What is the product of 12 and 32? Show your work.

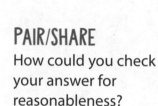

Solution ....

3 A deli is preparing trays of sandwiches. There are 48 trays. Each tray has 23 sandwiches. How many sandwiches are there?

Ⓐ 240

Ⓑ 824

Ⓒ 1,104

Ⓓ 1,932

Nathan chose Ⓐ as the correct answer. How did he get that answer?

4 A person blinks about 16 times per minute. About how many times does a person blink in 3 hours? [*Hint:* 1 hour = 60 minutes]

Ⓐ 48

Ⓑ 96

Ⓒ 960

Ⓓ 2,880

5 What is the product of 47 and 91?

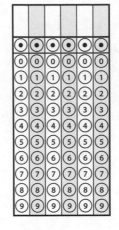

6 Which models below could represent the solution to the problem 45 × 15?

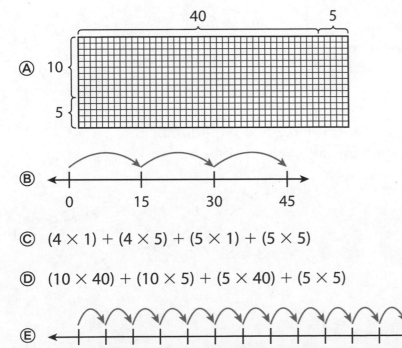

Ⓐ

Ⓑ

Ⓒ (4 × 1) + (4 × 5) + (5 × 1) + (5 × 5)

Ⓓ (10 × 40) + (10 × 5) + (5 × 40) + (5 × 5)

Ⓔ

Lesson 12 Multiply by Two-Digit Numbers   **265**

7 Complete each equation below using a factor between 20 and 30 so that:

- The missing factor in Ian's equation will give the greatest possible three-digit product.

- The missing factor in Tia's equation will give the least possible four-digit product.

Ian's equation: 43 × .... = ...

Tia's equation: 43 × .... = ...

8 Mo has 14 tutoring sessions. Each session is 35 minutes long. How many minutes does Mo spend in the 14 sessions? Show your work.

Solution ....

9 **MATH JOURNAL**

Write a word problem you can solve by multiplying 2 two-digit numbers. Solve the problem and show how to find the answer.

☑ **SELF CHECK** Go back to the Unit 3 Opener and see what you can check off.

Use Multiplication to Convert Measurements

Dear Family,

This week your child is learning to use multiplication to convert measurements.

When you **convert** from a larger unit, such as a pound, to a smaller unit, such as an ounce, you use multiplication.

Knowing that there are 16 ounces in 1 pound, you can find the number of ounces in a number of pounds by multiplying the number of pounds by 16. For example, to find how many ounces are in 10 pounds, you multiply 10 by 16.

When your child is converting larger units to smaller units, he or she is not only becoming more familiar with the relative sizes of units, but is also getting practice with multiplication!

Sometimes it is convenient to use a table to convert measurements. The diagram below shows that each pound is the same as 16 ounces.

10 pounds (lb)

1 lb	1 lb	1 lb	1 lb	1 lb	1 lb	1 lb	1 lb	1 lb	1 lb
16 oz	16 oz	16 oz	16 oz	16 oz	16 oz	16 oz	16 oz	16 oz	16 oz

160 ounces (oz)

The table below shows how many ounces are in a number of pounds.

Pounds (lb)	1	2	3	4	5	6	7	8	9	10
Ounces (oz)	16	32	48	64	80	96	112	128	144	160

When your child writes $p \times 16$ to tell how many ounces are in p pounds, he or she is applying the skill of writing an expression. The expression gives the formula for converting any number of pounds to ounces.

Invite your child to share what he or she knows about converting measurements by doing the following activity together.

ACTIVITY USING MULTIPLICATION TO CONVERT MEASUREMENTS

Do this activity with your child to use multiplication to convert measurements.

Materials ruler or yardstick

• Measure the stride of your child. Put a mark at your child's toe to identify a "starting point."

• Ask your child to take a long step and put another mark at the toe of the foot taking the step.

• Measure the distance in *feet* between the marks. Round the measurement to the nearest foot.

• Now, find the measure of your child's stride in inches by converting feet to inches. There are 12 inches in one foot.

• Talk with your child about different ways you could convert the measurement, such as using a diagram or a table, drawing a picture, or writing an expression. Ask: *How could you use a different way to convert the measurement?*

• Now, measure the stride of another family member. First, find the measure in feet and then convert it to inches. Compare the length of this stride to the length of your child's stride. Who has a longer stride? Who has a shorter stride?

Explore Using Multiplication to Convert Measurements

You have used basic units of measure such as hours and minutes. Now you will learn how to express the same measurement using different units in order to solve problems. Use what you know to try to solve the problem below.

Learning Target
- Know relative sizes of measurement units within one system of units including km, m, cm; kg, g; lb, oz.; l, ml; hr, min, sec. Within a single system of measurement, express measurements in a larger unit in terms of a smaller unit. Record measurement equivalents in a two-column table.

SMP 1, 2, 3, 4, 5, 6, 7

Lidia hears the announcer on a TV show say, "We will return in 240 seconds." It takes Lidia 5 minutes to wash the dishes. Does Lidia have enough time to wash the dishes before the TV show returns?

Change the number of minutes it takes Lidia to wash the dishes to a number of seconds to find out.

Units of Time
1 minute = 60 seconds
1 hour = 60 minutes
1 day = 24 hours
1 year = 365 days
1 year = about 52 weeks

TRY IT

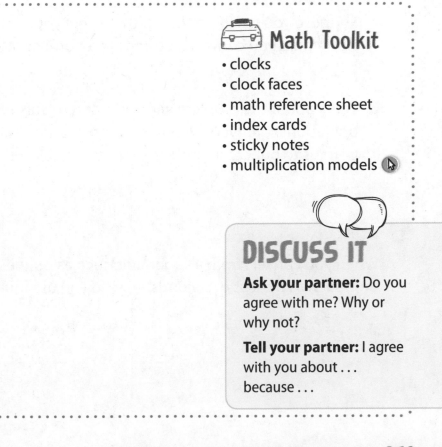

Math Toolkit
- clocks
- clock faces
- math reference sheet
- index cards
- sticky notes
- multiplication models

DISCUSS IT

Ask your partner: Do you agree with me? Why or why not?

Tell your partner: I agree with you about . . . because . . .

CONNECT IT

 LOOK BACK

Explain how you found out if Lidia has enough time to wash the dishes.

 LOOK AHEAD

You already solved a problem about converting units of time from a larger unit to a smaller unit. You can **convert** from larger to smaller units in other systems of measurement, such as length, mass, weight, and liquid volume. Look at the table that shows customary units of weight.

Customary Units of Weight
1 pound = 16 ounces
1 ton = 2,000 pounds

a. Name an object that is about 1 pound.

b. About how many ounces is that object? ....

c. Suppose you had 5 pounds of the object you wrote in problem 2a. How could you convert 5 pounds to a number of ounces?

d. Think about the problem with Lidia and the dishes. Do you use the same operation to convert from minutes to seconds as you use to convert from pounds to ounces in problem 2c? Explain.

③ REFLECT

When you convert from a larger unit, such as pounds or minutes, to a smaller unit, such as ounces or seconds, why do you use multiplication?

Prepare for Using Multiplication to Convert Measurements

1 Think about what you know about measurements. Fill in each box. Use words, numbers, and pictures. Show as many ideas as you can.

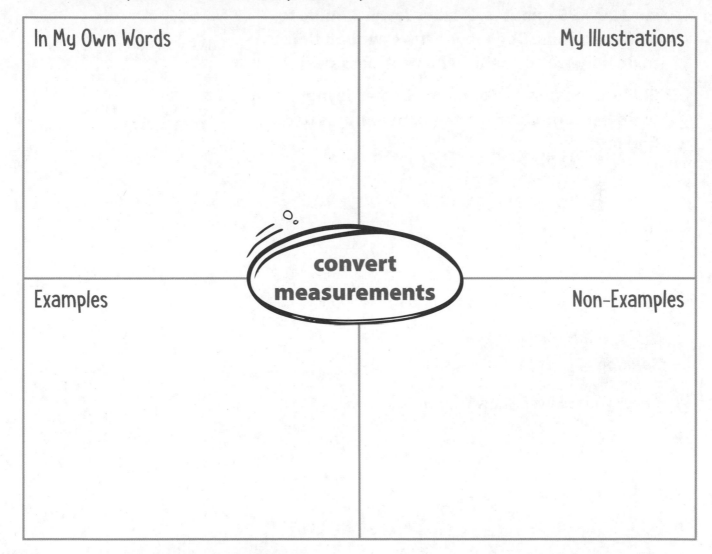

In My Own Words	My Illustrations

convert measurements

Examples	Non-Examples

2 How does the table at the right show converting from larger to smaller units of measurement?

Customary Units of Weight
1 pound = 16 ounces
1 ton = 2,000 pounds

3 Solve the problem. Show your work.

Jayne misses an exercise class. She wants to know if she has enough time to do her errands before the next exercise class. The next class starts in 195 minutes. It takes Jayne 3 hours to do her errands. Does Jayne have enough time to do her errands before the next class starts?

Change the number of hours it takes Jayne to do her errands to a number of minutes to find out.

Units of Time
1 minute = 60 seconds
1 hour = 60 minutes
1 day = 24 hours
1 year = 365 days
1 year = about 52 weeks

Solution

4 Check your answer. Show your work.

Develop Converting Units of Weight and Mass

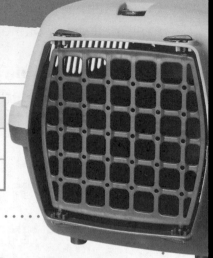

Read and try to solve the problem below.

> Wanda is shopping for a pet carrier for her cat. One small carrier can hold 240 ounces. Her cat weighs 12 pounds. Can the carrier hold her cat?

Customary Units of Weight
1 pound = 16 ounces
1 ton = 2,000 pounds

TRY IT

 **Math Toolkit**
- math reference sheet
- grid paper
- index cards
- sticky notes
- multiplication models

DISCUSS IT

Ask your partner: How did you get started?

Tell your partner: A model I used was . . . It helped me . . .

Explore different ways to understand converting from a larger unit of measurement to a smaller unit of measurement.

> Wanda is shopping for a pet carrier for her cat. One small carrier can hold 240 ounces. Her cat weighs 12 pounds. Can the carrier hold her cat?

Customary Units of Weight
1 pound = 16 ounces
1 ton = 2,000 pounds

MODEL IT

You can use a diagram to convert from a larger unit to a smaller unit.

The diagram shows that there are 16 ounces in 1 pound.

12 pounds (lb)

1 lb	1 lb	1 lb	1 lb	1 lb	1 lb	1 lb	1 lb	1 lb	1 lb	1 lb	1 lb
16 oz	16 oz	16 oz	16 oz	16 oz	16 oz	16 oz	16 oz	16 oz	16 oz	16 oz	16 oz

? ounces (oz)

Find the number of ounces in 12 pounds: $12 \times 16 = ?$

MODEL IT

You can use a table to convert from a larger unit to a smaller unit.

This table shows how many ounces are in different numbers of pounds.

Pounds (lb)	1	2	3	4	5	6	7	8	9	10	11	12
Ounces (oz)	16	32	48	64	80	96	112	128	144	?	?	?

The number of ounces in each column is equal to the number of pounds multiplied by 16.

CONNECT IT

Now you will use the problem from the previous page to help you understand how to convert larger measurement units to smaller measurement units.

 The diagram in the first Model It shows that 1 pound is equal to

how many ounces? ....

 What do you multiply the number of pounds by to find the number of ounces?

 Write an expression that shows how to convert any number of pounds to

ounces. Use *p* to stand for the number of pounds. ....

 Use the expression to solve the problem from the previous page.
Can the carrier hold the cat? Show your work.

 Describe how to convert from a larger unit to a smaller unit.

 REFLECT

Look back at your Try It, strategies by classmates, and Model Its. Which models or strategies do you like best for converting from a larger unit of measurement to a smaller unit of measurement? Explain.

....

....

....

....

Lesson 13 Use Multiplication to Convert Measurements   **275**

APPLY IT

Use what you just learned to solve these problems.

7 Steve buys 14 ounces of kiwis and 2 pounds of peaches. How many more ounces do the peaches weigh than the kiwis? Show your work. (1 pound = 16 ounces)

Solution

8 An empty suitcase has a mass of 2 kilograms. Draw a diagram to find its mass in grams. Show your work.

Metric Units of Mass
1 gram = 1,000 milligrams
1 kilogram = 1,000 grams

Solution

9 The table shows the mass of two boxes of raisins, in grams. Complete the table to show the mass of each box, in milligrams. Show your work.

	Mass in Grams	Mass in Milligrams
Box 1	9	
Box 2	7	

Practice Converting Units of Weight and Mass

Study the Example showing how to convert from a larger unit to a smaller unit of weight. Then solve problems 1–7.

EXAMPLE

Eleanor buys a 3-pound watermelon and 32 ounces of strawberries. How much more does the watermelon weigh than the strawberries? (1 pound = 16 ounces)

Write an expression to convert pounds to ounces. Let p stand for the number of pounds.

$p \times 16$

Find the weight of the watermelon in ounces. The watermelon weighs 48 ounces.

Substitute 3 for p.
$3 \times 16 = 48$

Find the difference between the weight of the watermelon and strawberries.

$48 - 32 = 16$

The watermelon weighs 16 ounces more than the strawberries.

1   Isaiah has a watermelon with a mass of 3 kilograms. Complete the diagram. Then write the mass of the watermelon in grams.

3 kilograms (kg)

1 kg	1 kg	
1,000 g	1,000 g	

.... grams (g)

2   Write an expression that shows how to convert kilograms to grams. Use k to stand for the number of kilograms.

3   Convert the units of mass.

2 kg = ... g   4 kg = ... g

> **Vocabulary**
>
> **convert** to write an equivalent measurement using a different unit.
>
> 1 kilogram = 1,000 grams
>
> ↑   ↑
> unit   unit

4 Complete the table to convert from a larger unit to a smaller unit of weight.

Pounds (lb)	1	2	3	4	5	6	7
Ounces (oz)	16		48				112

5 Neil has 2 pounds of grapes. He uses some to make a fruit salad. Now Neil has 8 ounces of grapes. How many ounces of grapes does Neil use for the fruit salad? Look at the table in problem 4 to help you answer the question. Show your work.

Solution ....

6 Select all the objects that weigh about 1 pound.

Ⓐ a flat-screen TV

Ⓑ three bananas

Ⓒ a house key

Ⓓ a can of soup

Ⓔ a bicycle helmet

7 An adult bottlenose dolphin has a mass of 200 kilograms. What is the mass of an adult bottlenose dolphin in grams? Show your work. (1 kilogram = 1,000 grams)

Solution ....

Develop Converting Units of Liquid Volume

Read and try to solve the problem below.

> Julie makes 4 liters of orange juice.
> How many milliliters of orange juice
> does Julie make?

Metric Units of Liquid Volume
1 liter = 1,000 milliliters

TRY IT

 **Math Toolkit**
- math reference sheet
- grid paper
- index cards
- sticky notes
- multiplication models

DISCUSS IT

Ask your partner: Can you explain that again?

Tell your partner: I am not sure how to find the answer because . . .

Explore different ways to understand converting from a larger unit to a smaller unit of liquid volume.

> Julie makes 4 liters of orange juice. How many milliliters of orange juice does Julie make?

Metric Units of Liquid Volume
1 liter = 1,000 milliliters

PICTURE IT

You can use a picture to help convert from a larger unit to a smaller unit of liquid volume.

Each beaker shows that 1 liter (L) is equal to 1,000 milliliters (mL).

MODEL IT

You can use a table to help convert from a larger unit to a smaller unit of liquid volume.

The table below shows that there are 1,000 milliliters in one liter. It also shows how many milliliters are in 2, 3, 4, and 5 liters.

Liters (L)	1	2	3	4	5
Milliliters (mL)	1,000	2,000	3,000	4,000	5,000

CONNECT IT

Now you will use the problem from the previous page to help you understand how to convert larger units to smaller units of liquid volume.

 Look at the beakers in **Picture It**. How many milliliters are in 1 liter? ....

 Look at the number pairs in each column of the table in **Model It**. Each number of milliliters is how many times the number of liters?

Write an equation to describe the relationship between each pair of numbers in the table.

3 Use the equation to find the number of milliliters in 4 liters.

How many milliliters of orange juice does Julie make? ....

4 Explain why the number of milliliters is always greater than the number of liters for each number pair in the table.

 REFLECT

Look back at your **Try It**, strategies by classmates, and **Picture It** and **Model It**. Which models or strategies do you like best for converting from a larger unit to a smaller unit of liquid volume? Explain.

....

....

....

....

APPLY IT

Use what you just learned to solve these problems.

6 Awan buys 3 liters of apple juice. He drinks 2,500 milliliters of the apple juice over a few days. How many milliliters of apple juice does Awan have left? Show your work. (1 liter = 1,000 milliliters)

Solution ....

7 Aliya makes 8 quarts of punch for a party. Make a table or write an equation to find the number of cups of punch she makes. Show your work.

Customary Units of Liquid Volume
1 cup = 8 fluid ounces
1 pint = 2 cups
1 quart = 2 pints
1 quart = 4 cups
1 gallon = 4 quarts

Solution ....

8 How many quarts are in 6 gallons? Use the table above.

Ⓐ 64

Ⓑ 24

Ⓒ 16

Ⓓ 10

Practice Converting Units of Liquid Volume

Study the Example showing how to convert from a larger unit to a smaller unit of liquid volume. Then solve problems 1–7.

EXAMPLE

Josie makes 4 quarts of iced tea for a family picnic. Her sister makes 14 cups of punch for the picnic. Who makes a greater amount of beverage?

Use a table to convert quarts to cups.

Quarts	1	2	3	4	5
Cups	4	8	12	16	20

Josie makes 4 quarts, or 16 cups of iced tea.
   $16 > 14$

Josie makes a greater amount of beverage.

1. The soccer coach has a container that holds 5 liters of water. How many milliliters of water does the container hold? Fill in the table to answer the question.

Liters (L)	1	2	3	4	5
Milliliters (mL)	1,000		3,000		

The container holds .... of water.

2. Write an expression that shows how to convert liters to milliliters. Use *L* to stand for the number of liters.

3. Convert the units of liquid volume.

   6 L = ... mL   9 L = ... mL

4   Carla has 2 liters of juice. She pours the juice into another container that has 500 milliliters of juice in it. How many milliliters of juice does the container have in all? Show your work. (1 liter = 1,000 milliliters)

Solution ....

5   Select all the objects that can hold about 1 gallon of liquid when filled.

Ⓐ   a paint can

Ⓑ   a paper cup

Ⓒ   a bathtub

Ⓓ   a large jug of milk

Ⓔ   a swimming pool

6   A small bottle contains 2 cups of juice. Do 5 small bottles of juice have a greater amount of juice than a 1-quart bottle of juice? Explain. (1 quart = 4 cups)

7   Rachel has a 4-liter jug of water. She uses it to fill 3 small vases each with 900 mL of water. How much water does Rachel use to fill the vases? How much water is left in the jug? Show your work. (1 liter = 1,000 milliliters)

Solution ....

Refine Using Multiplication to Convert Measurements

Complete the Example below. Then solve problems 1–9 using the Math Reference Sheet as necessary.

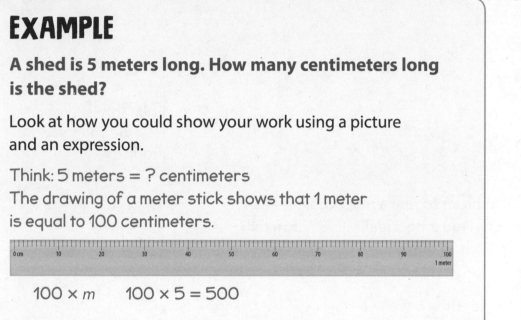

EXAMPLE

A shed is 5 meters long. How many centimeters long is the shed?

Look at how you could show your work using a picture and an expression.

Think: 5 meters = ? centimeters
The drawing of a meter stick shows that 1 meter is equal to 100 centimeters.

100 × m   100 × 5 = 500

Solution ....

The student substituted 5 for *m*: 100 × 5 = 500.

PAIR/SHARE
How else could you solve this problem?

APPLY IT

1 **a.** A bag of potatoes weighs 5 pounds. The bag is placed on a scale. The unit on the scale is ounces. What weight does the scale show? Show your work.

There are 16 ounces in 1 pound.

Solution ....

b. Two pounds of potatoes are taken out of the bag. What weight does the scale show now? Show your work.

PAIR/SHARE
How could you use a table to solve this problem?

Solution ....

2 The amount of liquid in three containers is shown below. Order the liquid measurements from least to greatest. Show your work.

2 gallons   3 quarts   15 cups

There are 4 quarts in 1 gallon. There are 4 cups in 1 quart.

PAIR/SHARE
How did you solve the problem?

Solution ....

3 Aaron is 63 inches tall. In order to ride a roller coaster at an amusement park, a person must be 5 feet tall. Is Aaron tall enough to ride a roller coaster? How many inches shorter or taller is he than 5 feet?

Ⓐ Yes. He is 3 inches taller than 5 feet.

Ⓑ Yes. He is 13 inches taller than 5 feet.

Ⓒ No. He is 7 inches shorter than 5 feet.

Ⓓ No. He is 17 inches shorter than 5 feet.

Tina chose Ⓐ as the correct answer. How did she get that answer?

There are 12 inches in a foot.

PAIR/SHARE
How can you check your answer?

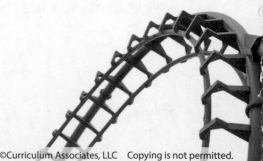

4 Ming buys a watermelon with a mass of 6 kilograms. She cuts off the rind. The remaining watermelon has a mass of 2,500 grams. What is the mass of the rind?

Ⓐ 15,000 grams

Ⓑ 4,500 grams

Ⓒ 3,500 grams

Ⓓ 500 grams

5 Tell whether each measurement is equal to 2 yards, 1 foot.

	Yes	No
4 feet	Ⓐ	Ⓑ
84 inches	Ⓒ	Ⓓ
7 feet	Ⓔ	Ⓕ
1 yard, 2 feet, 24 inches	Ⓖ	Ⓗ

6 Suzie is measuring furniture for her bedroom. She does not have a tape measure or a ruler. Instead, she uses her book. She knows that the length of her book is 8 inches.

The table below shows the total number of book lengths that Suzie uses to measure each object. Complete the table.

Object	Number of Book Lengths	Number of Inches
Bed	11	
Dresser	6	
Bookcase	4	

7 Ramon has an 8-liter jug filled with water. He uses it to fill nine 750-milliliter pitchers with water. How much water does Ramon have left in the jug?

Ⓐ 250 mL

Ⓑ 500 mL

Ⓒ 1,000 mL

Ⓓ 1,250 mL

8 Simone jogs 5 kilometers. How many meters does she jog?
Show your work.

Simone jogs .... meters.

9 MATH JOURNAL

Name an object that is about 3 feet long. Explain how to find the length of the object in inches.

✓ **SELF CHECK** Go back to the Unit 3 Opener and see what you can check off.

Divide Three-Digit Numbers

Dear Family,

This week your child is learning to divide three-digit numbers by one-digit numbers.

Your child is learning about division. He or she is also learning terminology related to division. You may hear your child use the terms dividend, divisor, and quotient. The **dividend** is the number being divided, the **divisor** is the number by which the dividend is divided, and the quotient is the result of the division. If the dividend is not a whole number multiple of the divisor, the amount left is called the remainder.

Your child is learning to divide a three-digit number by a one-digit number. One way your child can divide is by using an area model. With this strategy, your child divides by breaking apart the problem into smaller parts and using repeated subtraction. The problem below shows how to divide 138 by 6.

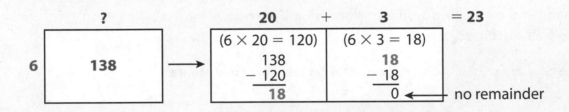

Altogether, there are 20 + 3, or 23, groups of 6 in 138, so **138 ÷ 6 = 23**. Your child is also learning to check the answer by multiplying the quotient, **23**, by the divisor, **6**, to make sure that the product is equal to the dividend of 138. Check: **23 × 6 = 138**, so the answer is correct.

Invite your child to share what he or she knows about dividing three-digit numbers by doing the following activity together.

ACTIVITY DIVIDING THREE-DIGIT NUMBERS

Do this activity with your child to divide three-digit numbers.

Materials book with a number of pages in the hundreds

- With your child, choose a favorite book and look at the number of pages it has.

- Tell your child that you want to read the entire book in 1 week. Ask your child to help you figure out how many pages you would need to read each day to finish the book in 1 week.

- Have your child use division to find the answer. For example, if the book has 157 pages, your child would divide 157 by 7. (157 ÷ 7 = 22 R 3, which means that there are 22 groups of 7 in 157 and a remainder of 3.)

- You and your child can check the answer to the division problem by using multiplication. If you have a remainder, remember to add the remainder to the product.

- Decide what to do if you have a remainder. Will you read one page each day for the number of days shown by the remainder, or will you read all the remaining pages on the last day?

- Repeat this activity with other favorite books at least three more times.

Explore Dividing Three-Digit Numbers

You have learned about division as equal sharing and about the relationship between multiplication and division. Use what you know to try to solve the problem below.

▼ **What is 78 ÷ 3?**

TRY IT

Learning Target

- Find whole-number quotients and remainders with up to four-digit dividends and one-digit divisors, using strategies based on place value, the properties of operations, and/or the relationship between multiplication and division. Illustrate and explain the calculation by using equations, rectangular arrays, and/or area models.

SMP 1, 2, 3, 4, 5, 6, 7, 8

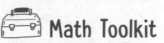 **Math Toolkit**
- base-ten blocks
- counters
- bowls
- paper plates
- grid paper
- multiplication models

DISCUSS IT

Ask your partner: How did you get started?

Tell your partner: At first, I thought . . .

CONNECT IT

 LOOK BACK

Explain how you found the quotient of 78 ÷ 3.

2 LOOK AHEAD

You can solve division problems in many ways. You can use place value, rectangular arrays, area models, equations, and the relationship between multiplication and division. The area model below shows 200 ÷ 4.

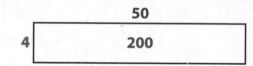

An area model shows both multiplication (**4 × 50 = 200**) and division (**200 ÷ 4 = 50**). You can also use area models to break apart a problem into smaller parts. Fill in the missing labels on two other area models for 200 ÷ 4.

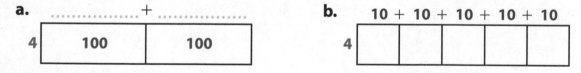

a.

.... + ...

| 4 | 100 | 100 |

b.   10 + 10 + 10 + 10 + 10

** a.** Sometimes there is a remainder left over when you divide. Fill in the remainder for 21 ÷ 4 in the box at the right.

5 R ☐
4)21

b. The **dividend** is .... , the number you are dividing.

c. The **divisor** is .... , the number you are dividing by.

d. The quotient is .... , the result of the division problem.

4 REFLECT

Explain how an area model shows both multiplication and division.

Prepare for Dividing Three-Digit Numbers

1 Think about what you know about division. Fill in each box. Use words, numbers, and pictures. Show as many ideas as you can.

Word	In My Own Words	Example
division		
dividend		
divisor		
quotient		
remainder		

2 Use the term *equal groups* to describe the division problem shown below.

$$123 \div 5 = 24 \text{ R } 3$$

Solve the problem. Show your work.

What is 68 ÷ 4?

Solution ....

4 Check your answer. Show your work.

Develop Dividing with Arrays and Area Models

Read and try to solve the problem below.

What is 136 ÷ 4?

TRY IT

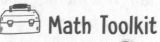 **Math Toolkit**
- base-ten blocks
- counters
- bowls
- paper plates
- grid paper
- multiplication models

DISCUSS IT

Ask your partner: Why did you choose that strategy?

Tell your partner: I do not understand how . . .

Explore different ways to understand dividing three-digit numbers by one-digit numbers.

What is 136 ÷ 4?

MODEL IT

You can use a rectangular array to help you break apart the problem into smaller parts.

The array shows a rectangle divided into 136 squares in 4 rows.

You can use what you know about multiplication and subtraction to break apart 136 and divide the lesser numbers by 4.

	Part 1		**Part 2**		**Part 3**		**Part 4**	
	10	+	10	+	10	+	4	= ?

4

(4 × 10 = 40)	(4 × 10 = 40)	(4 × 10 = 40)	(4 × 4 = 16)
136	96	56	16
− 40	− 40	− 40	− 16
96	56	16	0

MODEL IT

You can use an area model to help you break apart the problem into smaller parts.

This area model uses multiplication and repeated subtraction. You can break apart 136 and divide the lesser numbers by 4.

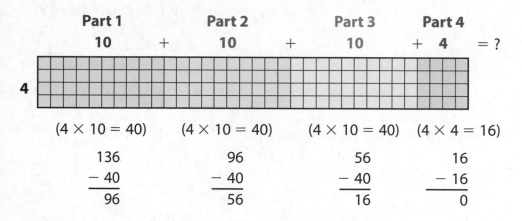

	?		10	+	10	+	10	+	4	= ?

| 4 | 136 | → | 4 | (4 × 10 = 40) 136 − 40 96 | (4 × 10 = 40) 96 − 40 56 | (4 × 10 = 40) 56 − 40 16 | (4 × 4 = 16) 16 − 16 0 |

CONNECT IT

Now you will use the problem from the previous page to help you understand how to use a rectangular array and an area model to divide a three-digit number by a one-digit number.

1 Look at the first **Model It**. Why do you think Parts 1, 2, and 3 of the array show multiplying the divisor, 4, by 10?

2 Why is the area model in the second **Model It** broken into four parts?

3 What is 136 ÷ 4? .... How do both **Model Its** show how to find the quotient of 136 ÷ 4 in a similar way?

4 Explain how using an array and an area model can help you divide.

5 How can you use multiplication to check that your answer is correct?

6 REFLECT

Look back at your **Try It**, strategies by classmates, and **Model Its**. Which models or strategies do you like best for dividing a three-digit number by a one-digit number? Explain.

APPLY IT

Use what you just learned to solve these problems.

7 Complete the area model below to find 132 ÷ 3.

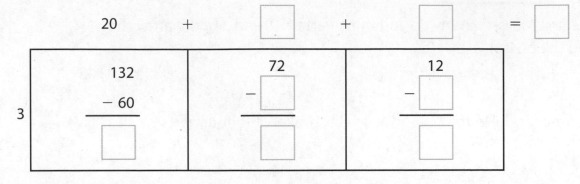

20 + ☐ + ☐ = ☐

Solution ....

8 Complete the array to find 198 ÷ 6. Use multiplication to check your answer. Show your work.

10

6

Solution ....

9 What is 224 divided by 7?

Ⓐ 30

Ⓑ 31

Ⓒ 32

Ⓓ 42

Practice Dividing with Arrays and Area Models

Study the Example showing one way to divide a three-digit number by a one-digit number. Then solve problems 1–5.

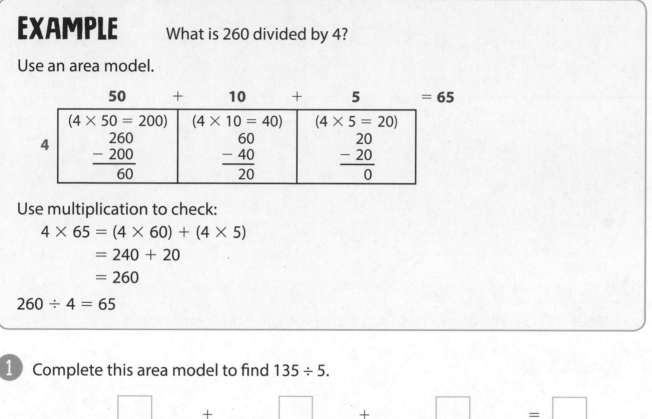

EXAMPLE What is 260 divided by 4?

Use an area model.

	50 +	**10** +	**5** = **65**
4	(4 × 50 = 200) 260 − 200 / 60	(4 × 10 = 40) 60 − 40 / 20	(4 × 5 = 20) 20 − 20 / 0

Use multiplication to check:

$$4 \times 65 = (4 \times 60) + (4 \times 5)$$
$$= 240 + 20$$
$$= 260$$

$$260 \div 4 = 65$$

1 Complete this area model to find 135 ÷ 5.

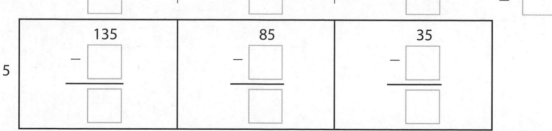

Solution ....

2 Identify the dividend, divisor, and quotient.

a. 900 ÷ 3 = 300

dividend: .... divisor: .... quotient: ....

b. 120 = 600 ÷ 5

dividend: .... divisor: .... quotient: ....

3 Complete the array to find 208 ÷ 8. Show your work.

10

8

Solution ....

4 What is 476 ÷ 7? Use an area model to solve the problem. Show your work.

Solution ....

5 Explain how to use multiplication to check your answer in problem 4.

Develop Dividing with Estimation and Area Models

Read and try to solve the problem below.

> There are 232 people waiting in line for an amusement park ride. Each car on the ride will be filled with 5 people. How many cars are needed to hold all the people waiting in line?

TRY IT

 **Math Toolkit**
- base-ten blocks
- grid paper
- multiplication models

DISCUSS IT

Ask your partner: Do you agree with me? Why or why not?

Tell your partner: I disagree with this part because . . .

Explore how to estimate a quotient and how to use the estimate to divide with an area model.

> **There are 232 people waiting in line for an amusement park ride. Each car on the ride will be filled with 5 people. How many cars are needed to hold all the people waiting in line?**

MODEL IT

You can use the relationship between multiplication and division to estimate the quotient in a division problem with a one-digit divisor.

$232 \div 5 = ?$ and $5 \times ? = 232$

Find the products of 5 and multiples of 10. Make a table.

Number of Cars	10	20	30	40	50
Number of People	50	100	150	200	250

The dividend 232 is between **200** and **250**, so the quotient is between **40** and **50**.

MODEL IT

You can use an area model to solve a division problem with a one-digit divisor.

The estimate shows the quotient is between 40 and 50.
Begin the area model by multiplying 40 by 5.

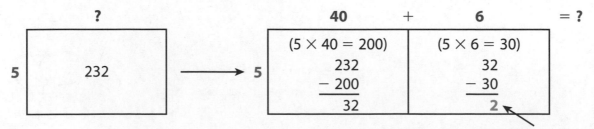

Use multiplication to check:
$$5 \times 46 = (5 \times 40) + (5 \times 6)$$
$$= 200 + 30$$
$$= 230 \qquad\qquad 230 + 2 = 232$$

CONNECT IT

Now you will use the problem from the previous page to help you understand how to estimate a quotient and use the estimate to divide with an area model.

 In the first **Model It**, why do you multiply 5 by multiples of 10?

 Look at the second **Model It**. How can you find the number of cars that are each filled with 5 people?

 What does the remainder mean in this problem?

4 How many cars are needed to hold all the people waiting in line? Explain.

5 How can you break apart a division problem with an area model in order to solve the problem?

 REFLECT

Look back at your **Try It**, strategies by classmates, and **Model Its**. Which models or strategies do you like best for estimating a quotient and for dividing a three-digit number by a one-digit number? Explain.

....

....

....

....

APPLY IT

Use what you just learned to solve these problems.

7 A store orders 315 hats. The hats are shipped in boxes of 8. How many boxes are needed to ship all the hats? First, find which two multiples of 10 the quotient is between. Then find the quotient using an area model. Show your work.

Number of Boxes				
Number of Hats				

Solution ....

8 What is 174 divided by 3? Use multiplication to check your answer. Show your work.

Solution ....

9 Find 456 ÷ 6. Show your work.

Solution ....

Practice Dividing with Estimation and Area Models

Study the Example showing one way to divide a three-digit number by a one-digit number. Then solve problems 1–6.

EXAMPLE

There are 650 flowers to arrange in vases. Each vase holds 6 flowers. How many vases can each be filled with 6 flowers? Are there any flowers left over?

Find $650 \div 6$.
Use an area model.

```
           100          +           8          = 108
     ┌─────────────────────┬─────────────────────┐
     │ (6 × 100 = 600)     │ (6 × 8 = 48)        │
     │         650         │          50         │
  6  │       − 600         │        − 48         │
     │       ─────         │        ─────        │
     │          50         │           2         │
     └─────────────────────┴─────────────────────┘
```

$650 \div 6 = 108 \text{ R } 2$

108 vases can each be filled with 6 flowers. There are 2 flowers left over.

1 The table lists the products of 7 and multiples of 10. Use the table to help estimate the quotient of $253 \div 7$.

10	20	30	40	50
70	140	210	280	350

The quotient is between .... and ....

2 Use the estimate in problem 1 to find the quotient of $253 \div 7$.
Complete the area model to solve the problem.

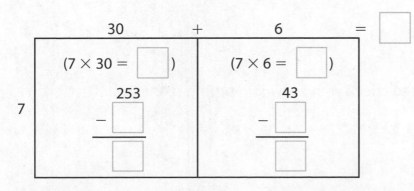

Solution ....

3　Explain how to check whether the answer to the division problem below is correct.

134 ÷ 5 = 26 R 4

4　Mike has 876 toy building pieces to share among himself and 2 friends. He wants each person to have an equal number of pieces. How many pieces does each person get? Show your work.

Solution

5　Look at how you solved problem 4. Explain how you could use estimation before you divide in order to know whether your answer is reasonable.

6　Explain how to use multiplication to check your answer in problem 4.

Refine Dividing Three-Digit Numbers

Complete the Example below. Then solve problems 1–9.

EXAMPLE

In art class, 8 students share 104 pieces of felt. Each student gets the same number of pieces. How many pieces of felt does each student get?

Look at how you could show your work using an area model.

```
        ?                    10      +      3     =  13
   ┌─────────┐         ┌──────────────┬──────────────┐
   │         │         │ (8 × 10 = 80)│ (8 × 3 = 24) │
 8 │   104   │  →   8  │     104      │      24      │
   │         │         │    − 80      │    − 24      │
   └─────────┘         │    ────      │    ────      │
                       │      24      │       0      │
                       └──────────────┴──────────────┘
```

Solution ....

The student first multiplied 8 × 10. After subtracting 80 from 104, there were still 24 left.

PAIR/SHARE
How else could you solve this problem?

APPLY IT

1 Find 641 ÷ 3. Use multiplication to check your answer. Show your work.

How can you estimate to find how many digits the quotient will have?

PAIR/SHARE
How do you know if there is a remainder in this problem?

Solution ....

2 What is 738 divided by 9? Show your work.

> How could you use an area model to help solve this problem?

Solution ....

PAIR/SHARE
How could you use multiplication to check your answer?

3 The Prize Place has 252 toys to divide equally among 6 piñatas. How many toys go into each piñata?

Ⓐ 32

Ⓑ 41 R 4

Ⓒ 42

Ⓓ 420

Erin chose Ⓓ as the correct answer. How did she get that answer?

> Will there be any toys left over?

PAIR/SHARE
How can you tell that Erin's answer does not make sense?

4 Select all the true division equations.

Ⓐ $255 \div 8 = 31$

Ⓑ $493 \div 7 = 73$

Ⓒ $320 \div 4 = 8$

Ⓓ $675 \div 5 = 135$

Ⓔ $318 \div 6 = 53$

5 Select all the expressions that have a value of 25.

Ⓐ $225 \div 8$

Ⓑ $180 \div 7$

Ⓒ $150 \div 6$

Ⓓ $130 \div 5$

Ⓔ $100 \div 4$

6 Together, Aiden and his two sisters save 720 quarters. They divide the quarters equally. Aiden puts his quarters into 3 equal piles. How many quarters does Aiden put in each pile?

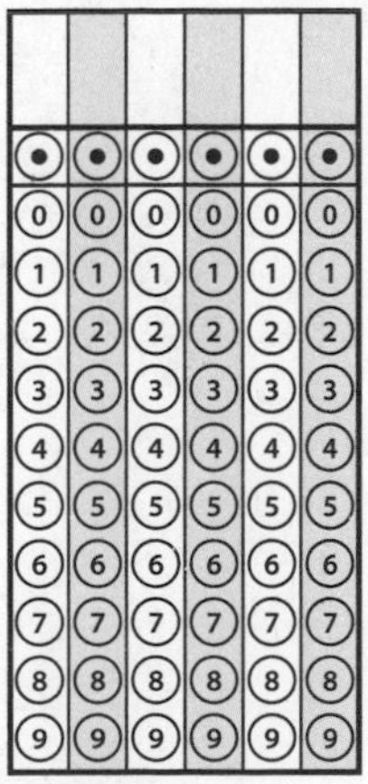

7 James, Micah, and Rebecca work at a restaurant. There is $115 in the tip jar. They decide to divide the tips equally among them and leave any extra money in the jar. How much money do they leave in the jar?

Ⓐ $1

Ⓑ $2

Ⓒ $38

Ⓓ $39

8 Mrs. Long makes 7 snack bags. She uses 175 almonds and shares them evenly among the bags. How many almonds are in each bag? How many almonds are left over? Show your work.

There are .... almonds in each bag.

There are .... almonds left over.

9 MATH JOURNAL

Look at the expression 228 ÷ 6. What two multiples of 10 is the quotient between? Explain how you know.

☑ **SELF CHECK** Go back to the Unit 3 Opener and see what you can check off.

Divide Four-Digit Numbers

Dear Family,

This week your child is learning to divide four-digit numbers by one-digit numbers.

Your child is learning to divide a four-digit number by a one-digit number.

One way your child can solve a division problem is to find **partial quotients**. With this strategy, your child divides by breaking the dividend into parts.

Below shows one way to divide 2,113 by 4 by finding partial quotients.

```
        3
       25
      500
    4)2,113  ◄── How many groups of 4 in 2,000? 500
    − 2,000  ◄── Subtract 500 groups of 4.
        113  ◄── How many groups of 4 in 100? 25
      − 100  ◄── Subtract 25 groups of 4.
         13  ◄── How many groups of 4 in 13? 3
       − 12  ◄── Subtract 3 groups of 4.
          1
```

The partial quotients are **500**, **25**, and **3**. The remainder is **1**.

Altogether, there are **500** + **25** + **3**, or **528**, groups of 4 in 2,113, with 1 left over.

2,113 ÷ 4 = **528 R 1**

Invite your child to share what he or she knows about dividing four-digit numbers by doing the following activity together.

Lesson 15 Divide Four-Digit Numbers

ACTIVITY DIVIDING FOUR-DIGIT NUMBERS

Do this activity with your child to divide four-digit numbers.

Materials 1 number cube (or dot cube)

- Have your child roll a number cube five times to make a division problem with a four-digit number and a one-digit number.

- The first four rolls form the four-digit number in the order of the rolls. The first roll is the thousands digit. The last roll is the divisor.

    Example: Your child rolls a 4, 2, 6, 1, and 3.
    The division problem is 4,261 ÷ 3.

- Have your child find the quotient. There may or may not be a remainder.

    Example: 4,261 ÷ 3 = 1,420 R 1

- Then you multiply to check your child's answer.

    Example: 3 × 1,420 = 4,260
    4,260 + 1 = 4,261
    Your child's answer is correct!

- Switch roles and repeat the activity with you doing the division and your child using multiplication to check the answer.

- The player with the greater quotient wins the round.

- Play three rounds.

Explore Dividing Four-Digit Numbers

Previously, you learned about dividing three-digit numbers by one-digit numbers. Use what you know to try to solve the problem below.

▼ **What is 1,400 ÷ 4?**

TRY IT

🧰 Math Toolkit

- base-ten blocks
- grid paper
- multiplication models 🖱

DISCUSS IT

Ask your partner: Can you explain that again?

Tell your partner: I started by . . .

CONNECT IT

1 LOOK BACK

Explain how you found the quotient of 1,400 ÷ 4.

2 LOOK AHEAD

You can divide four-digit numbers in many ways.

a. Complete the area model to show 3,200 ÷ 5.

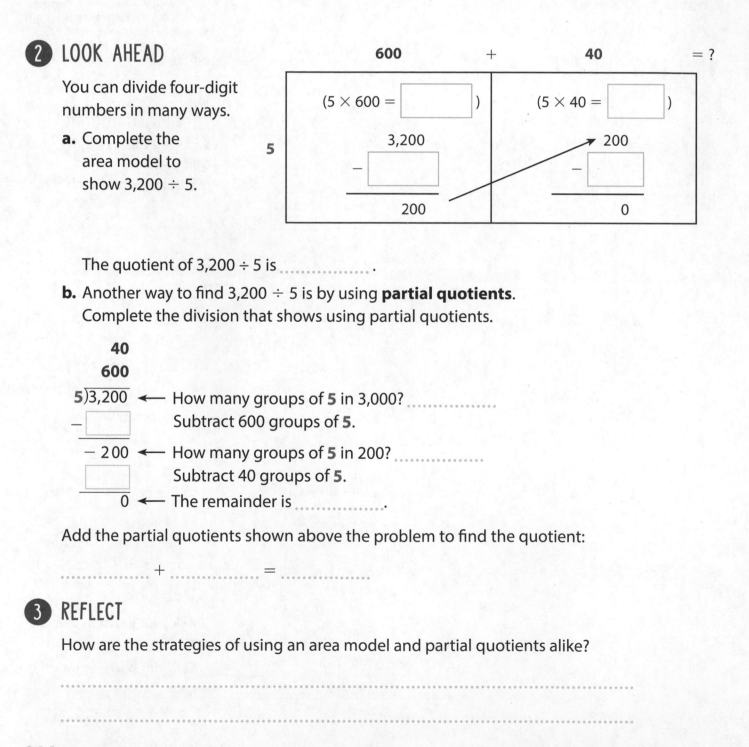

The quotient of 3,200 ÷ 5 is ....

b. Another way to find 3,200 ÷ 5 is by using **partial quotients**. Complete the division that shows using partial quotients.

```
        40
       600
   5)3,200  ⟵ How many groups of 5 in 3,000? .................
   – ___
     – 200  ⟵ How many groups of 5 in 200? .................
     ___
       0  ⟵ The remainder is ................. .
```

Add the partial quotients shown above the problem to find the quotient:

.... + ... = ...

3 REFLECT

How are the strategies of using an area model and partial quotients alike?

....

....

Prepare for Dividing Four-Digit Numbers

1 Think about what you know about division. Fill in each box. Use words, numbers, and pictures. Show as many ideas as you can.

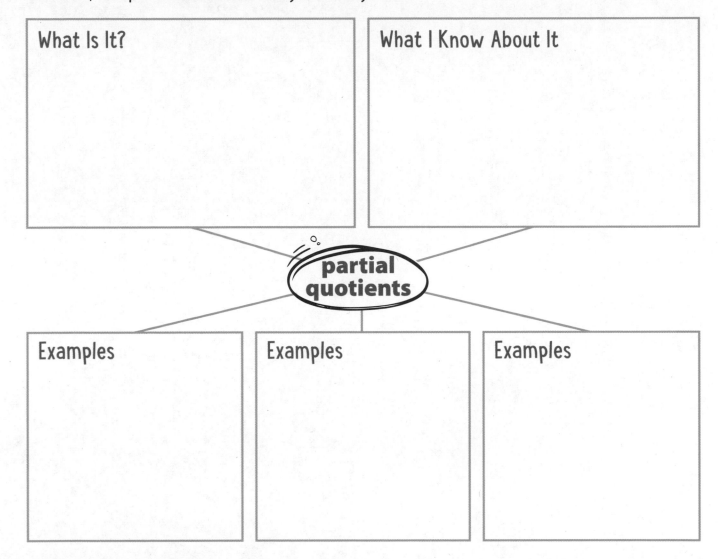

What Is It?	What I Know About It

partial quotients

Examples	Examples	Examples

2 Complete the area model to show 2,200 ÷ 8. Add the partial quotients to solve the division problem.

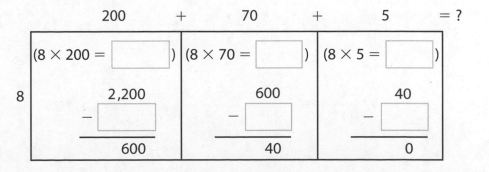

200   +   70   +   5   = ?

8	(8 × 200 = ☐)	(8 × 70 = ☐)	(8 × 5 = ☐)
	2,200	600	40
	− ☐	− ☐	− ☐
	600	40	0

3 Solve the problem. Show your work.

What is 1,500 ÷ 6?

Solution ....

4 Check your answer. Show your work.

Develop Dividing Four-Digit Numbers

Read and try to solve the problem below.

> **A factory has 2,125 tablets to ship to stores.**
> **It can ship 4 tablets in each box.**
> **How many full boxes can the factory ship?**

TRY IT

Math Toolkit
- base-ten blocks
- grid paper
- multiplication models

DISCUSS IT

Ask your partner: Do you agree with me? Why or why not?

Tell your partner: I agree with you about . . . because . . .

Explore different ways to understand dividing a four-digit number by a one-digit number.

> A factory has 2,125 tablets to ship to stores. It can ship 4 tablets in each box. How many full boxes can the factory ship?

MODEL IT

You can use an area model to break apart the problem into smaller parts.

The area model shows how to use multiplication and repeated subtraction to divide 2,125 by 4.

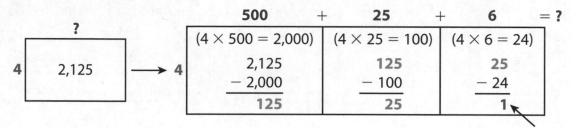

remainder

MODEL IT

You can also find partial quotients to divide.

Divide each place value of 2,125 by 4.

```
          6
         25
        500
     4)2,125   ←  How many groups of 4 in 2,000? 500
     − 2,000      Subtract 500 groups of 4.
         125   ←  How many groups of 4 in 100? 25
       − 100      Subtract 25 groups of 4.
          25   ←  How many groups of 4 in 25? 6
        − 24      Subtract 6 groups of 4.
           1
```

The partial quotients are **500**, **25**, and **6**.

The quotient includes both the sum of the partial quotients and the remainder, the amount left over.

CONNECT IT

Now you will use the problem from the previous page to help you understand how to use an area model and partial quotients to divide a four-digit number by a one-digit number.

 1 Look at the first Model It. How can you find the number of full boxes the factory can ship?

2 What does the remainder mean in this problem?

 3 Look at the second Model It. How does using the partial quotients strategy help you find the quotient of 2,125 ÷ 4?

4 Explain how using an area model and partial quotients can help you divide a four-digit number by a one-digit number.

5 How can you check that your answer is correct?

 6 REFLECT

Look back at your Try It, strategies by classmates, and Model Its. Which models or strategies do you like best for dividing a four-digit number by a one-digit number? Explain.

....

....

APPLY IT

Use what you just learned to solve these problems.

7 Find 1,010 ÷ 9. Show your work.

Solution ....

8 Find 1,458 ÷ 3. Use multiplication to check your answer. Show your work.

Solution ....

9 What is 5,783 divided by 6?

   Ⓐ 963

   Ⓑ 963 R 5

   Ⓒ 964 R 5

   Ⓓ 968

Practice Dividing Four-Digit Numbers

Study the Example showing how to divide a four-digit number by a one-digit number. Then solve problems 1–5.

EXAMPLE

A group of hikers plan to take 3 hours to hike a trail 5,380 meters long. They want to hike the same distance each hour. How many meters do they plan to hike each hour?

$$5,380 \div 3 = \mathbf{1,793\ R\ 1}$$

The hikers plan to hike 1,793 meters each hour. Then they will need to hike 1 more meter to reach the end of the trail.

```
        3
       90
      700
    1,000
  3)5,380   ←— There are 1,000 groups of 3 in 5,000.
   - 3,000      Subtract 1,000 groups of 3.
     2,380   ←— There are 700 groups of 3 in 2,380.
   - 2,100      Subtract 700 groups of 3.
       280   ←— There are 90 groups of 3 in 280.
     - 270      Subtract 90 groups of 3.
        10   ←— There are 3 groups of 3 in 10.
       - 9      Subtract 3 groups of 3.
         1
```

1 Complete the division problem using partial quotients.

8,235 ÷ 5 = ...

```
5)8, 2 3 5
```

2 Complete the division problem using partial quotients.

4,507 ÷ 4 = ...

```
4)4, 5 0 7
```

3 One week has 7 days. How many weeks do 1,230 days make? What does the remainder mean? Show your work.

Solution ....

4 Mugs can be packed with up to 6 mugs in each box. How many boxes are needed to pack 1,528 mugs? Show your work.

Solution ....

5 Use estimation to select all the true division equations.

Ⓐ 4,960 ÷ 2 = 9,920

Ⓑ 7,095 ÷ 5 = 1,419

Ⓒ 9,621 ÷ 3 = 230 R 7

Ⓓ 3,875 ÷ 6 = 645 R 5

Ⓔ 5,004 ÷ 4 = 251

> ## Vocabulary
>
> **remainder** the amount left over when one number does not divide another number a whole number of times.
>
> 5,380 ÷ 8 = 672 R 4
>
> ↑
> remainder

©Curriculum Associates, LLC   Copying is not permitted.

Refine Dividing Four-Digit Numbers

Complete the Example below. Then solve problems 1–9.

EXAMPLE

What is 7,824 divided by 3?

Look at how you could show your work using partial quotients.

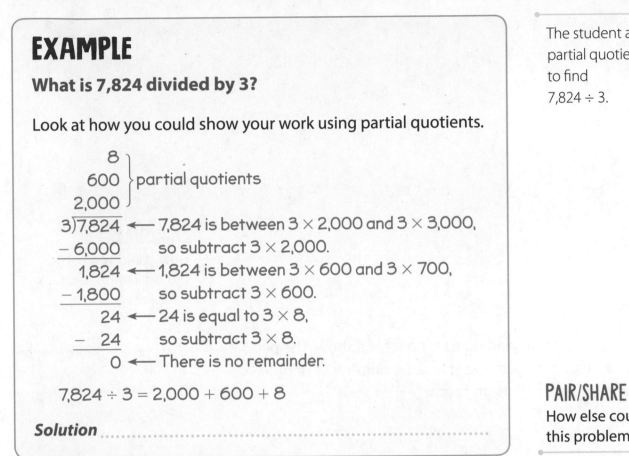

$$
\begin{array}{r}
8 \\
600 \\
2{,}000
\end{array} \left. \right\} \text{partial quotients}
$$

$$
\begin{array}{r}
3\overline{)7{,}824} \quad \longleftarrow \text{ 7,824 is between } 3 \times 2{,}000 \text{ and } 3 \times 3{,}000, \\
-\ 6{,}000 \qquad \text{ so subtract } 3 \times 2{,}000. \\
\hline
1{,}824 \quad \longleftarrow \text{ 1,824 is between } 3 \times 600 \text{ and } 3 \times 700, \\
-\ 1{,}800 \qquad \text{ so subtract } 3 \times 600. \\
\hline
24 \quad \longleftarrow \text{ 24 is equal to } 3 \times 8, \\
-\ 24 \qquad \text{ so subtract } 3 \times 8. \\
\hline
0 \quad \longleftarrow \text{ There is no remainder.}
\end{array}
$$

$7{,}824 \div 3 = 2{,}000 + 600 + 8$

Solution ....

> The student added the partial quotients to find $7{,}824 \div 3$.

APPLY IT

1 Find $1{,}359 \div 4$. Use multiplication to check your answer. Show your work.

Solution ....

> How many digits will the quotient have?

2 Rogelio has 2,490 stamps in his collection. He divides his stamps equally among his 6 children. How many stamps does each child get? Show your work.

How could you use partial quotients to solve this problem?

PAIR/SHARE
How could you use multiplication to check your answer?

Solution

3 There are 1,275 people waiting to try out for a show. The people wait in 5 rooms. Each room has the same number of people. How many people are in each room?

Ⓐ 111

Ⓑ 251

Ⓒ 255

Ⓓ 1,270

Awan chose Ⓓ as the correct answer. How did he get that answer?

Can you use multiplication to help solve the problem?

PAIR/SHARE
How can you tell that Awan's answer does not make sense?

4 Mariah finds 4,048 ÷ 8 using partial quotients as shown at the right. What partial quotient goes in the box?

Ⓐ 6

Ⓑ 7

Ⓒ 60

Ⓓ 70

```
        □
        500
   8)4,048
   − 4,000
        48
      − 48
         0
```

5 A tailor has 1,495 yards of fabric to make costumes. He needs 7 yards of fabric for each costume. How many costumes can the tailor make? Is there any fabric left over? Show your work.

Solution ....

6 Jack uses partial quotients to solve 6,035 ÷ 5 as shown by the area model.

	1,000	+ 200 + 35	
5	5,000	1,000	35

Jack says the quotient is 1,235 because 1,000 + 200 + 35 = 1,235. What did Jack do wrong?

Ⓐ Jack broke apart 6,035 incorrectly.

Ⓑ Jack wrote the incorrect partial quotient above 1,000.

Ⓒ Jack should have subtracted 35 from 1,000 + 200.

Ⓓ Jack wrote the incorrect partial quotient above 35.

7 Find 2,259 ÷ 3.

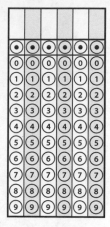

8 Trina has a box of 1,132 beads to make necklaces. She wants to use as many of the beads as possible to make 9 necklaces. She uses the same number of beads for each necklace. How many beads are on each necklace? How many beads are left over? Show your work.

There are _____ beads on each necklace.

There are _____ beads left over.

9 MATH JOURNAL

Explain how to divide 3,625 by 4 using partial quotients.

 SELF CHECK Go back to the Unit 3 Opener and see what you can check off.

Find Perimeter and Area

Dear Family,

This week your child is learning about perimeter and area.

Some real-world situations that involve perimeter and area are installing a fence around a yard and determining how much flooring is needed for a room.

To find the perimeter of a rectangle, find the total length of all the sides. One way to do this is by adding together the lengths of all the sides.

For example, to find the length of fencing that is needed to enclose a rectangular yard like the one shown, add the 4 side lengths.

Perimeter = length + length + width + width
           = 20 feet + 20 feet + 14 feet + 14 feet
           = 68 feet

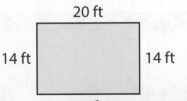

20 ft

14 ft   14 ft

20 ft

Another way to find the perimeter of a rectangle is to use a **formula**.
P stands for perimeter, ℓ stands for length, and w stands for width.

$P = 2\ell + 2w$	or	$P = 2(\ell + w)$
$= 2(20) + 2(14)$		$= 2(20 + 14)$
$= 40 + 28$		$= 2 \times 34$
$= 68$		$= 68$

You need 68 feet of fencing to enclose the yard.

To find the area of a rectangle, use the area formula.
    Area = length $\times$ width $A = \ell \times w$

20 ft

14 ft   14 ft

20 ft

The area of the rectangle at the right is:
20 feet $\times$ 14 feet = 280 square feet

If you were covering the rectangular yard with pavers, you would need enough pavers to cover 280 square feet.

Invite your child to share what he or she knows about perimeter and area by doing the following activity together.

ACTIVITY FINDING PERIMETER AND AREA

Do this activity with your child to find perimeter and area.

Materials ruler or yardstick

- Look around your home for items that are shaped like a rectangle.
  For example: a TV or computer screen, a table top, a rug, the floor of a room

- Help your child measure each side of the rectangular item. Have your child write the measurements. Be sure to use the same units of measurement, such as inches or feet, for each side.

- Have your child use the measurements to find the perimeter of the item.

- Now measure a different rectangular-shaped item and find its perimeter. Is the perimeter greater or less than the perimeter of the first item you measured?

- Next, find area. Suppose you want to cover a rectangular window with a shade. Choose a window and measure each side. Have your child find the area and tell how many square inches or square feet of shade are needed to cover the window.

- Find the area of other rectangular items in your home, such as different-sized windows or floors.

Look for other real-world opportunities to find perimeter and area with your child.

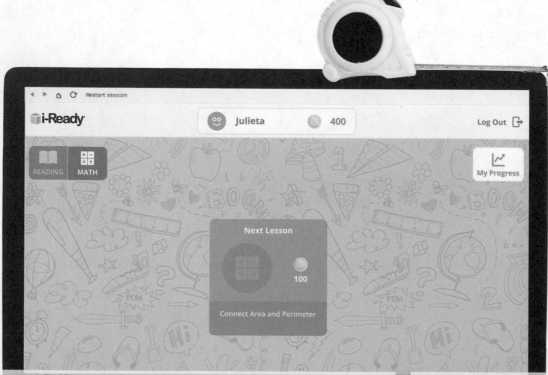

Explore Finding Perimeter

You have learned that you can find the perimeter of a rectangle by adding the lengths of the sides. Use what you know to try to solve the problem below.

> **Marissa uses 64 feet of fence to make a border around a rectangular flower garden. The length of the garden is 20 feet. What is the width of the garden?**

TRY IT

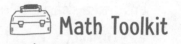 **Math Toolkit**
• rulers
• grid paper
• perimeter and area tool ⬦
• multiplication models ⬦

DISCUSS IT

Ask your partner: How did you get started?

Tell your partner: I started by …

CONNECT IT

 LOOK BACK

Explain how you can find the width of the garden.

 LOOK AHEAD

You can find the perimeter, or distance around a shape, in different ways.

10 yd

5 yd | 5 yd

10 yd

a. Complete the addition equation to find the perimeter of the rectangle.

Perimeter = ... + ... + ... + ...

The perimeter is .... yards.

b. The perimeter **formula** at the right uses multiplication and addition to find perimeter. Use the formula to find the perimeter of the rectangle.

$P = (2 \times \ell) + (2 \times w)$

$= (2 \times \underset{\text{length}}{\underline{\hspace{2cm}}}) + (2 \times \underset{\text{width}}{\underline{\hspace{2cm}}})$

$= \underline{\hspace{2cm}} + \underline{\hspace{2cm}}$

The perimeter is .... yards.

c. You can also find perimeter with the formula shown at the right. Use this formula to find the perimeter of the rectangle.

$P = 2 \times (\ell + w)$

$= 2 \times (\underset{\text{length}}{\underline{\hspace{2cm}}} + \underset{\text{width}}{\underline{\hspace{2cm}}})$

$= 2 \times \underline{\hspace{2cm}}$

The perimeter is .... yards.

③ **REFLECT**

A formula for the perimeter of a square with a side length of s is $P = 4s$. Explain why this formula works.

....

....

Prepare for Finding Perimeter

1   Think about what you know about measurement. Fill in each box. Use words, numbers, and pictures. Show as many ideas as you can.

Word	In My Own Words	Example
length		
width		
perimeter		

2   Complete the addition equation to find the perimeter of the rectangle.

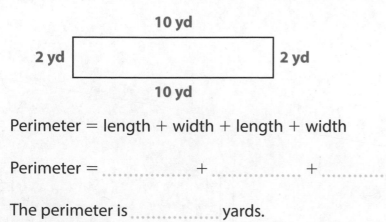

Perimeter = length + width + length + width

Perimeter = ... + ... + ... + ...

The perimeter is .... yards.

Lesson 16 Find Perimeter and Area   **331**

3 Solve the problem. Show your work.

Khan uses 78 feet of fence to make a rectangular pen for his pet rabbit. The length of the pen is 25 feet. What is the width of the rectangular pen?

Solution ....

4 Check your answer. Show your work.

Develop Finding Perimeter

Read and try to solve the problem below.

Keegan builds a fence to make a rectangular dog pen in his backyard.
The pen is 30 feet long and 24 feet wide. How much fence does
Keegan use to make the dog pen?

TRY IT

🧰 **Math Toolkit**
- rulers
- math reference sheet
- grid paper
- perimeter and area
  tool 🖱
- multiplication models 🖱

DISCUSS IT

Ask your partner: Why did
you choose that strategy?

Tell your partner: I knew . . .
so I . . .

Explore different ways to find the perimeter of a rectangle.

> **Keegan builds a fence to make a rectangular dog pen in his backyard. The pen is 30 feet long and 24 feet wide. How much fence does Keegan use to make the dog pen?**

PICTURE IT

You can use pictures to help find the perimeter of a rectangle.

Draw a picture to represent the fence.

You can use color to highlight the sides that have the same length.

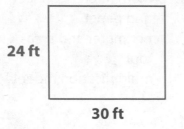

24 ft

30 ft

Add the lengths to find how much fence Keegan uses.

30 feet + 24 feet + 30 feet + 24 feet

MODEL IT

You can also use a formula to help find the perimeter of a rectangle.

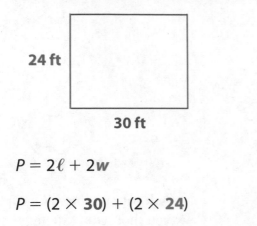

24 ft

30 ft

$P = 2\ell + 2w$

$P = (2 \times 30) + (2 \times 24)$

CONNECT IT

Now you will use the problem from the previous page to help you understand how to find the perimeter of a rectangle.

1 Use the formula in **Model It** to find how much fence Keegan uses to make the dog pen.

2 Keegan uses the formula $P = 2(\ell + w)$ to find how much fence he needs. Does Keegan's formula work? Why or why not?

3 Which formula do you think is easier? Why?

4 How are the methods for finding the perimeter of a rectangle in **Picture It** and **Model It** alike?

5 REFLECT

Look back at your **Try It**, strategies by classmates, and **Picture It** and **Model It**. Which models or strategies do you like best for finding the perimeter of a rectangle? Explain.

....

....

....

....

APPLY IT

Use what you just learned to solve these problems.

6 Bianca puts a fence around a rectangular garden. The garden is 15 feet long by 10 feet wide. How much fence does Bianca use? Show your work.

Solution ....

7 Michael glues craft sticks around the edges of a rectangular poster. He uses a total of 14 craft sticks. He uses 5 craft sticks on each long side of the poster. How many craft sticks does he use for each short side of the poster? Show your work.

Solution ....

8 A rectangle has a length of 17 inches and a width of 13 inches. What is the perimeter, in inches, of the rectangle? Show your work.

Solution ....

Practice Finding Perimeter

Study the Example showing how to find the perimeter of a rectangle. Then solve problems 1–5.

EXAMPLE

The community center has a rectangular kiddie pool. The length of the pool is 25 feet. The width is 15 feet. What is the perimeter of the kiddie pool?

Use a formula for the perimeter of a rectangle.

$$P = 2\ell + 2w \qquad\qquad P = 2(\ell + w)$$
$$= (2 \times 25) + (2 \times 15) \qquad = 2(25 + 15)$$
$$= 50 + 30 \qquad\qquad = 2(40)$$
$$= 80 \qquad\qquad\qquad = 80$$

25 ft

15 ft

The perimeter of the kiddie pool is 80 feet.

1 A rectangular photo has a length of 10 inches and a width of 8 inches. Fill in the blanks to show two ways to find the perimeter of the photo.

$$P = \qquad 2\ell \qquad + \qquad 2w \qquad\qquad P = 2(\ell + w)$$

$$P = (2 \times \text{..........}) + (2 \times \text{..........}) \qquad P = 2(\text{..........} + \text{..........})$$

$$= \qquad \text{..........} \quad + \quad \text{..........} \qquad\qquad = 2(\text{..........})$$

$$= \qquad \text{..........} \qquad\qquad\qquad\qquad = \text{..........}$$

The perimeter is .... inches.

2 Jason's rectangular computer screen is 50 centimeters across and 36 centimeters high. What is its perimeter? Show your work.

$$P = \text{...............} \text{ centimeters}$$

3 A rectangular garden has a width of 90 feet. The perimeter of the garden is 500 feet. What is the length of the garden?

$$500 = (2 \times \ell) + (\text{..............} \times \text{..............})$$

$$500 = 2\ell + \text{..............}$$

$$\text{..............} = 2\ell$$

$$\text{..............} \div 2 = \ell$$

$$\text{..............} = \ell$$

The length of the garden is .... feet.

4 Amy has a ribbon that is 36 inches long. Tell whether she has enough ribbon to wrap around the perimeter of a picture frame for each frame with the given shape and size.

	Yes	No
square, side lengths of 9 inches	Ⓐ	Ⓑ
rectangle, 18 inches by 10 inches	Ⓒ	Ⓓ
rectangle, 12 inches by 24 inches	Ⓔ	Ⓕ
square, side lengths of 6 inches	Ⓖ	Ⓗ

5 The square and the rectangle at the right each have a perimeter of 200 centimeters. What are the side lengths of the square and rectangle? (*Hint*: First, find the side length of the square.) Show your work.

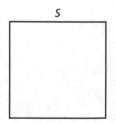

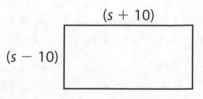

Square: side length .... cm **Rectangle:** length .... cm width .... cm

Develop Finding Area

Read and try to solve the problem below.

> Kevin makes a rectangular mural with colored tiles. He has enough
> tiles to cover 112 square feet. He uses all the tiles. The mural is
> 8 feet wide. How long is the mural?

TRY IT

Math Toolkit
- rulers
- math reference sheet
- grid paper
- perimeter and area
  tool ↻
- multiplication models ↻

DISCUSS IT

Ask your partner: Do you
agree with me? Why or
why not?

Tell your partner: I agree
with you about . . .
because . . .

Explore different ways to understand solving area problems.

> **Kevin makes a rectangular mural with colored tiles. He has enough tiles to cover 112 square feet. He uses all the tiles. The mural is 8 feet wide. How long is the mural?**

PICTURE IT

You can use a picture to help solve area problems.

Make a sketch of the mural.

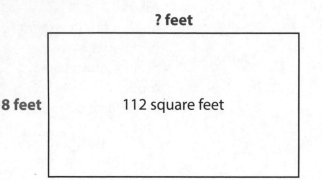

? feet

8 feet | 112 square feet

Since you multiply the length and width of a rectangle to find the area, think: **8 × ? = 112**.

MODEL IT

You can use the formula for the area of a rectangle to help understand the problem.

$A = \ell \times w$

area of the mural = **length** × **width**

The area of the mural is 112 square feet.

It can be covered by 8 rows of square units that each have an area of 1 square foot.

The number of square units in each row is also the number of feet in the length of the mural.

CONNECT IT

Now you will use the problem from the previous page to help you understand how to solve area problems.

 Write an equation to represent the area of the mural.

 Describe how you can find the length of the mural.

 What is the length of the mural? ....

4 Kevin notices another package of tiles. This package can make a rectangular mural with an area of 152 square feet. Suppose Kevin wants to use these tiles to make another mural that is 8 feet wide. Write an equation that can help you find the length of this mural.

5 Find the length of the rectangular mural Kevin can make with the package of tiles that covers an area of 152 square feet.

6 Suppose that you know the length and area of a rectangle. How would you find the width?

7 REFLECT

Look back at your **Try It**, strategies by classmates, and **Picture It** and **Model It**. Which models or strategies do you like best for solving area problems? Explain.

....

....

....

....

APPLY IT

Use what you just learned to solve these problems.

 Carla has a rectangular garden in her backyard. The width of the garden is 9 meters. The area of the garden is 360 square meters. What is the length of the garden? Show your work.

Solution ....

9 Bill builds a rectangular deck with a length of 15 feet and a width of 7 feet. What is the area of Bill's deck? Show your work.

Solution ....

10 A rectangle has an area of 65 square centimeters and a width of 5 centimeters. What is the length of the rectangle? Show your work.

Solution ....

Practice Finding Area

Study the Example showing how to solve a problem about the area of a rectangle. Then solve problems 1–6.

EXAMPLE

Michelle uses bricks to make a rectangular patio. She covers an area of 63 square feet with the bricks. The length of the patio is 9 feet. How wide is the patio?

Use the formula for the area of a rectangle.

$$A = \ell \times w$$
$$A = 9 \times w$$
$$63 = 9 \times w$$
$$63 \div 9 = w$$
$$7 = w$$

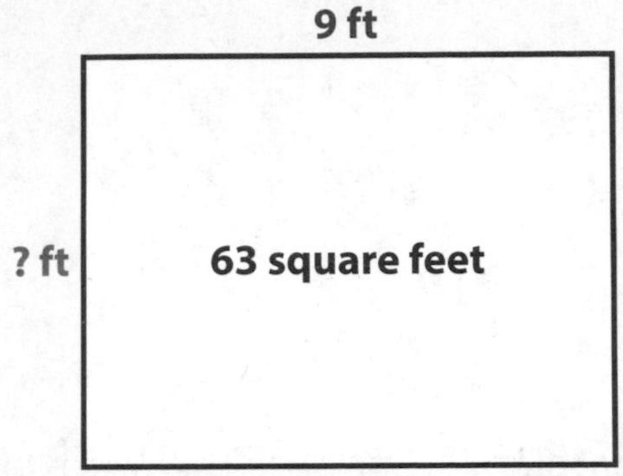

The patio is 7 feet wide.

9 ft

? ft | **63 square feet**

1 Juan puts new flooring in a rectangular room. The picture shows the length and width of the room. How many square feet of flooring does Juan use?

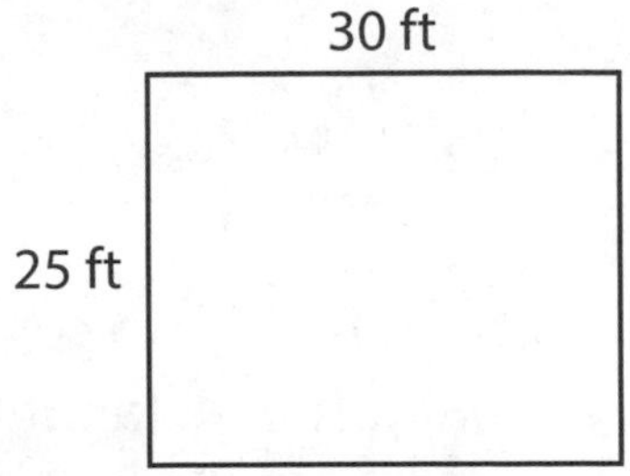

$A =$ .... $\times$ ....

$A =$ ....

30 ft

25 ft

Juan uses .... square feet of flooring.

2 Look at the picture below. Alyssa wants to tile a rectangular room with an area of 160 square feet. The width of the room is 8 feet. What is the length of the room?

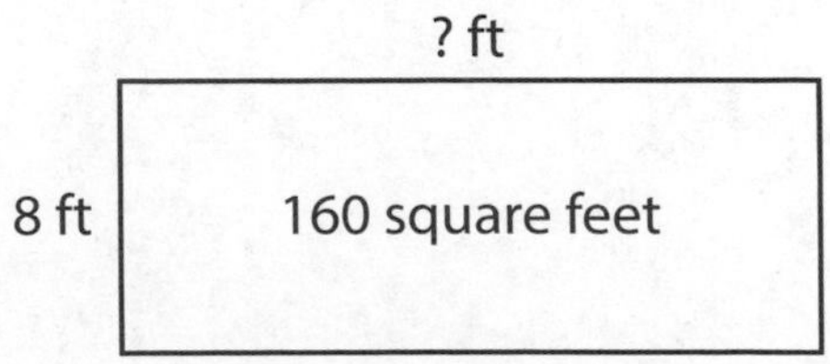

.... $= \ell \times$ ....

.... $\div$ .... $= \ell$

.... $= \ell$

? ft

8 ft | 160 square feet

The length of the room is .... feet.

3 Jim paints the surface of a shelf. The rectangular surface has an area of 90 square inches. The width of the shelf is 6 inches. What is the length of the shelf? Show your work.

Solution

4 A rectangular exercise mat has an area of 48 square meters. Its length is 8 meters. What is the width of the mat? Show your work.

Solution

5 Look at problem 4. Suppose the width of the rectangular exercise mat is 2 meters longer. What is another name for the shape of this exercise mat? Explain how you know.

Solution

6 Melissa has enough paint to cover an area of 250 square feet. She wants to paint two walls. The rectangular wall is 9 feet high and 20 feet wide. The square wall has a height of 9 feet. Does Melissa have enough paint to cover the area of both walls? Show your work.

Solution

Refine Finding Perimeter and Area

Complete the Example below. Then solve problems 1–8, using the Math Reference Sheet as necessary.

EXAMPLE

Jen draws a rectangle with a length of 12 inches and a width of 10 inches. Then she draws another rectangle by doubling the length and width of the first one. What is the perimeter of the second rectangle?

Look at how you could show your work using a formula for the perimeter of a rectangle.

$P = 2(\ell + w)$

length and width of first rectangle:
$\ell = 12$ inches and $w = 10$ inches

length and width of second rectangle:
$\ell = 12 \times 2$, or 24, inches $w = 10 \times 2$, or 20, inches

Perimeter of second rectangle $= 2(24 + 20)$
$$P = 2 \times 44$$

Solution ....

The student uses a formula for the perimeter of a rectangle and labels the work to keep it organized.

PAIR/SHARE
How else could you solve the problem?

APPLY IT

1 A designer puts a tile border around the edge of a rectangular swimming pool. The length of the pool is 52 meters, and the width is 26 meters. How long is the tile border? Show your work.

Are you looking for the perimeter or the area of the pool?

PAIR/SHARE
How did you solve the problem? Why did you choose that method?

Solution ....

2 Zachary has new carpet on his bedroom floor. The dimensions of his rectangular room are 9 feet by 13 feet. How much carpet is used to cover the whole floor? Show your work.

Are you finding the perimeter or the area of the room?

Solution ....

PAIR/SHARE
How do the units in the answer tell whether you found area or perimeter?

3 Tricia wants to make a rectangular path using pebbles. She has 8 bags of pebbles. Each bag covers an area of 6 square feet. Tricia wants to make the path 2 feet wide. How long can she make the path?

Ⓐ 3 feet

Ⓑ 22 feet

Ⓒ 24 feet

Ⓓ 48 feet

Laura chose Ⓐ as the correct answer. How did she get that answer?

How much area can Tricia cover with all the bags of pebbles?

PAIR/SHARE
Does Laura's answer make sense?

4 A playground in the park is rectangular and has a length of 18 yards. The width of the playground is half the length. What is the area of the playground?

Ⓐ 27 square yards

Ⓑ 54 square yards

Ⓒ 92 square yards

Ⓓ 162 square yards

5 Maya is finding the perimeter of the rectangle at the right. Which expressions can be used to find the perimeter?

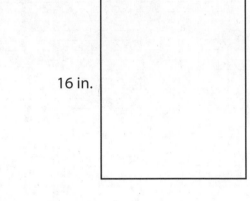

12 in.

16 in.

Ⓐ $(2 \times 16) + (2 \times 12)$

Ⓑ $2 \times 16 + 12$

Ⓒ $2(16 + 12)$

Ⓓ 16×12

Ⓔ $16 + 12 + 16 + 12$

6 A rectangle is 22 feet long and has a perimeter of 56 feet. What is the width of the rectangle? Show your work.

Solution ....

7 Ms. Leone's plan for a raised garden bed includes the following:

- It is in the shape of a rectangle.

- The sides of the bed use a total of 30 feet of cedar boards.

- Each side is longer than 1 foot.

- The length and width have measurements in whole feet.

Part A Use the grid below to draw three different rectangles that can each represent Ms. Leone's garden bed. Be sure to use all 30 feet of cedar boards for each bed.

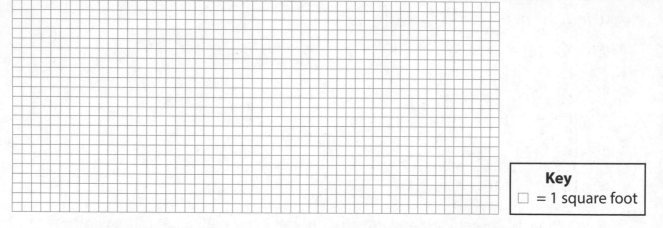

Key
☐ = 1 square foot

Part B Write the length and width of each garden bed you drew. Then find the area of each garden bed.

Garden Bed 1:

Length: ....

Width: ....

Area: ....

Garden Bed 2:

Length: ....

Width: ....

Area: ....

Garden Bed 3:

Length: ....

Width: ....

Area: ....

8 MATH JOURNAL

Draw a rectangle. Label its length and width. Explain how to find the perimeter and area of your rectangle. Use perimeter and area formulas in your explanation.

☑ **SELF CHECK** Go back to the Unit 3 Opener and see what you can check off.

In this unit you learned to ...

Skill	Lesson
Multiply a four-digit number by a one-digit number, for example: 2,810 × 3 = 8,430.	11
Multiply a two-digit number by a two-digit number, for example: 62 × 33 = 2,046.	12
Use multiplication to convert measurements.	13
Divide a three-digit number by a one-digit number, for example: 348 ÷ 6 = 58.	14
Divide a four-digit number by a one-digit number, for example: 6,328 ÷ 4 = 1,582.	15
Use the perimeter formulas for rectangles, for example: $P = (2 \times 12) + (2 \times 5)$ for a rectangle with length of 12 feet and width of 5 feet.	16
Use the area formula for rectangles, for example: $A = 9 \times 3$ for a rectangle with length of 9 feet and width of 3 feet.	16

Think about what you learned.

Use words, numbers, and drawings.

1 The math I could use in my everyday life is .... because ...

2 I worked hardest to learn how to ...

3 One thing I could do better is ...

Multiply and Divide Multi-Digit Numbers

Study an Example Problem and Solution

SMP 1 Make sense of problems and persevere in solving them.

Read this problem about perimeter and area. Then look at Beau's solution to this problem.

Birdcages

The zoo is planning to build a new area for birds. The zoo is going to use recycled materials. There will be three different-size rectangular cages as shown below.

Small cage: floor area of 12 square feet

Medium cage: floor area of 24 square feet

Large cage: floor area of 36 square feet

Beau needs to find a possible length and width for the rectangular floor of each size cage. What is a possible length, width, and perimeter for each cage's floor?

Read the sample solution on the next page. Then look at the checklist below. Find and mark parts of the solution that match the checklist.

✓ PROBLEM-SOLVING CHECKLIST

☐ Tell what is known.

☐ Tell what the problem is asking.

☐ Show all your work.

☐ Show that the solution works.

a. Circle something that is known.

b. Underline something that you need to find.

c. Draw a box around what you do to solve the problem.

d. Put a checkmark next to the part that shows the solution works.

BEAU'S SOLUTION

- **I already know** the area of each cage floor in square feet. The area of a rectangle is length times width.

- **I need to find** two factors that can be multiplied to get the area of each rectangle. These factors can be the length and width of the rectangle.

- **I can use multiplication facts to find possible lengths and widths.**

  $6 \times 2 = 12$
  $8 \times 3 = 24$
  $9 \times 4 = 36$

- **I can use the perimeter formula to find the perimeter of each rectangle.**

  Perimeter = $(2 \times \text{length}) + (2 \times \text{width})$

Hi, I'm Beau. Here's how I solved this problem.

I only wrote one fact for each area but there are others.

I sketched the cages to help keep my answer organized.

small cage	medium cage	large cage
Length = 6 feet	Length = 8 feet	Length = 9 feet
Width = 2 feet	Width = 3 feet	Width = 4 feet
Perimeter = 16 feet	Perimeter = 22 feet	Perimeter = 26 feet

- **I can also find the perimeters by adding the length and width, then multiplying by 2.**

Here's my final answer.

For the small cage, the sum of the length and width is 8 feet. So, the perimeter is 2×8 feet = 16 feet.

For the medium cage, the sum of the length and width is 11 feet. So, the perimeter is 2×11 feet = 22 feet.

For the large cage, the sum of the length and width is 13 feet. So, the perimeter is 2×13 feet = 26 feet.

Try Another Approach

There are many ways to solve problems. Think about how you might solve the Birdcages problem in a different way.

Birdcages

The zoo is planning to build a new area for birds. The zoo is going to use recycled materials. There will be three different-size rectangular cages as shown below.

Small cage: floor area of 12 square feet

Medium cage: floor area of 24 square feet

Large cage: floor area of 36 square feet

Beau needs to find a possible length and width for the rectangular floor of each size cage. What is a possible length, width, and perimeter for each cage's floor?

PLAN IT

Answer these questions to help you start thinking about a plan.

A. What are all the factor pairs of 12? 24? 36?

B. Think about each factor pair as the length and width of a rectangle. Which factor pairs do you think would make the best rectangular shapes for the birdcages? Explain.

SOLVE IT

Find a different solution for the Birdcages problem. Show all your work on a separate sheet of paper.

You may want to use the Problem-Solving Tips to get started.

PROBLEM-SOLVING TIPS

- **Tools**

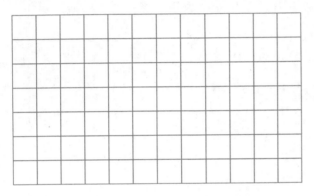

- **Word Bank**

factor	length	area
factor pair	width	perimeter
multiply	product	formula

- **Sentence Starters**
  - The factors of _____
  - To find the area _____

REFLECT

Use Mathematical Practices As you work through the problem, discuss these questions with a partner.

- **Persevere** How can you use your answers to the **Plan It** questions to decide on a solution path?
- **Use Tools** How can you use the grid paper to draw rectangles with the given areas?

Discuss Models and Strategies

Read the problem. Write a solution on a separate sheet of paper. Remember, there are lots of ways to solve a problem!

Recycle It

Because of his work with the zoo, Beau decides to start other recycling projects. He wants to promote recycling in his neighborhood. This is the slogan he will use to start a recycling campaign.

Everyone can recycle at least 30 pounds of waste in 3 months!

Beau weighs different items that can be recycled. Here are some items he found that weigh about 1 pound:

- 3 medium-sized cardboard boxes
- 105 sheets of printer paper
- 24 empty plastic bottles
- 32 empty aluminum cans

Help Beau write a report to show ways people can recycle 30 pounds of waste in 3 months.

PLAN IT AND SOLVE IT

Find a solution to the Recycle It problem.

Use Beau's information.

- Use a combination of at least two of the items on the list.
- Explain how a person could recycle at least 30 pounds of waste in 3 months with these items.

You may want to use the Problem-Solving Tips to get started.

PROBLEM-SOLVING TIPS

- **Questions**
  - What are some different ways you can combine two or three weights to have a sum of 30 pounds?
  - How can you find the number of a type of item it takes to make each of these weights?

- **Sentence Starters**
  - If you recycle _____ plastic bottles, you _____
  - If you add the weights of all the items, _____

☑ **PROBLEM-SOLVING CHECKLIST**

Make sure that you . . .
- ☐ tell what you know.
- ☐ tell what you need to do.
- ☐ show all your work.
- ☐ show that the solution works.

REFLECT

Use Mathematical Practices As you work through the problem, discuss these questions with a partner.

- **Use Tools** What methods can you use to find the numbers you need in your solution?
- **Be Precise** How can you make sure that your solution shows the meaning of all the numbers in it?

Persevere On Your Own

Read the problems. Write a solution on a separate sheet of paper.

Rainwater Recycling

Beau's report about recycling was very popular. He decides to write a similar report about recycling rainwater. He will post both reports on the bulletin board at the Community Center. Here is some information Beau found about this topic.

Information About Recycling Rainwater

- A 1,000 square foot roof on a typical house can collect 620 gallons of water when 1 inch of rain falls.
- The typical rainfall in our area is 3 inches per month.

It takes about . . .

- 50 gallons to water a 200 square foot garden.
- 62 gallons to water a 100 square foot area of lawn.
- 55 gallons of water to wash a car.

What should Beau include in his report to convince people in the area to collect rainwater?

SOLVE IT

Help Beau write a report about recycling rainwater.

- Find the amount of water that a homeowner could collect in one month.
- Write a short report to convince people to save water.
- Tell at least two things that could be done with the rainwater.

REFLECT

Use Mathematical Practices After you complete the task, choose one of these questions to discuss with a partner.

- **Use a Model** How could you use equations to find the numbers you need for the report?

- **Be Precise** How did you make sure that readers will see the different measurements in your report?

Recycled Robots

Beau started his first recycling project with broken robots. He recycles the broken parts and keeps the good parts. Beau needs to sort the good parts and put them into storage bins.

Beau does not want to mix any of the parts in the same bin. He wants each bin to have no more than 100 items in it. Beau also wants to have close to the same number of items in each bin.

My Robot Parts

Fuses 216

Switches 178

Pieces of Wire 332

Screws 426

How could Beau sort his parts into the bins?

fuse   switch

wire   screw

SOLVE IT

Suggest a way that Beau could arrange the robot parts in bins.

• Find how many bins are needed for each type of part.

• Tell how many parts to put in each bin.

• Show that your arrangement includes every kind of part and the total number of parts on the list.

REFLECT

Use Mathematical Practices After you complete the task, choose one of these questions to discuss with a partner.

• **Use Structure** Beau wants to have close to the same number of items in each bin. How did you decide how many this should be?

• **Make Sense of Problems** How could you use estimation to check that your answer is reasonable?

1 The marching band sells 1,036 shirts as a fundraiser. Each shirt sells for $5. Which expression can be used to find the total amount of sales in dollars?

Ⓐ $(1,000 \times 5) + (300 \times 5) + (6 \times 5)$ Ⓑ $(1,000 \times 5) + (30 \times 5) + (6 \times 5)$

Ⓒ $(1,000 + 30 + 60) \times 5$ Ⓓ $(1 \times 5) + (0 \times 5) + (3 \times 5) + (6 \times 5)$

2 Alek gives 18 flowers to each person at his office. There are 42 people at his office. How many flowers does he give away? Show your work.

Solution

3 What is $9,260 \div 4$? Record your answer on the grid. Then fill in the bubbles.

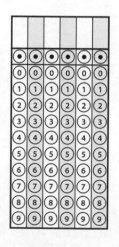

4 Maria solves the division problem below. Explain how to check whether her answer is correct.

$318 \div 4 = 79\,\text{R}\,2$

For problems 5–7, use the Math Reference Sheet as necessary.

5 A square has a perimeter of 24 meters and an area of 36 square meters. What is the side length of the square? Show your work.

The side length of the square is .... meters.

6 How many seconds are in different numbers of minutes? Complete the table. Write your answers in the blanks.

Minutes	1	2	3	4	5
Seconds			180		

7 Carl runs in a 5 kilometer race. He has 1 kilometer left to run. Decide if each statement about the race is true or false.

Choose *True* or *False* for each statement.

	True	False
Carl has run 4 meters so far.	Ⓐ	Ⓑ
The equation $5 \times 1,000 = m$ can be used to find the total length of the race in meters.	Ⓒ	Ⓓ
The race is 500 meters long.	Ⓔ	Ⓕ
Carl has 1,000 meters left to run.	Ⓖ	Ⓗ

Performance Task

Answer the questions and show all your work on separate paper.

Zander is in charge of filling goodie bags for the school party. He plans to order items to fill the goodie bags from an online party store. The store sells items by the gross. (1 gross = 144)

Zander expects 225 guests to be at the party. He plans on having 8 items in each goodie bag. Use the list of items below to put together an order for Zander. Explain how you know that your order has enough items.

Item	Price	Quantity
Finger Puppets (1 gross)	$11	
Bookmarks (1 gross)	$27	
Assorted Pencils (2 gross)	$15	
Animal Erasers (1 gross)	$16	
Foam Craft Kits (1 gross)	$125	
Glow-in-the-Dark Stickers (1 gross)	$110	

REFLECT

Use Mathematical Practices After you complete the task, choose one of the following questions to answer.

- **Model** Which operations did you use in order to solve the problem?

- **Be Precise** Could you use the word *dozen* instead of *gross* to describe the number of items on the order form? Explain. (1 dozen = 12)

Draw or write to show examples for each term. Then draw or write to show other math words in the unit.

convert to write an equivalent measurement using a different unit.

My Example

dividend the number that is divided by another number.

My Example

divisor the number by which another number is divided.

My Example

formula a mathematical relationship that is expressed in the form of an equation. For example, $A = \ell \times w$.

My Example

partial products the products you get in each step of the partial-products strategy. You use place value to find partial products. For example, the partial products for 124×3 are 3×100 or 300, 3×20 or 60, and 3×4 or 12.

My Example

partial quotients the quotients you get in each step of the partial-quotient strategy. You use place value to find partial quotients. For example, the partial quotients for $2,124 \div 4$ could be $2,000 \div 4$ or 500, $100 \div 4$ or 25, and $24 \div 4$ or 6.

My Example

My Word: _____

_____

_____

My Example

My Word: _____

_____

_____

My Example

My Word: _____

_____

_____

My Example

My Word: _____

_____

_____

My Example

My Word: _____

_____

_____

My Example

My Word: _____

_____

_____

My Example

Set 1: Multiply and Divide

Solve the problems. Multiply or divide.

1 3 × 5 = ...

2 4 × 6 = ...

3 7 × 3 = ...

4 36 ÷ 6 = ...

5 28 ÷ 4 = ...

6 64 ÷ 8 = ...

7 Write 4 equations using the fact family with the numbers 7, 8, and 56.

_____ × _____ = _____   _____ × _____ = _____

_____ ÷ _____ = _____   _____ ÷ _____ = _____

Set 2: Use Properties to Multiply

Fill in the blanks to make each equation true.

1 4 × 2 × 5 = ... × 4 × 5

2 8 × 6 = ... × 8

3 3 × (2 × 4) = 3 × ....

4 2 × (................. × 4) = 2 × 12

5 2 × 18 = 2 × .... × 2

6 .... × 7 = (2 × 2) × 7

Set 3: Use Patterns

Solve the problems. Fill in the blanks to complete the patterns. Then finish naming the rule.

1 8, 16, 24, 32, _____, _____, 56   Rule: Add _____

2 3, 6, 9, _____, 15, _____   Rule: Multiply by _____

3 The table shows a pattern in addends that have a sum of 10.

Identify the pattern by completing the statement below.

Write your answers in the blanks.

As one addend increases by _____, the other addend decreases by _____

Addend	Addend	Sum
0	10	10
2	8	10
4	6	10
6	4	10

Set 4: Area

Write the area of each shape in square units.

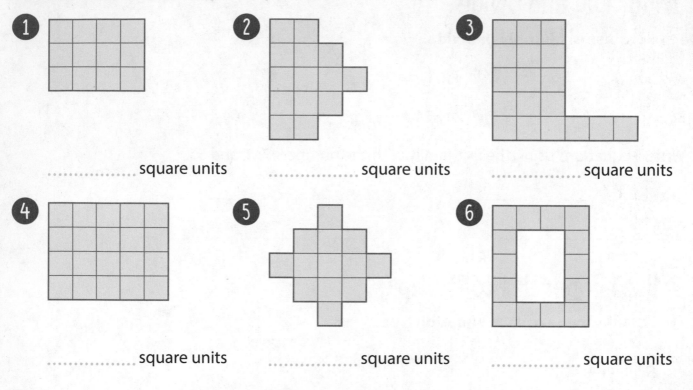

1 .... square units

2 .... square units

3 .... square units

4 .... square units

5 .... square units

6 .... square units

Set 5: Two-Step Word Problems

Write equation(s) for the unknown in each problem. Then solve.

1 Bree wants to save $40 to buy dance shoes. She earns $5 per hour babysitting for 5 hours. How much more money will she need to reach her goal?

2 The school band has 45 members. The members will work in groups of 5 to raise money for new uniforms. Each group will raise $100. How much money will the band raise?

3 Ms. Danforth needs to use all the playground balls in the school for field day. She asks each of the 9 classrooms for their 4 playground balls. The balls will be shared equally among 6 teams. How many balls will each team have?

Set 6: Equivalent Fractions

Write the missing numerator or denominator to make equivalent fractions.

1 $\frac{2}{3} = \frac{4}{\boxed{}}$

2 $\frac{4}{\boxed{}} = \frac{1}{2}$

3 $\frac{3}{9} = \frac{1}{\boxed{}}$

4 $\frac{1}{4} = \frac{\boxed{}}{8}$

5 $\frac{3}{6} = \frac{\boxed{}}{12}$

6 $\frac{1}{3} = \frac{2}{\boxed{}}$

7 Circle all the fractions that are equivalent to $\frac{3}{4}$:

$\frac{4}{3}$ $\frac{6}{12}$ $\frac{6}{8}$ $\frac{6}{9}$ $\frac{9}{12}$ $\frac{4}{5}$ $\frac{7}{10}$

Set 7: Compare Fractions

Solve the problems.

1 Label the fractions $\frac{3}{4}$ and $\frac{3}{6}$ on the number lines.

Circle the fraction that is less.

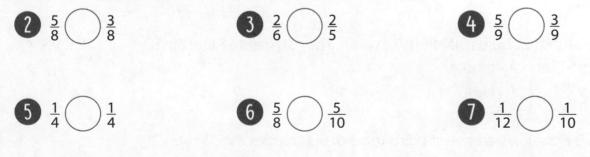

Write >, <, or = in each circle to compare the fractions.

2 $\frac{5}{8} \bigcirc \frac{3}{8}$

3 $\frac{2}{6} \bigcirc \frac{2}{5}$

4 $\frac{5}{9} \bigcirc \frac{3}{9}$

5 $\frac{1}{4} \bigcirc \frac{1}{4}$

6 $\frac{5}{8} \bigcirc \frac{5}{10}$

7 $\frac{1}{12} \bigcirc \frac{1}{10}$

Set 8: Tell Time

Solve the problems. Show your work for problems 3 and 4.

1 Write the time shown on the clock.

2 Draw hands on the clock to show 4:15.

....

3 Sarai's favorite show comes on at 8 PM. She starts her homework at 7:15 PM. She works for 20 minutes. Then she cleans her room for 28 minutes. Is she done in time to see the beginning of her show?

4 Jin arrives at a meeting at 7:00. She waits at the bus stop for 12 minutes. She rides the bus for 25 minutes to the meeting. What time did she leave?

Set 9: Mass and Liquid Volume

Solve. Show your work.

1 Stan has a bath tub that holds 300 liters of water. The tub has 167 liters in it. How many more liters can it hold?

2 Mr. Brantz has 3 erasers. Each eraser has a mass of 30 grams. What is the mass of the 3 erasers?

Cumulative Practice

Name: _____

Set 1: Place Value

Fill in the blanks to make each statement true.

1 The value of the 4 in 54,298 is ....

2 The value of the 2 in 490,200 is .... times the value of the 2 in 649,120.

3 In the number 88,845, the value of the 8 in the thousands place is 10 times

the value of the 8 in the .... place.

Set 2: Read and Write Whole Numbers

Write each number in standard form in problems 1–4.

1 Eight hundred thousand, eight

....

2 Forty-five thousand, twelve

....

3 2,000 + 200 + 2

....

4 10,000 + 800

....

Write the numbers in word form in problems 5 and 6.

5 20,490 =

6 48,016 =

Set 3: Compare Whole Numbers

Write <, >, or = in each circle to compare the numbers.

1 15,076 ◯ 9,628

2 7,648 ◯ 7,648

3 66,666 ◯ 666,666

4 11,154 ◯ 101,114

5 520,605 ◯ 520,650

6 22,004 ◯ 21,998

Set 4: Round to the Nearest Ten

Round each number to the nearest ten for problems 1–9.

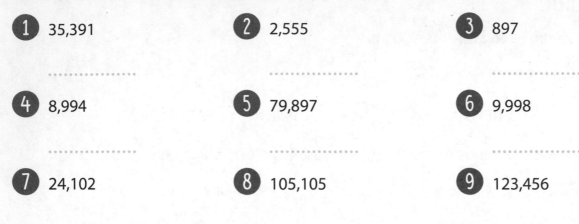

1 35,391

2 2,555

3 897

4 8,994

5 79,897

6 9,998

7 24,102

8 105,105

9 123,456

Fill in the missing digit that makes the statement correct for problems 10–13.

10 The value of 2 ☐ 4 rounded to the nearest ten is 250.

11 The value of 9,9 ☐ 9 rounded to the nearest ten is 9,990.

12 The value of 45,8 ☐ 7 rounded to the nearest ten is 45,840.

13 The value of 4,9 ☐ 5 rounded to the nearest ten is 5,000.

Set 5: Round to the Nearest Hundred

Round each number to the nearest hundred.

1 84,968

2 61

3 6,549

4 4,444

5 72,894

6 65,598

7 654,456

8 89,024

9 49,951

Set 6: Round to the Nearest Thousand

Fill in the missing digit that makes the statement correct for problems 1–3.

1 The value of 2☐,514 rounded to the nearest thousand is 25,000.

2 The value of ☐9,712 rounded to the nearest thousand is 100,000.

3 The value of 8☐,135 rounded to the nearest thousand is 82,000.

Round each number to the nearest thousand for problems 4–6.

4 24,489

5 79,564

6 5,849

Set 7: Round to the Nearest Ten Thousand

Round each number to the nearest ten thousand.

1 14,899

2 525,600

3 188,201

4 994,758

5 48,051

6 98,492

7 4,808

8 8,156

9 268,143

Fill in the blanks to make the sentences true.

10 The closest ten thousands to the number 562,548 are .... and

.... Since 562,548 is closer to ...., the value of 562,548

rounded to the nearest ten thousand is ....

Set 8: Add Whole Numbers

Find the sum in problems 1–3. Show your work.

1   25,305
    + 64,888

2   5,154
    + 2,132

3   561
    + 1,084

Fill in the missing digits that make the sums correct in problems 4–6.

4   4 , 1 8 ☐
    + 2 , 3 5 ☐
      6 , 5 4 8

5   1 8 , 7 ☐ 3
    +   6 , 1 5 ☐
      2 4 , 8 7 1

6   2 4 , ☐ 7 7
    + 2 7 , ☐ 2 5
      5 1 , 1 0 2

Set 9: Subtract Whole Numbers

Find the difference in problems 1–3. Show your work.

1   42,154
    − 35,726

2   12,976
    − 1,744

3   5,061
    − 4,784

Fill in the missing digits that make the differences correct in problems 4–6.

4   6 5 , 2 ☐ 6
    − 2 ☐ , 4 7 3
      4 1 , 7 6 3

5   1 2 , ☐ ☐ 8
    −   1 , 3 1 9
      1 0 , 6 8 9

6   7 4 , ☐ 2 7
    − 6 8 , 6 1 ☐
       6 , 3 0 8

Cumulative Practice

Name: _____

Set 1: Multiplication as a Comparison

Fill in the blanks.

 What two comparisons does the equation 5 × 6 = 30 show?

.... is .... times as many as ....

.... is .... times as many as ....

2 What two equations does the comparison *24 is 6 times as many as 4* represent?

.... × .... = ... × .... = ...

3 What two equations does the comparison *32 is 4 times as many as 8* represent?

.... × .... = ... × .... = ...

Set 2: Multiplication and Division in Word Problems

Solve the problems. Show your work.

1 Marcus picks 4 times as many blueberries as Tim. Marcus picks 20 cups of blueberries. How many cups of blueberries does Tim pick?

 Ceramic tiles come in packs of 9. Jillian needs 4 times that amount to tile her bathroom floor. How many tiles does Jillian need?

Set 3: Multi-step Word Problems

**Write and solve an equation with a variable for each word problem.
Show your work.**

 Aman sells clay flowerpots for $6 each. He has earned $36 so far. How many
more clay flowerpots does Aman need to sell to earn enough money to
buy a pair of shoes that costs $55?

 A city had 62 millimeters of rain in January. That is twice the amount of
rain the city had in February. How much rain did the city have altogether
in January and February?

 In a video game, Tara collects 5 tokens on each of the first four levels
and 8 tokens on each of the other three levels. How many tokens does
Tara collect in all seven levels?

 Tommy makes lanyards that he sells for $3 each. He sells 6 lanyards.
Then he spends $5 on materials to make more lanyards and $2 on a drink.
How much money does Tommy have left?

Name: _____

Set 4: Place Value

Describe how each place is related to the place next to it.

1 10 tens is 1 ....

2 10 thousands is 1 ....

3 10 .... is 1 ten.

4 10 .... is 1 hundred.

5 10 ten thousands is 1 ....

6 10 .... is 1 thousand.

Set 5: Compare Whole Numbers

Write the symbol (>, <, =) that makes each statement true.

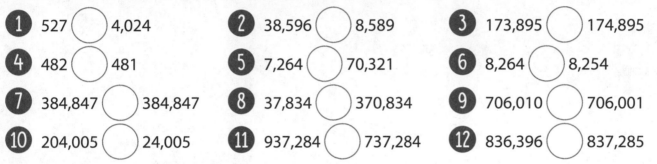

1 527 ◯ 4,024

2 38,596 ◯ 8,589

3 173,895 ◯ 174,895

4 482 ◯ 481

5 7,264 ◯ 70,321

6 8,264 ◯ 8,254

7 384,847 ◯ 384,847

8 37,834 ◯ 370,834

9 706,010 ◯ 706,001

10 204,005 ◯ 24,005

11 937,284 ◯ 737,284

12 836,396 ◯ 837,285

Set 6: Round Multi-Digit Whole Numbers

Round each number.

1 Round 4,752 to the nearest thousand: ....

2 Round 524 to the nearest ten: ....

3 Round 35,758 to the nearest ten thousand: ....

4 Round 55 to the nearest hundred: ....

5 Round 28,461 to the nearest ten: ....

6 Round 8,274 to the nearest hundred: ....

7 Round 173,593 to the nearest thousand: ....

8 Round 704,368 to the nearest ten thousand: ....

9 Round 105,238 to the nearest thousand: ....

10 Round 185,320 to the nearest ten thousand: ....

Set 7: Add Whole Numbers

Find the sum using the standard algorithm. Show your work.

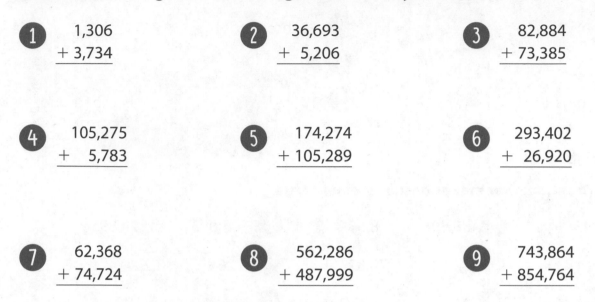

1   1,306
       + 3,734

2   36,693
       + 5,206

3   82,884
       + 73,385

4   105,275
       +   5,783

5   174,274
       + 105,289

6   293,402
       + 26,920

7   62,368
       + 74,724

8   562,286
       + 487,999

9   743,864
       + 854,764

Set 8: Subtract Whole Numbers

Find the difference using the standard algorithm. Show your work.

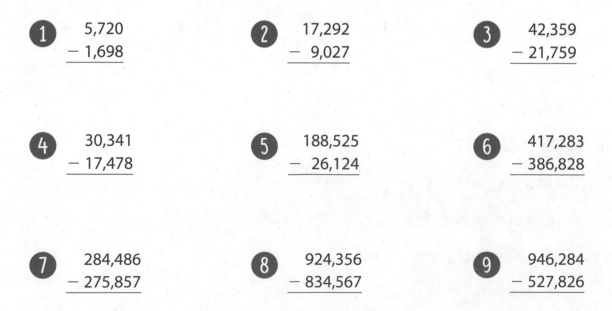

1   5,720
       − 1,698

2   17,292
       − 9,027

3   42,359
       − 21,759

4   30,341
       − 17,478

5   188,525
       − 26,124

6   417,283
       − 386,828

7   284,486
       − 275,857

8   924,356
       − 834,567

9   946,284
       − 527,826

Glossary/Glosario

English	Español	Example/Ejemplo

Aa

acute angle an angle that measures more than 0° but less than 90°.

ángulo agudo ángulo que mide más de 0° pero menos de 90°.

acute triangle a triangle that has three acute angles.

triángulo acutángulo triángulo que tiene tres ángulos agudos.

addend a number being added.

sumando número que se suma.

$24 + 35 = 59$

addends

algorithm a set of routine steps used to solve problems.

algoritmo conjunto de pasos que se siguen rutinariamente para resolver problemas.

$$\begin{array}{r} {}^{2}26 \\ \times\ 14 \\ \hline 104 \\ +\ 260 \\ \hline 364 \end{array}$$

AM the time from midnight until before noon.

a. m. el tiempo que transcurre desde la medianoche hasta el mediodía.

AM 7:20

angle a geometric shape formed by two rays, lines, or line segments that meet at a common point.

ángulo figura geométrica formada por dos semirrectas, rectas, o segmentos de recta que se encuentran en un punto.

English	Español	Example/Ejemplo
area the amount of space inside a closed two-dimensional figure. Area is measured in square units such as square centimeters.	**área** cantidad de espacio dentro de una figura bidimensional cerrada. El área se mide en unidades cuadradas, como los centímetros cuadrados.	Area = 4 square units
array a set of objects arranged in equal rows and equal columns.	**matriz** conjunto de objetos agrupados en filas y columnas iguales.	
associative property of addition when the grouping of three or more addends is changed, the total does not change.	**propiedad asociativa de la suma** cambiar la agrupación de tres o más sumandos no cambia el total.	$(2 + 3) + 4 = 2 + (3 + 4)$
associative property of multiplication changing the grouping of three or more factors does not change the product.	**propiedad asociativa de la multiplicación** cambiar la agrupación de tres o más factores no cambia el producto.	$(2 \times 4) \times 3 = 2 \times (4 \times 3)$
attribute any characteristic of an object or shape, such as number of sides or angles, lengths of sides, or angle measures.	**atributo** característica de un objeto o una figura, como el número de lados o ángulos, la longitud de los lados, o la medida de los ángulos.	attributes of a square: • 4 square corners • 4 sides of equal length

Bb

English	Español	Example/Ejemplo
benchmark fraction a common fraction that you might compare other fractions to.	**fracción de referencia** fracción común que se puede comparar con otras fracciones.	$\frac{1}{4}$, $\frac{1}{2}$, $\frac{2}{3}$, and $\frac{3}{4}$ are often used as benchmark fractions.

Cc

English	Español	Example/Ejemplo
capacity the amount a container can hold. Capacity can be measured in the same units as liquid volume.	**capacidad** cantidad que cabe en un recipiente. La capacidad se mide en las mismas unidades que el volumen líquido.	capacity of 2 liters

English	Español	Example/Ejemplo
centimeter (cm) a unit of length. There are 100 centimeters in 1 meter.	**centímetro (cm)** unidad de longitud. 100 centímetros equivalen a 1 metro.	Your little finger is about 1 **centimeter** (cm) across.
column a vertical line of objects or numbers, such as in an array or table.	**columna** línea vertical de objetos o números, como las de una matriz o una tabla.	
common denominator a number that is a common multiple of the denominators of two or more fractions.	**denominadores comunes** número que es común múltiplo de los denominadores de dos o más fracciones.	$2 \times 3 = 6$, so 6 is a common denominator for $3\frac{1}{2}$ and $1\frac{1}{3}$.
commutative property of addition changing the order of addends does not change the total.	**propiedad conmutativa de la suma** cambiar el orden de los sumandos no cambia el total.	$3 + 4 = 4 + 3$
commutative property of multiplication changing the order of the factors does not change the product.	**propiedad conmutativa de la multiplicación** cambiar el orden de los factores no cambia el producto.	$3 \times 2 = 2 \times 3$
compare to decide if numbers, amounts, or sizes are greater than, less than, or equal to each other.	**comparar** determinar si un número, una cantidad, o un tamaño es mayor que, menor que o igual a otro número, otra cantidad u otro tamaño.	$6{,}131 > 5{,}113$

English	Español	Example/Ejemplo
compose to make by combining parts. You can put together numbers to make a greater number or shapes to make a new shape.	**componer** combinar partes para formar algo. Se pueden combinar números para formar un número mayor o figuras para formar otra figura.	The three 50° angles compose the larger angle.
composite number a number that has more than one pair of factors.	**número compuesto** número que tiene más de un par de factores.	16 is a composite number.
convert to write an equivalent measurement using a different unit.	**convertir** expresar una medida equivalente en una unidad diferente.	5 feet = 60 inches
cup (c) a liquid volume in the customary system. 4 cups is equivalent to 1 quart.	**taza (tz)** unidad de volumen líquido del sistema usual. Cuatro tazas equivalen a 1 cuarto.	
customary system the measurement system commonly used in the United States that measures length in inches, feet, yards, and miles; liquid volume in cups, pints, quarts, and gallons; and weight in ounces and pounds.	**sistema usual** sistema de medición comúnmente usado en Estados Unidos. La longitud se mide en pulgadas, pies, yardas, y millas; el volumen líquido, en tazas, pintas, cuartos, y galones; y el peso, en onzas y libras.	

Length
1 foot = 12 inches
1 yard = 3 feet
1 mile = 5,280 feet

Weight
1 pound = 16 ounces

Liquid Volume
1 quart = 2 pints
1 quart = 4 cups
1 gallon = 4 quarts

English	Español	Example/Ejemplo

Dd

English	Español	Example/Ejemplo
data a set of collected information. Often numerical information such as a list of measurements.	**datos** conjunto de información reunida. A menudo es información numérica, tal como una lista de mediciones.	earthworm lengths (in inches) $4\frac{1}{2}, 5, 5, 5, 5\frac{1}{4}, 5\frac{1}{4}, 5\frac{1}{4}, 6, 6\frac{1}{4}$
decimal a number containing a decimal point that separates a whole from fractional place values (tenths, hundredths, thousandths, and so on).	**número decimal** número que contiene un punto decimal que separa la posición de las unidades de las posiciones fraccionarias (décimas, centésimas, milésimas, etc.).	1.293
decimal point the dot used in a decimal that separates the ones place from the tenths place.	**punto decimal** punto que se usa en un número decimal para separar la posición de las unidades de la posición de las décimas.	1.65 ↑ decimal point
decompose to break into parts. You can break apart numbers and shapes.	**descomponer** separar en partes. Se pueden separar en partes números y figuras.	$\frac{3}{8} = \frac{1}{8} + \frac{1}{8} + \frac{1}{8}$
degree (°) a unit of measure for angles. There are 360° in a circle.	**grado** (°) unidad de medida para ángulos. Hay 360° en un círculo.	There are 360° in a circle.
denominator the number below the line in a fraction that tells the number of equal parts in the whole.	**denominador** número que está debajo de la línea de una fracción. Dice cuántas partes iguales hay en el entero.	$\frac{2}{3}$
difference the result of subtraction.	**diferencia** el resultado de la resta.	$\frac{3}{4} - \frac{1}{4} = \frac{2}{4}$
digit a symbol used to write numbers.	**dígito** símbolo que se usa para escribir números.	The digits are 0, 1, 2, 3, 4, 5, 6, 7, 8, and 9.
dimension length in one direction. A figure may have one, two, or three dimensions.	**dimensión** longitud en una dirección. Una figura puede tener una, dos, o tres dimensiones.	5 in. 2 in. 3 in.

English	Español	Example/Ejemplo
distributive property when one of the factors of a product is written as a sum, multiplying each addend by the other factor before adding does not change the product.	**propiedad distributiva** cuando uno de los factores de un producto se escribe como suma, multiplicar cada sumando por el otro factor antes de sumar no cambia el producto.	$2 \times (3 + 6) = (2 \times 3) + (2 \times 6)$
divide to separate into equal groups and find the number in each group or the number of groups.	**dividir** separar en grupos iguales y hallar cuántos hay en cada grupo o el número de grupos.	$2{,}850 \div 38 = 75$
dividend the number that is divided by another number.	**dividendo** el número que se divide por otro número.	$15 \div 3 = 5$
division an operation used to separate a number of items into equal-sized groups.	**división** operación que se usa para separar una cantidad de objetos en grupos iguales.	**Division** $12 \div 3 = 4$ total · number of groups · number in each group
divisor the number by which another number is divided.	**divisor** el número por el que se divide otro número.	$15 \div 3 = 15$

Ee

edge a line segment where two faces meet in a three-dimensional shape.	**arista** segmento de recta donde se encuentran dos caras de una figura tridimensional.	edge

English	Español	Example/Ejemplo
elapsed time the amount of time that has passed between a start time and an end time.	**tiempo transcurrido** tiempo que ha pasado entre el momento de inicio y el fin.	The elapsed time from 2:00 PM to 3:00 PM is 1 hour.
equal having the same value, same size, or same amount.	**igual** que tiene el mismo valor, el mismo tamaño o la misma cantidad.	$25 + 15 = 40$ $25 + 15$ **is equal to** 40.
equal sign (=) a symbol that means *is the same value as*.	**signo de igual (=)** símbolo que significa *tiene el mismo valor que*.	$12 + 4 = 16$
equation a mathematical statement that uses an equal sign (=) to show that two expressions have the same value.	**ecuación** enunciado matemático que tiene un signo de igual (=) para mostrar que dos expresiones tienen el mismo valor.	$25 - 15 = 10$
equilateral triangle a triangle that has all three sides the same length.	**triángulo equilátero** triángulo que tiene los tres lados de igual longitud.	8 in. /\ 8 in. 8 in.
equivalent fractions two or more different fractions that name the same part of a whole or the same point on a number line.	**fracciones equivalentes** dos o más fracciones diferentes que nombran la misma parte de un entero y el mismo punto en una recta numérica.	$\frac{2}{4} = \frac{1}{2}$ $\frac{5}{10} = \frac{1}{2}$
estimate (noun) a close guess made using mathematical thinking.	**estimación** suposición aproximada que se hace usando el razonamiento matemático.	$28 + 21 = ?$ $30 + 20 = 50$ 50 is an estimate of the sum.

English	Español	Example/Ejemplo
estimate (verb) to make a close guess based on mathematical thinking.	**estimar / hacer una estimación** hacer una suposición aproximada usando el razonamiento matemático.	11×40 is about 400.
even number a whole number that always has 0, 2, 4, 6, or 8 in the ones place. An even number of objects can be put into pairs or into two equal groups without any leftovers.	**número par** número entero que siempre tiene 0, 2, 4, 6, o 8 en la posición de las unidades. Un número par de objetos puede agruparse en pares o en dos grupos iguales sin que queden sobrantes.	20, 22, 24, 26, and 28 are even numbers.
expanded form the way a number is written to show the place value of each digit.	**forma desarrollada** manera de escribir un número para mostrar el valor posicional de cada dígito.	$249 = 200 + 40 + 9$
expression one or more numbers, unknown numbers, and/or operation symbols that represents a quantity.	**expresión** uno o más números, números desconocidos o símbolos de operaciones que representan una cantidad.	3×4 or $5 + b$

Ff

English	Español	Example/Ejemplo
face a flat surface of a solid shape.	**cara** superficie plana de una figura sólida.	face
fact family a group of related equations that use the same numbers, but in a different order, and two different operation symbols. A fact family can show the relationship between addition and subtraction or between multiplication and division.	**familia de datos** grupo de ecuaciones relacionadas que tienen los mismos números, ordenados de distinta manera, y dos símbolos de operaciones diferentes. Una familia de datos puede mostrar la relación que existe entre la multiplicación y la división.	$5 \times 4 = 20$ $4 \times 5 = 20$ $20 \div 4 = 5$ $20 \div 5 = 4$

English	Español	Example/Ejemplo
factor a number that is multiplied.	**factor** número que se multiplica.	$4 \times 5 = 20$ factors
factor pair two numbers that are multiplied together to give a product.	**pares de factores** dos números que se multiplican para obtener un producto.	$4 \times 5 = 20$ factor pair
factors of a number whole numbers that multiply together to get the given number.	**factores de un número** números enteros que se multiplican para obtener el número dado.	$4 \times 5 = 20$ **4** and **5** are factors of 20.
foot (ft) a unit of length in the customary system. There are 12 inches in 1 foot.	**pie (ft)** unidad de longitud del sistema usual. 1 pie equivale a 12 pulgadas.	12 inches = 1 foot
formula a mathematical relationship that is expressed in the form of an equation.	**fórmula** relación matemática que se expresa en forma de ecuación.	$A = \ell \times w$
fourths the parts formed when a whole is divided into four equal parts.	**cuartos** partes que se forman cuando se divide un entero en cuatro partes iguales.	fourths 4 equal parts
fraction a number that names equal parts of a whole. A fraction names a point on the number line.	**fracción** número que nombra partes iguales de un entero. Una fracción nombra un punto en una recta numérica.	$\frac{3}{4}$

English	Español	Example/Ejemplo

Gg

English	Español	Example/Ejemplo
gallon (gal) a unit of liquid volume in the customary system. There are 4 quarts in 1 gallon.	**galón (gal)** unidad de volumen liquido del sistema usual. Un galón es igual a 4 cuartos.	4 quarts = 1 gallon
gram (g) a unit of mass in the metric system. A paper clip has a mass of about 1 gram. There are 1,000 grams in 1 kilogram.	**gramo (g)** unidad de masa del sistema métrico. Un clip tiene una masa de aproximadamente 1 gramo. 1,000 gramos equivalen a 1 kilogramo.	1,000 grams = 1 kilogram
greater than symbol (>) a symbol used to compare two numbers when the first is greater than the second.	**símbolo de mayor que (>)** símbolo que se usa para comparar dos números cuando el primero es mayor que el segundo.	6,131 > 5,113

Hh

English	Español	Example/Ejemplo
halves the parts formed when a whole is divided into two equal parts.	**medios** partes que se obtienen cuando se divide un entero en dos partes iguales.	halves 2 equal parts
hexagon a polygon with exactly 6 sides and 6 angles.	**hexágono** polígono que tiene exactamente 6 lados y 6 ángulos.	
hour (h) a unit of time. There are 60 minutes in 1 hour.	**hora (h)** unidad de tiempo. 1 hora equivale a 60 minutos.	60 minutes = 1 hour
hundredths the parts formed when a whole is divided into 100 equal parts.	**centésimos (fracciones)/ centésimas (decimales)** partes que se forman cuando un entero se divide en 100 partes iguales.	

English	Español	Example/Ejemplo
obtuse triangle a triangle that has one obtuse angle.	**triángulo obtusángulo** triángulo que tiene un ángulo obtuso.	
odd number a whole number that always has 1, 3, 5, 7, or 9 in the ones place. An odd number of objects cannot be put into pairs or into two equal groups without a leftover.	**número impar** número entero que siempre tiene el dígito 1, 3, 5, 7, o 9 en la posición de las unidades. Los números impares no pueden ordenarse en pares o en dos grupos iguales sin que queden sobrantes.	21, 23, 25, 27, and 29 are odd numbers.
operation a mathematical action such as addition, subtraction, multiplication, or division.	**operación** acción matemática como la suma, la resta, la multiplicación y la división.	$15 + 5 = 20$ $20 - 5 = 15$ $4 \times 6 = 24$ $24 \div 6 = 4$
ounce (oz) a unit of weight in the customary system. A slice of bread weighs about 1 ounce. There are 16 ounces in 1 pound.	**onza (oz)** unidad de peso del sistema usual. Una rebanada de pan pesa aproximadamente 1 onza. 16 onzas equivalen a 1 libra.	16 ounces = 1 pound

Pp

English	Español	Example/Ejemplo
parallel lines lines that are always the same distance apart and never cross.	**rectas paralelas** rectas que siempre están a la misma distancia y nunca se cruzan.	
parallelogram a quadrilateral with opposite sides parallel and equal in length.	**paralelogramo** cuadrilátero que tiene lados opuestos paralelos e iguales en longitud.	
partial products the products you get in each step of the partial-products strategy. You use place value to find partial products.	**productos parciales** los productos que se obtienen en cada paso de la estrategia de productos parciales. Se usa el valor posicional para hallar productos parciales.	The partial products for 124×3 are 3×100 or 300, 3×20 or 60, and 3×4 or 12.

English	Español	Example/Ejemplo
partial quotients the quotients you get in each step of the partial-quotients strategy. You use place value to find partial quotients.	**cocientes parciales** los cocientes que se obtienen en cada paso de la estrategia de cocientes parciales. Se usa el valor posicional para hallar cocientes parciales.	The partial quotients for $2{,}124 \div 4$ could be $2{,}000 \div 4$ or 500, $100 \div 4$ or 25, and $24 \div 4$ or 6.
partial sums the sums you get in each step of the partial-sums strategy. You use place value to find partial sums.	**sumas parciales** las sumas que se obtienen en cada paso de la estrategia de sumas parciales. Se usa el valor posicional para hallar sumas parciales.	The partial sums for $124 + 234$ are $100 + 200$ or 300, $20 + 30$ or 50, and $4 + 4$ or 8.
partial-products strategy a strategy used to multiply multi-digit numbers.	**estrategia de productos parciales** estrategia que se usa para multiplicar números de varios dígitos.	$$\begin{array}{r} 218 \\ \times\, 6 \\ \hline \mathbf{48} \quad (6 \times 8 \text{ ones}) \\ \mathbf{60} \quad (6 \times 1 \text{ ten}) \\ +\, \mathbf{1200} \quad (6 \times 2 \text{ hundreds}) \\ \hline 1308 \end{array}$$ The partial products for 218×6 are 6×200 or 1,200, 6×10 or 60, and 6×8 or 48.
partial-quotients strategy a strategy used to divide multi-digit numbers.	**estrategia de cocientes parciales** estrategia que se usa para dividir números de varios dígitos.	$$\begin{array}{r} 6 \\ 25 \\ 500 \\ \hline 4\,\overline{)\,2{,}125} \\ -\,2{,}000 \\ \hline 125 \\ -\,100 \\ \hline 25 \\ -\,24 \\ \hline 1 \end{array}$$ The partial quotients are 500, 25, and 6. The quotient, 531, is the sum of the partial quotients. The remainder is 1.

English	Español	Example/Ejemplo
partial-sums strategy a strategy used to add multi-digit numbers.	**estrategia de sumas parciales** estrategia que se usa para sumar números de varios dígitos.	312 +235 **Add the hundreds.** 500 **Add the tens.** 40 **Add the ones.** + 7 547
pattern a series of numbers or shapes that follow a rule to repeat or change.	**patrón** serie de números o figuras que siguen una regla para repetirse o cambiar.	▲ ■ ▲ ■ ▲ ■
pentagon a two-dimensional closed shape with exactly 5 sides and 5 angles.	**pentágono** figura bidimensional cerrada que tiene exactamente 5 lados y 5 ángulos.	
perimeter the distance around a two-dimensional shape. The perimeter is equal to the sum of the lengths of the sides.	**perímetro** longitud del contorno de una figura bidimensional. El perímetro es igual al total de las longitudes de los lados.	**60 yards** **40 yards** ⬚ **40 yards** **60 yards** The perimeter of the soccer field is 200 yards. (60 yd + 40 yd + 60 yd + 40 yd)
period a group of three places in a number, usually separated by commas. The first three periods are the ones period, the thousands period, and the millions period.	**período** grupo de tres valores posicionales de un número, generalmente separados por comas. Los primeros tres períodos son el período de las unidades, el período de los millares y el período de los millones.	321,987 987 is the first period.
perpendicular lines two lines that meet to form a right angle, or a 90° angle.	**rectas perpendiculares** dos rectas que se unen para formar un ángulo recto, o un ángulo de 90°.	
pint (pt) a unit of liquid volume in the customary system. There are 2 cups in 1 pint.	**pinta (pt)** unidad de volumen líquido del sistema usual. 1 pinta equivale a 2 tazas.	2 cups = 1 pint

English	Español	Example/Ejemplo

place value the value assigned to a digit based on its position in a number.

valor posicional valor de un dígito según su posición en un número.

Hundreds	Tens	Ones
4	4	4

| 400 | 40 | 4 |

plane figure a two-dimensional figure, such as a circle, triangle, or rectangle.

figura plana figura bidimensional, como un círculo, triángulo, o rectángulo.

PM the time from noon until before midnight.

p. m. tiempo que transcurre desde el mediodía hasta la medianoche.

PM 5:10

point a single location in space.

punto ubicación única en el espacio.

A
•

polygon a two-dimensional closed figure made with three or more straight line segments that do not cross over each other.

polígono figura bidimensional cerrada formada que tiene tres o más segmentos de recta que no se cruzan.

Polygons	Not Polygons

pound (lb) a unit of weight in the customary system. There are 16 ounces in 1 pound.

libra (lb) unidad de peso del sistema usual. 1 libra equivale a 16 onzas.

16 ounces = 1 pound

prime number a whole number greater than 1 whose only factors are 1 and itself.

número primo número entero mayor que 1 cuyos únicos factores son 1 y él mismo.

2, 3, 5, 7, 11, 13, 17, 19 are prime numbers.

product the result of multiplication.

producto el resultado de la multiplicación.

$5 \times 3 = 15$

English	Español	Example/Ejemplo
protractor a tool used to measure angles.	**transportador** herramienta que se usa para medir ángulos.	

Qq

quadrilateral a polygon with exactly 4 sides and 4 angles.	**cuadrilátero** polígono que tiene exactamente 4 lados y 4 ángulos.	
quart (qt) a unit of liquid volume in the customary system. There are 4 cups in 1 quart.	**cuarto (ct)** unidad de volumen líquido del sistema usual. 1 cuarto equivale a 4 tazas.	4 cups = 1 quart
quotient the result of division.	**cociente** el resultado de la división.	$15 \div 3 = \mathbf{5}$ ⟵ quotient

Rr

ray a straight row of points that starts at one point and goes on forever in one direction.	**semirrecta** fila recta de puntos que comienza en un punto y continúa infinitamente en una dirección.	
reasonable something that makes sense when given facts are taken into account.	**razonable** algo que tiene sentido cuando se tienen en cuenta los datos dados.	You can estimate to make sure an answer is reasonable. 29 + 22 = 51 30 + 20 = 50
rectangle a quadrilateral with 4 right angles. Opposite sides of a rectangle are the same length.	**rectángulo** paralelogramo que tiene 4 ángulos rectos. Los lados opuestos de un rectángulo tienen la misma longitud.	
regroup to put together or break apart ones, tens, or hundreds.	**reagrupar** unir o separar unidades, decenas, o centenas.	10 ones can be regrouped as 1 ten, or 1 hundred can be regrouped as 10 tens.

English	Español	Example/Ejemplo
remainder the amount left over when one number does not divide another number a whole number of times.	**residuo** en la división, la cantidad que queda después de haber formado grupos iguales.	Remainder $17 \div 5 = 3\,R\,2$
rhombus a quadrilateral with all sides the same length.	**rombo** cuadrilátero que tiene todos los lados de la misma longitud.	
right angle an angle that looks like a square corner and measures 90°.	**ángulo recto** ángulo que parece la esquina de un cuadrado y mide 90°.	90°
right triangle a triangle that has one right angle.	**triángulo rectángulo** triángulo con un ángulo recto.	90°
round to find a number that is close in value to a given number by finding the nearest ten, hundred, or other place value.	**redondear** hallar un número que es cercano en valor al número dado hallando la decena, la centena, o otro valor posicional más cercano.	48 rounded to the nearest ten is 50.
row a horizontal line of objects or numbers, such as in an array or table.	**fila** línea horizontal de objetos o números, tal como las que aparecen en una matriz o una tabla.	
rule a procedure that is followed to go from one number or shape to the next in a pattern.	**regla** procedimiento que se sigue para ir de un número o una figura al número o la figura siguiente de un patrón.	17, 22, 27, 32, 37, 42 rule: add 5

English	Español	Example/Ejemplo

Ss

scale (on a graph) the value represented by the distance between one tickmark and the next on a number line.

escala (en una gráfica) el valor que representa la distancia entre una marca y la marca siguiente de una recta numérica. la relación entre los valores de los ejes de una gráfica.

Points Scored During the Game

Students: Alan, Cate, Gary, Mae

Number of Points Scored: 0 2 4 6 8

---

scalene triangle a triangle that has no sides the same length.

triángulo escaleno triángulo que no tiene lados de igual longitud.

---

second (s) a unit of time. There are 60 seconds in 1 minute.

segundo (s) unidad de tiempo. 60 segundos equivalen a 1 minuto.

60 seconds = 1 minute

---

side a line segment that forms part of a two-dimensional shape.

lado segmento de recta que forma parte de una figura bidimensional.

side

---

square a quadrilateral with 4 square corners and 4 sides of equal length.

cuadrado cuadrilátero que tiene 4 esquinas cuadradas y 4 lados de igual longitud.

---

square unit the area of a square with side lengths of 1 unit.

unidad cuadrada el área de un cuadrado que tiene lados de 1 unidad de longitud.

1 unit
1 unit   1 unit
1 unit

---

standard form the way a number is written with numerals.

forma estándar manera de escribir un número usando dígitos.

The standard form of *twelve* is 12.

English	Español	Example/Ejemplo
sum the result of addition.	**suma** el resultado de la suma.	$34 + 25 = \mathbf{59}$
symbol a character, such as a letter or question mark, that can be used to stand for an unknown number in an equation.	**símbolo** cualquier marca o dibujo, tal como una letra o un signo de interrogación, que puede usarse para representar un número desconocido en una ecuación.	$18 - \mathbf{?} = 9$

Tt

English	Español	Example/Ejemplo
tenths the parts formed when a whole is divided into 10 equal parts.	**décimos (fracciones)/ décimas (decimales)** partes que se forman cuando se divide un entero en 10 partes iguales.	
thirds the parts formed when a whole is divided into three equal parts.	**tercios** partes que se forman cuando se divide un entero en tres partes iguales.	thirds 3 equal parts
three-dimensional solid, or having length, width, and height. For example, a cube is three-dimensional.	**tridimensional** sólido, o que tiene longitud, ancho, y altura. Por ejemplo, los cubos son tridimensionales.	
trapezoid (exclusive) a quadrilateral with exactly one pair of parallel sides.	**trapecio** cuadrilátero que tiene exactamente un par de lados paralelos.	

English	Español	Example/Ejemplo
trapezoid (inclusive) a quadrilateral with at least one pair of parallel sides.	**trapecio** cuadrilátero que tiene al menos un par de lados paralelos.	
triangle a polygon with exactly 3 sides and 3 angles.	**triángulo** polígono que tiene exactamente 3 lados y 3 ángulos.	
two-dimensional flat, or having measurement in two directions, like length and width. For example, a rectangle is two-dimensional.	**bidimensional** plano, o que tiene medidas en dos direcciones, como la longitud y el ancho. Por ejemplo, un rectángulo es bidimensional.	

Uu

English	Español	Example/Ejemplo
unit fraction a fraction with a numerator of 1. Other fractions are built from unit fractions.	**fracción unitaria** fracción cuyo numerador es 1. Otras fracciones se construyen a partir de fracciones unitarias.	$\frac{1}{4}$
unknown the value you need to find to solve a problem.	**desconocido** el valor que se debe hallar para resolver un problema.	$18 - ? = 9$

Vv

English	Español	Example/Ejemplo
vertex the point where two rays, lines, or line segments meet to form an angle.	**vértice** punto donde dos semirrectas, rectas, o segmentos de recta se unen y forman un ángulo.	vertex

English	Español	Example/Ejemplo

Ww

weight the measurement that tells how heavy an object is. Units of weight include ounces and pounds.

peso medición que dice cuán pesado es un objeto. Las onzas y las libras son unidades de peso.

Weight
1 pound = 16 ounces

word form the way a number is written with words or said aloud.

en palabras manera en que se escribe o se dice en voz alta un número usando palabras.

467,882
four hundred sixty-seven thousand, **eight hundred eighty-two**

Yy

yard (yd) a unit of length in the customary system. There are 3 feet, or 36 inches, in 1 yard.

yarda (yd) unidad de longitud del sistema usual de Estados Unidos. 1 yarda equivale a 3 pies o a 36 pulgadas.

3 feet = 1 yard
36 inches = 1 yard

Acknowledgments

Common Core State Standards © 2010. National Governors Association Center for Best Practices and Council of Chief State School Officers. All rights reserved.

Photography Credits

United States coin images (unless otherwise indicated) from the United States Mint

Images used under license from **Shutterstock.com**.

iii Racheal Grazias, David Herraez Calzada; **iv** Antonia Giroux, tratong; **v** 2happy, Allen McDavid Stoddard; **vi** Gordana Sermek, Thitima Boonnak; **vii** d100, Photoonlife; **1** S. Bonaime; **3** Alex Staroseltsev; **4** Alex Staroseltsev, KaiMook Studio 99, Lano4ka, Mhatzapa; **8** Mhatzapa, NikoNomad; **13** Mhatzapa, Peter Sobolev; **15** Alexsandr Sadkov, Art'n'Lera, Marssanya; **16** Aleksandr Sadkov, Art'n'Lera; **17** piotr_pabijan; **18** Authentic Creations, Pixfiction; **19** Pixfiction; **20** Cheryl Casey; **21** David Lee; **22** Brocreative; **24** Lyekaterina, Super Prin; **29** Khunnoo; **30** Butsaya; **31** Africa Studio; **32** Stratos Giannikos; **33** Africa Studio; **34** Andregric, EkaC; **36** Roman Samokhin; **37** Neveshkin Nikolay; **40** Thodonal88; **44** Antpkr; **45** Kzww; **47** Ann Stryzhekin, dmitro2009, In-Finity, Jason Patrick Ross, Jo Crebbin; **49** Digidreamgrafix, In-Finity, StacieStauffSmith Photos, Steve Bower; **52** Pixeldreams.eu, Zmiter; **53** Racheal Grazias, Redchocolate; **56** Songsak P; **58** Electra, Flipser, Spacaj; **60** Hannamariah; **63** Liskus, Normana Karia; **71** Ekaterina Kondratova, Lotus Images; **74** Bryan Solomon; **75** Ewais; **76** Ericlefrancais; **78** Aperturesound; **79** Dmitry Petrenko; **87** David Herraez Calzada; **89** V J Matthew; **90** Ivonne Wierink; **96** Naruedom Yaempongsa, 3000ad; **105** Lotus_studio; **108** Thodonal88; **115** Cathleen A Clapper; **116** Javier Brosch, olnik_y; **117** olnik_y, Sofiaworld; **118** marssanya, PERLA BERANT WILDER; **119** Efetova Anna; **120** Igor Sirbu, Peyker; **121** tratong; **124** blue67design, Jag_cz; **125–126** Nataliia Pyzhova; **128** Amawasri Pakdara; **130** Denis Belyaevskiy; **131** Elena Schweitzer; **132** Subbotina Anna; **134** Dan Thornberg; **138** Africa Studio, Wonderful Future World; **141** humbak; **142** Sanzhar Murzin; **143** blue67design, Leigh Prather; **146** Eans; **147** Sarah Marchan; **148** ILEISH ANNA, Kaiskynet Studio; **149** Jiri Hera; **150** Good Shop Background; **152** Nata-Lia; **153–154** Narong Jongsirikul; **159** James Steidl; **160** elbud; **169** Kaspri, LDDesign, Maaike Boot, Travelview, Vibe Images; **170** PowerUp; **171** T Cassidy; **175** design56, Kolopach; **176** Ostill; **178** Elena Voynova; **179** Nataliia Pyzhova, RedHead_Anna, Venus Angel; **181–182** Antonia Giroux; **191** Julie Vader; **192** Nikita Biserov; **196** OmniArt, TeddyandMia; **197** EDMAVR, FernPat; **198** Mon Nakornthab; **201** Erik Lam; **202** Vladyslav Starozhylov; **203** Billion Photos; **204** Issarawat Tattong, Levent Konuk; **206** Axio Images; **208** alfocome; **210** Mlorenz; **211** Dmitry Petrenko; **214, 216** Domnitsky; **218** Videowokart, Koncz, Arsentyeva E, Barbol, oksana2010, tr3gin, Pavel Vakhrushev, Stephen B. Goodwin; **220** Evgenyi; **221** Marilyn Barbone, Smspsy, I'm Friday, Temastadnyk; **227** eyal granith; **229** Allen McDavid Stoddard; **230** Owatta, Pandapaw; **241** ravl; **242** Orla; **248** Sashkin; **249** David Franklin, WhiteDragon; **250** Ewapee; **252** PrimaStockPhoto; **257** vdimage; **258** Room27; **261** RemarkEliza; **262** ZanyZeus; **264** Elena Elisseeva; **268** ConstantinosZ, IB Photography; **270** 2happy; **272** Denis Rozhnovsky; **273** Africa Studio; **274** 5 second Studio, Natasha Pankina; **276** Roman Samokhin, Subject Photo; **278** M. Unal Ozmen; **279** Igor Polyakov; **280** Potapov Alexander; **282** Daniela Barreto, Evgeny Karandaev; **284** Beata Becla; **286** GoBOb, Ponsawan saelim; **287** SOMMAI; **288** kolopach; **290** Artem Shadrin; **301** Lori Martin;

304 YolLusZam1802; **306** Ravl; **308** Philip Lange; **309** Heymo; **310** Hong Vo; **312** Art24hrDesign; **317** Alexey Boldin; **322** Sosika; **325** Seregam; **326** Andrei Dubadzel; **327** Jiang Zhongyan; **328** Marco Scisetti, v.s.anandhakrishna; **329** Graph, Vasily Kovalev; **332** JIANG HONGYAN, olnik_y, Visual Generation; **333** Cynoclub, Monica Click; **334** Eric Isselee, olnik_y, Natasha Pankina, Visual Generation; **336** Stephen Orsillo; **339–340** horiyan; **344** Peter Wollinga; **346** Worraket; **348** Lucy Liu, olnik_y, Vilax; **350** Eric Isselee; **352** Igor Zh; **354** Rtimages; **356** Maerzkind; **357** Bas Nastassia, Marekusz, WachiraS, vovan, Vlabo; **363** Ocskay Bence; **365** Tim UR; **366** Gayvoronskaya_Yana; **377** Tatyana Vyc; **378** DenisNata; **379** Andy Dean Photography; **382** HelgaLin, Mark Herreid, Padma Sanjaya; **383** Protasov AN; **384** happymay; **386** Madlen; **389** Africa Studio; **390** kolopach; **397** Davidoff777; **398** Images.etc; **399** PhotoMediaGroup; **400** Iurii Kackkovskyi; **401** Theo Fitzhugh; **402** IB Photography; **405** Naruedom Yaempongsa; **409** Duplass, Stephen Mcsweeny; **410** cynoclub; **411** LittlePigPower; **412** MaraZe, Rodrigobark, Wealthylady; **413** Victor Habbick, Aphelleon, Marc Ward, Niko Nomad, NASA, NASA/JPL-Caltech, NASA/JPL/Cornell University/ Maas Digital, NASA/JPL, NASA, ESA, and M. Livio and the Hubble 20th Anniversary Team (STScI), NASA/Ames **414** Bestv, blue67design; **416** Christian Musat, Don Mammoser, Florida Stock, Gary powell, Jayne Carney, Moosehenderson, Sandy Hedgepeth, Schalke fotografie | Melissa Schalke, Steven Blandin; **417–418** Sergej Razvodovskij; **419** blue67design, Gino Santa Maria; **420** Bernashafo; **421** Africa Studio, Ffolas, Strannik_fox; **422** blue67design, Halfpoint; **423** 3777190317; **424** Mariyana M; **425** Kolopach; **426** Robert_s; **427** Jaroslav74; **428** Africa Studio; **429** Hong Vo; **433** RusGri; **437** John Kasawa; **438** Carlos E. Santa Maria; **439** CameraOnHand; **440** Butterfly Hunter, Lucky-photographer, Luria; **441** Danielle Balderas; **442** showcake; **444** HelloRF Zcool, Wonderful Future World, Yellow Cat; **445** Photo Melon; **446** Lunatictm; **448** bonchan; **449** Gordana Sermek; **451** Zheltyshev; **452** ZoranOrcik; **455** Nattika; **456** Viktar Malyshchyts, Wonderful Future World; **457** Inhabitant; **459** Hurst Photo; **460** Tiger Images, Wintakorn Choemnarong; **461** bonchan; **462** Alfocome; **463** Nataly Studio; **464** Kzww; **466** Gita Kulinitch Studio, smilewithjul; **467** Valentina Razumova; **468** Wk1003mike; **470** Bonchan; **472** Natasha Pankina, Scorpp; **474** Aopsan; **476** olnik_y; **477** Aleksandr Simonov; **479, 480, 482** Manbetta; **483** kolopach; **487** Kalamurzing; **488** Africa Studio; **490** Elizabeth A. Cummings; **499** Sarah Marchant; **501** EG_, RedHead_Anna; **502** gowithstock, M. Unal Ozmen, Padma Sanjaya; **503** Richard Peterson; **506** lineartestpilot, Yellow Cat; **507** Tyler Olson; **508** Sevenke, Thitima Boonnak; **511** Pockygallery; **512** Baishev, RedHead_Anna; **514** Billion Photos; **515** victoriaKh; **516** Mtsaride; **517** Aperture51; **519** Luminis; **522** Daniela Barreto, Gelpi; **523** Jeffrey Sheldon; **526** Ivinni; **527** Matt Benoit; **530** schankz; **532** C-You, hchjjl; **535** Aperture51; **536** Thodonal88; **538** Sharon Day; **539** Daniela Barreto, Jezper; **545** Andrey Yurlov, Eugene Onischenko, ostill; **546** Eugene Onischenko; **549** Natalia D.; **553** 3D_creation,

Front Cover Credits

©Bill Reitzel/Digital Vision/Getty Images

Maaike Boot; **556** HstrongART, Ljupco Smokovski; **557** design56; **558** Bborriss.67; **560** baibaz; **561** karen roach; **565** Tim UR; **566** Africa Studio; **567** Dionisvera, irin-k; **568** irin-k, Trofimov Denis; **571** Tiger Images; **574** PrimaStockPhoto; **577** Coprid; **578** Heymo, Monticello; **579** Elena Elisseeva; **582** Jaroslava V; **583** Sasha_Ivv, Myimages-Micha; **586** picamaniac; **588** Mega Pixel; **589** Motorolka; **590** Fotoksa, nimon, Pete Spiro; **592** Africa Studio; **594** Chones, Keith Wilson; **597** CWIS; **598** Evangelos, Gemenacom; **600** Montego; **601** Swardian; **602** Swardian; **605** Garantiopa; **606** Olga Nayashkova; **608** Africa Studio; **610** Eugene Onischenko; **611** GrigoryL; **612** Minur; **614** KarSol; **616** Fascinadora; **617** Heymo; **618** Ulrike Welsch; **620** VAV; **622** New Africa; **626** Peter Zvonar; **627** Steve Mann; **628** Deniza 40x; **630** Marieke Feenstra; **631** Deniza 40x; **632** Sanit Fuangnakhon, OnlyZoia; **633** Vilaiporn Chatchawal; **634** Ksokolowska; **635** JoemanjiArts; **638** Anastasia Sergeeva, M. Unal Ozmen, Hurst Photo, Gts, design56; **641** carlos castilla; **644** Akura Yochi, Ann_ saowaluk, Megaflopp, YK; **654** Photoonlife; **656** Optimarc; **659** Ian Scammell, liskus; **661** Mega Pixel; **665** d100, denisik11; **666** PloyBuraphon; **668** equinoxvect; **671** Veniamin Kraskov; **672** MR. RAWIN TANPIN, photka, Sergiy Kuzmin; **677** Veniamin Kraskov; **683** Artem Shadrin; **684** Hayati Kayhan; **693** Veniamin Kraskov; **694** DiamondGT, Gmlykin; **702** Dmitry Naumov; **703** Twin Design; **704** Photo Melon; **705** Mtlapcevic; **708** kamnuan; **713** Arthito; **715** grmarc, Petr Malyshev; **717** Farah Sadikhova, Zsolt Biczo; **718** Shah Rohani; **724** Elnur, hchjjl; **730** Farah Sadikhova, Vitezslav Valka; **736** photogal; **738** YaniSinla; **742** Farah Sadikhova, RusGri; **743** Butterfly Hunter, Mr. Alien; **749** George_C; **750** Andrii Cherniakhov; **752** Claudio Divizia, Kriangx1234; **753** wacomka; **754** Murat Irfan Yalcin, Nata9; **757** Aleksangel; **759** Tatiana Popova; **760** Nico99; **762** Nortongo; **763** Laborant; **A3** Prostock-studio; **A11** Trinacria Photo

Student Handbook, appearing in Student Bookshelf and Teacher Guide only: HBi ArtMari, Rawpixel.com, Pixfiction, Disavorabuth; **HB1** Africa Studio, opicobello; **HB2** iadams; **HB3** Palabra; **HB5** Havepino; **HB6** Tatiana Popova; **HB8** Chiyacat; **HB9** Kyselova Inna, Markus Mainka; **HB10** ArtMari; **HB11** Disavorabuth; **HB12** ArtMari, Disavorabuth; **HB13-HB14** ArtMari; **HB16** Rawpixel.com